The Invisible Lion

BENJAMIN FRY

Copyright © 2019 Benjamin Fry

All rights reserved. No part of this publication may be reproduced, distributed, or transmitted in any form or by any means, including photocopying, recording, or other electronic or mechanical methods, without the prior written permission of the publisher, except in the case of brief quotations embodied in critical reviews and certain other non-commercial uses permitted by copyright law. For permission requests, write to the publisher, addressed "Attention: Permissions Coordinator," at the address below.

Printed in the United Kingdom

www.theinvisiblelion.com

First Edition, April 2019

978-1095674703

14 13 12 11 10 / 10 9 8 7 6 5 4 3 2 1

DEDICATION

To all of the clients of Khiron House past, present and future, and to the people who do and have worked there.

These ideas were explored with you all in countless workshops, groups and consultations. Thank you for making this possible.

CONTENTS

	Acknowledgements	i
	Prologue	1

Part One: How the Lion Was Born

1	A Little Bit of Evolution	13
2	The Cycle of a Threat Response	27
3	A Threat Response Interrupted	53

Part Two: What the Lion Feels Like

4	Health Problems in the Body	79
5	Health Problems in the Mind	89
6	Health Problems in Behaviour	103

Part Three: What the Lion Looks Like

7	When Nervous Systems Meet	149
8	How Nervous Systems Form Attachments	173
9	How Nervous Systems Fall in Love	183
10	Our Parts Personalities and Character	195

Part Four: How to Put the Lion to Sleep

11	Understanding	221
12	Reframing	227
13	Connecting	253
14	Discharging	261
	Epilogue	269
	Your 28-day Recovery Plan	277
	Clinical Case Studies	387
	Further Resources	435
	Index	439

ACKNOWLEDGMENTS

My last book ended with the clinic I was setting up being dismantled before my very eyes on the eve of its opening. By a series of miracles, the clinic found a way to open in an alternative property and survived this very peculiar baptism of fire. Exactly seven years on I am writing these words reflecting on the journey we have all taken since.

I have been very fortunate in this work to have travelled the world to attend conferences, workshops and events learning from the pioneers whose life's work have created a new understanding of our behaviour and our health. I've been lucky to spend time with many of them too. They are specialist in their own areas. My initial goal was to understand how their ideas related specifically to me. To do that I had to knit together everything I learned from them, make it work together and to become something which I could understand as being about one ordinary life.

So, this book is written for people, for a general audience. It is not trying to be academic or medical. It is born out of specialism and sits on the shoulders of some brilliant academics, clinicians and authors. Dr Bessel van der Kolk, Dr Stephen Porges, Dr Peter Levine, Dr Pat Ogden, Dr Janina Fisher, Dr Dan Seigel, Dr Richard Schwartz and Pia Mellody, are the architects of my understanding of this field, and I know that they would credit many others too.

Most of what follows is a synthesis of their ideas, which I hope I have represented reasonably and credited accurately. It will become a measure of how well we are as a planet to see how well-known these names become by future generations. I have included a further reading section at the end of the book to reference some of their seminal works. Thank you also to Colleen Derango and her team who first put these ideas together in practice for me and taught them to their grateful clients.

This is my interpretation of what I believe I have learned from my own work and experiences. Please don't hold anyone else but me to account for any failing you might find in this book. All errors, inaccuracies or omissions are entirely mine.

PROLOGUE

Meet The Lion

Imagine you are walking along, minding your own business, when across the road you see a man running. He's waving his arms wildly, screaming, turning this way and that, looking over his shoulder. He's dishevelled. He seems feral, wild. He's frightening.

People get out of his way. They avoid him, crossing the road as they see him coming. You feel the urge to do the same because this guy makes you feel really uncomfortable. You tell yourself that he is crazy, that you are not like him.

You are just about to look the other way when you see something.

Around the corner bounds a lion. A fully grown, roaring lion. And it's running after the man. Suddenly, you see the man differently. You understand that he is in danger. You want to help him. You are not alone. Other people see the danger. They also want to help.

No one thinks the man is crazy anymore. They are

no longer afraid of him.

The man has not changed. He is still running wildly, terrified, blind with panic. Yet everything else has changed. His behaviour is exactly the same as before. His body is doing exactly what it was doing before. And somehow he has gone from crazy to normal, from being avoided to being helped.

What if you are the same? What if everything you think is wrong with you is actually normal, but just belongs to a different context? What if you are not crazy, or difficult, or sick, but just can't see the lion?

The man's behaviour is normal. His body is working perfectly. His reaction and choices are sane. But without being able to see the lion, he becomes a problem to solve.

You are reading this book because you are running away from a lion you can no longer see.

Nobody's crazy. People want to help. They just can't see the lion.

My Lion

I've been in some threatening situations in my life. My mother died, over the course of six months, just before my first birthday.

Human babies aren't really ready for life. They need a close, nourishing relationship with a caregiver for up to three years before they are ready to flirt with independence. My first three years, on the other hand, were chaos.

After my mother died I went to live with her friend's young family for a year. Then my father re-married and I moved back from my adopted home to live with him and his new wife. Life settled down after that and I had a very privileged life, going to great schools and universities. But the legacy of those early years, that challenged my basic human need for safety appeared to have remained with me.

As an adult, I was plagued with anxiety. I found relationships difficult. It was hard for me to connect with people. I was emotionally distant from my family after ten years in boarding schools. I relied heavily on girlfriends to fill in the gap of human connection, but found I couldn't handle endings in relationships. Conversely, commitment was also overwhelmingly frightening. When I got engaged and my fiancée became pregnant, I was almost perpetually in a state of panic. It affected everything.

I also struggled to work effectively for these reasons. I would crater with anxiety about what I was doing, feel crippled by panic attacks and not want to go to the office or to meetings. Paradoxically, I lived what some people might see as a risky professional life, running entrepreneurial projects and avoiding mainstream conventional careers. I think I was able to handle risk because life felt terrifying to me anyway, so this didn't seem like too much extra to handle. People would probably say that I appeared pretty calm or cool, but really I had just learned to shut down. That's why I struggled with personal relationships too. I seemed aloof, but actually I was just afraid.

I survived like this. I set up companies. I got married and had children. But I was busking it. I had no plan, no strategy. I could not think long-term. I was just trying to get through the day. Fortunately, I was pretty good at that. I could be persuasive and charming, so selling came easily to me.

But, in the end, it wasn't enough. When the music

stopped, I was totally unprepared.

I had built a pyramid of debt, thinking I was clever, and invested in the Greek property market. It seemed like the next big boom, and I was hoping this might take care of my problems for good. But this was 2007 and not long after the markets all crashed, worse in Greece than anywhere else.

I was ruined. I had no job, no money, huge debts and a young family. Then my wife discovered she was pregnant with our fifth child. I did not cope well.

Slowly, painfully, inevitably, I had a breakdown. It started with fear, then panic, then not sleeping, and then really just losing my mind. It was like my body was on high alert all the time. It was pumping adrenaline and there was nothing that I or anyone else could do or think to make it stop. I was running from the lion twenty-four-seven. And, in the end, it made me very, very ill. I needed help.

As a trained psychotherapist, I thought to try some therapy. But that didn't even make a dent in the symptoms. I avoided doctors because I was afraid of medication. Instead, I did anything else; faith healing, the church, exercise, a job. People confidently predicted that I was on the right track and would recover, but nothing was working. I just got more and more unwell.

Finally, in the depths of despair, I brought out the big guns and checked myself into a well-known London psychiatric hospital. Such was its fame that I reasoned that it had to work.

It didn't. The medication was hard to bear, the doctors were dismissive and the way they spoke about my problem didn't help either. They just said I was depressed or anxious or both. But there was no real sense made of my story and what I was living through. It was all about the assumption that everything would be fine with a pill. It just didn't ring true for me.

I bounced on and off medication for a few more months until despair took me again. I knew I wouldn't survive if I stayed at home, but I couldn't bear to go back to that hospital or anything like it. It seemed so hard to find any well-informed useful help, but a friend told me about a hospital in Arizona. I got on a plane and went. That was a fairly dreadful experience too, but there was one psychiatrist there who literally nursed me back to health with very, very careful use of medication.

I then moved to their aftercare unit and it was there that I discovered a different world, seen through an entirely different lens. Everything I had been told before about my condition was swept away and replaced with a story that actually made sense to me. I didn't have some kind of mysterious disease called anxiety. I had a nervous system which was reacting as if I was in great danger. There would actually be nothing odd about my thoughts, feelings and experiences if I had been running away from a dangerous lion. The problem wasn't me; it was the invisible lion.

This transformed everything for me.

My treatment, based on this model, worked. It was hard and painful but I came through it and slowly set about rebuilding my life. I remained fascinated about what had happened.

The whole concept of mental and behavioural health was being inverted and put forward as a consequence of a problem that was actually in the body. But like all new developments, there have been difficulties and disagreements. The early pioneers of these ideas would fall out with one another, and followers would take their ideas and use them in one way at the expense of another. Very similar theories were put forward and rather than synthesise, they would compete. It was hard to take it all in.

But I tried because I wanted to. I wanted to understand my own experience. I had suffered damaging consequences in every area of my life and needed to make sense of it. Somehow, I had to understand how I had ended up sabotaging, destroying or ruining almost everything of value in my life; and what my nervous system had to do with it. It mattered to me.

I set up a clinic in England doing the same work I'd experienced in Arizona. Through that work, I met many more therapists, clinicians and pioneers in this field. I also met many people just like me, who were suffering with the same problems. They didn't come to our clinic for their first go at treatment, or even their second, or third, or fourth. Like me, they had seen many therapists and doctors or had spent time in clinics, rehabs and hospitals.

They came to us, as desperate as I had once been, for their last shot at treatment. What I tried to do for them first was to explain what was going on, trying to put everything I'd learned from my journey into simple concepts and language to help them to understand their journeys.

As my life started to recover, I began to be more outward looking myself. I engaged more with life outside of my narrow focus of family and work. I started to think about my other relationships, with family and friends. I took a greater interest in how the world was working too.

Everywhere I looked, I saw the same patterns. The explanations I would give to people in the consulting rooms and the lectures in the clinic became the same way I would talk to people about their non-clinical lives, about politics, about culture, about behaviour and even about the planet.

And so eventually I decided to write about it.

How To Use This Book

If you're running from an invisible lion, this book is for you. I'm going to show you how to find the lion and how to put your behaviour and experiences in context. Then we are going to try to put the lion to sleep.

This book is written for everyone. Although I have worked in mental health, it is not about mental health. And although I have worked in a residential clinic with some very severe and specialist cases and staff, it is not a specialist book, nor is it just for professionals. It is, in essence, a book about how being a human being is difficult.

The ideas and expertise in it trickle down from specialist healthcare work, but because they are about how the human being works, these ideas apply to everyone, everywhere. So, you can read this book however you like. It is designed to help you understand how your nervous system is shaping every aspect of your experience as a human.

To help with your learning, you will have a chance to answer a few multiple-choice questions on each chapter as part of your 28-day recovery plan. This is when you will start to put these ideas into practice for yourself.

Two words I will not be using in this book are "trauma" and "stress". These words have become so over-used in clinical work and in daily life that they have lost accurate meaning. Everything in this book will help you to understand what people are trying to talk about when they use these words.

Finally, you will find some very bad illustrations in this book. I am not an artist. These are drawings which I can do on a white board, or on a piece of paper. I could have had them turned into amazing graphic design, but I didn't want to. This is not to cheat you or to create a cheap-looking book, but to make it possible for you to recreate these drawings yourself.

They are so simple to do that anyone can draw them. I want you to be able to explain this work to your friends, family and colleagues with a few simple lines on a piece of paper. The originals are in four colours and so the text sometimes refers to these colours. If you are reading this on a black and white format, then have a look at the colour illustrations at www.theinvisiblelion.com. You can also buy them separately in a flip-book if you wish to use them more often, but once you have them in your head, you should be able to draw them anywhere, anytime, for anyone. So, they are simple for a reason. Just like the language in this book. I want these ideas to be known by everyone, not just by artists and professionals. Invisible lions are everywhere. Understanding how to cope with them is for everyone.

I want to move us towards a world where no one is afraid of the lion; a world where everyone sees the lion and where we all rush towards, not away from, those who are being chased. In that world, people help each other, and people get helped by each other.

I want to help you, to help others, and to help myself. I don't want to be alone with all these lions anymore.

PART ONE

HOW THE LION WAS BORN

1. A LITTLE BIT OF EVOLUTION

What You Will learn

To understand a person, it helps to know a little about their family. Just as to understand a country, it helps to be familiar with its history. In our case, to understand humans, it helps to understand their evolution.

Natural Selection

The idea of evolution is that there are small random changes that happen to an animal and these changes then affect its chances of survival. The resulting increase in numbers of the ones who survive better is called natural selection.

A famous example is a type of butterfly that is white, but sometimes randomly born black. In the wild, the black butterflies don't do so well because they are easier to see and therefore easier for predators to find and eat. It follows that there are then fewer of them around to make little baby butterflies, so the white ones then tend to dominate.

But things change. Once upon a time in an English industrial town, the buildings became blacker and blacker because of soot from the new factories. This provided new camouflage for the black butterflies and showed up the white ones. The black ones now survived longer and therefore had more baby butterflies because now the white ones were easy for predators to see and eat. Very soon they became the new dominant species. (Remember, the butterflies are doing this at random. They're not doing anything on purpose to survive. It just happens to work.)

It helps to look at the history of how animals have responded to threat because we are going to become very interested in understanding how we humans respond to threat. And few things are more important to natural selection than how we respond to threat. In people and animals, this is largely determined by the working of the nervous system.

If you don't know much about the nervous system, don't panic. You can just imagine the nervous system being like the hard-wiring of the body, and the particular parts we are interested in when it comes to our response to threat are the accelerator and the brake.

It's worth noting that both this accelerator and brake are parts of our bodies that function automatically without us having to decide what's going to happen. It's like your heartbeat. It has its own rhythm, independent of your decisions about it. You don't get to decide.

This can turn into a big problem later on as organisms get as complex as the human being, but, back in the day, things were still pretty simple.

Jawless Fish

Our modern nervous systems are dated back to fossils from over five hundred million years ago and the first sign of sophistication in this system comes in none less than a jawless fish. This was basically a prehistoric aquatic vacuum cleaner, swimming around with an open face, sucking in stuff to eat.

Imagine that you are a predator, say a shark, and you come across a school of these fish, lazily wandering around the warm blue ocean. You are hungry. And it's not too difficult just to swim up to them and eat as many as you like. These fish don't really do anything to defend themselves except keep swimming around. It's a big old ocean, and they just take their chances.

Now imagine that you are one of those fish. You see the shark coming. And for some random reason, instead of just carrying on as usual, you do nothing. Literally nothing. You freeze. This is a revolution. And to understand why, we need to have a look at what makes sharks sharks.

The shark's primary goal is simple, to find prey and to eat it. For that purpose, it has developed (not by design, but by accident and natural selection) really good eyes for seeing things that move. It's not so interested in rocks or plants; it's all about the fish. So, imagine what happens when the shark chances upon a school of fish swimming around the reef. All of its sensors light up and it sees lots and lots of lunch.

As it ploughs into this meandering meal, it continues to track and follow movement. Now, through an act of random genetic transformation, the one jawless fish's response to this danger is to stay stock still. So, the shark doesn't see it and passes on by.

The fish survives.

As we have seen, survival is the referee of natural selection. By developing this new behaviour, which we might call a freeze response, this fish has now become better able to survive predation. And in doing so, it is likely to reproduce and live for longer. This type of fish will have many more descendants than its non-freezing cousins. This will go on for a few generations and slowly, we begin to see a change in the population. More and more fish are freezing when attacked. They are changing as a species and surviving better as a result. This is the adaptation necessary to survive threat through natural selection.

But it doesn't go unnoticed. Or unpunished.

The Shark's Revenge

Now look at it from the shark's point of view. Over time, the shark is finding that there are fewer fish to eat. Well, they are all actually there, but the shark just can't see them because they all stop moving whenever the shark comes around for a snack. The sharks are hungry and begin to starve and die. Fewer sharks are reproducing and fewer of them are surviving. The shark population is in trouble.

Then another random thing happens. One shark develops the capacity to see the fish that freeze when sharks pass by. For this shark, the ocean is a glorious buffet of helpless, stationary fish. He doesn't even have to chase them to catch them! Lunch is everywhere. So, he prospers, reproduces and starts a whole new line of sharks with the ability to spot stationary fish. The other sharks are dying out, but his descendants are flourishing. Gradually, the whole population of sharks becomes better at seeing the stationary fish and finding food.

And so it goes on.

Learning To Run

The next adaptation is a fish who develops an even more sophisticated response to threat. By now, all the fish are freezing whenever a shark comes near, and the shark is just eating as many as she wants. Randomly, again, a fish develops a new mutation. This time, whenever a shark comes near, the fish takes off at high speed.

This is now a helpful response. As soon as a shark is anywhere near the fish, this lone jawless Speedy Gonzales puts on the afterburners and darts away while all his cousins freeze. He gets away and all the others get eaten. And so, he has more baby fish, they survive better and the population changes and, well, you get the idea. This is adaptation and natural selection in action.

But what does this tale of jawless fish teach us humans about ourselves?

Building The Brain

Over the course of millions of years, layers upon layers of adaptations were developed in all species, resulting in the diversity of life we see on Earth today. Even our own brains have been built up in these layers. We are the result of reptiles becoming mammals, and mammals becoming humans. We even have within our brain three distinct brains! One functions like our reptilian ancestors, one like the mammals and one like a human.

This is also a really good opportunity for me to showcase the quality of illustrations which I am going to give you in this book. A professional illustration of the brain is the one on the left. I want you to be able to draw these diagrams for yourself and others, so, from now on, you will have to put up with mine, on the right!

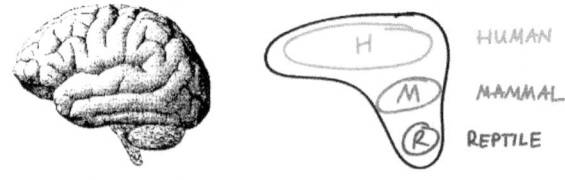

At this exact moment, I'm writing this book on a computer. A long time ago, it was an achievement of gigantic proportions just to get this computer to turn on. But, today, we take this for granted. There is a little pea-brained thing called a BIOS in every computer, which listens for the 'on' button when we think the whole system is asleep. Otherwise, how would it know that I'm pressing the button? A part of it has to be awake at all times.

This is like the original reptile brain still in us. It's very small, very simple and kind of on-off in its functions. It's not sophisticated. It won't do much other than turn you on and off, like putting you into a deep freeze if you are overwhelmed by great threat; such as being eaten by a lion.

Once this same computer is awake, it runs an operating system. This might be something like Windows or Linux. It's simply the software that makes the computer ready for us to use for our tasks. This layer is more like our mammal brain. It's pretty sophisticated. It gives us many complex ways to respond to stimuli of all kinds. But it doesn't really have a language. It gives us urges, like instincts or emotions, but there aren't any words. There are no plans to get stuff done.

To get the computer to do anything useful, I have to load a programme, like Word, which I'm using right now. Finally, with the help of this sophisticated programme, I can finally use my computer to do something I want to get done; I can now solve problems and complete tasks. This is like our human brain. It is much larger than the mammal brain, which, in turn, is larger than the reptile brain. It has language and complex connections. It tries to find interpretations, meaning and use from all of the other signals which come to it from all of our other brains, and all of our senses.

My Thinking Brain

My human brain makes things happen. It is the reason I'm sitting in a warm, dry room right now rather than a cave. It puts together cause and effect in the world, and then takes action to change the effect to something I want to cause. It allows me to wrestle some control from the otherwise seemingly rather random world that the mammal and reptile live in. The human brain can override nature and now seems to sit above it, making things the way we want them to be, rather than leaving nature to it.

But, just as a computer doesn't work without a BIOS or an operating system, I can't do any of this sophisticated stuff without all three of my brains. Everything is connected. If I can't turn on my computer, I can't use it to write. If my operating system won't recognise my computer monitor, I can't see what I'm writing. No matter how sophisticated my intended use is, these basics have to be functioning for me to do anything complicated at all. And so it is with us humans.

Unfortunately, this is also where the problems start for humans. We've now become so complex that the older software we are running in our reptile and mammal brains is in conflict with the layers and layers of new upgrades on top of it. Everyone knows what this feels like on a computer. You buy it and it works just great, then, years later, after all the installs and updates, it barely turns on in less than five minutes. Somehow the whole thing just clogs up under the weight of all of that added functionality.

So, you give up and buy a new one; and everything starts all over again. Your problem is that you are that computer, thousands of years later. And you can't just get a new one.

More Responses To Threat

So let's look at some of this more advanced functionality. Dr Peter Levine and Dr Stephen Porges have given us a glimpse into how this complexity of human evolution has affected where we find ourselves today.

The history of humans' response to threat comes all the way back from those prehistoric jawless fish, right up to the modern day. We can see a whole range of responses over time, but they are built in these layers. How they were developed is shown in the story above, but the story continues.

The first response developed by jawless fish to improve their reaction to a threat was to freeze. Then the dance of the fish and the shark began, and next the fish learned to run. Some slower fish maybe even thought they might be able to fight back when the sharks were catching up. After all, since the sharks had a lot of fish to go for, why bother with the feisty ones? So, by the time all the fish were doing a great job of running or fighting (what we think of as fight or flight), there wasn't any competitive advantage in doing either.

The next competitive advantage for a species was to develop a better radar for sharks, something we might call vigilance. Some fish knew the shark was coming earlier than others, so they were able to take off earlier, swimming away at the front of the pack from the shark. Again, they survived better so the whole population was naturally selected to do the same. And so on.

Let's skip through eons of time, because this pattern repeated itself in all kinds of species and gradually the activity of complex societies started to emerge in mammals. Once everyone's basic survival skills levelled out, nuance became a factor in who survived and who didn't. Everyone might run at the same time, so the fastest would be safest. Or everyone might fight at the same time, so the strongest would win. But if you were neither the fastest nor the strongest, what could you do? A great idea would be to be the best friend of the fastest and the strongest.

Becoming Human

Our complex societal rules were born out of exactly the same process and for all the same reasons as the very first jawless fish stopped in its tracks at shark-feeding time. The layers of adaptation just got more and more complicated. This is how we end up with time-honoured scenarios like the school playground, where there are bullies and mean girls and geeks and jocks. Or, in other words, a system of establishing influence via winners and losers. Then the whole pack is lined up, ready to deal with an attack and ordered for survival from top to bottom.

To compete in this order, we created a new response to threat called 'the social engagement system'. It's an odd response to threat, because it looks like being very friendly, sometimes with the very people who threaten us. But it bonds people together for exactly the same reason fish freeze or run; it gives them a competitive advantage in staying alive. So, human interaction is, in fact, the highest functioning level of response to threat, and it is where we as humans, ideally, would want to be spending our time. It means we are keeping ourselves as safe as possible and that feels great.

The Gears Of Evolution

These kinds of responses to threat are extremely sophisticated. Telling a joke at a party to attempt to endear yourself to a bunch of strangers is very different to running for your life or fighting to the death. It requires the mind and body to work in a new way. Stephen Porges' Polyvagal Theory shows how the anatomy even grew new pathways in its nervous system to do this.

It turns out that each of our possible responses to threat is the legacy of a different layer of evolution. And that's why they each belong to different parts of the brain, which, itself, was built up in different layers during evolution.

The reptile runs the freeze response. This is basic, a kind of on-off response. The mammal runs the fight or flight response. This is more sophisticated and requires some judgement of whether or not a fight can be won, or whether running is required. The human runs the social engagement response. It makes friends, builds alliances, greets people, gains influence. The human connects.

You can (and should) do all three. The question is in which order?

Think of them as a stack of pancakes, built from the bottom up. You start with the jawless fish, which you could not be more bored of by now, and so on. This gives you a stack of pancakes which looks like this.

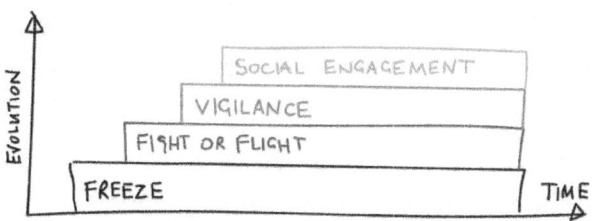

Since the top layers were built last, they are the ones which are easiest to access. It turns out that the body will start there and eat its way down the stack of pancakes if each sequential response to threat is not enough to solve the problem. Basically, we are going back in time. If our new-fangled way of dealing with things doesn't work, we go more basic, and so on.

Think about it like this. You walk into a party. What is your first line of defence against this sea of potentially dangerous mammals? Social engagement. You chat, you flirt, you find things you have in common with people. Then you hear a commotion. You notice that all your senses orientate towards the source of the noise. You lose interest in the conversation you are in the middle of and the person you are talking to. You are now more vigilant for a specific threat.

Your vigilance was a good idea! Turning to the source of the noise, you see a masked man running into the room and panicked party-goers scattering left and right. You change gear again and you run. You take off towards the back of the room, where there is a fire exit, confident of your escape, but it is blocked. You turn around. The masked man is approaching you menacingly. You abandon your flight and remember your boxing lessons. You swing for him.

He dodges your punch and expertly flips you to the floor. He pulls out a large gun and is joined by four other assassins. You are on the floor, in a corner, out-gunned and outnumbered. You freeze. You are in the last pancake.

It seems like a pretty good system. You have a range of responses to threat and as the threat increases you can go through the gears, back down into earlier evolved layers of responses, to try to solve the problem. It seems to work for our mammal friends in the wild.

Glitch In The Matrix

But what if the software glitches? And things get out of sequence? Or your three brains start fighting each other and can't agree on what to do and when? That would be bad.

When life feels really easy, clear and good, regardless of whether you are chatting, fighting or freezing, it is probably because your three brains are lining up correctly. They all agree on what to do and you just flow. It feels organic and natural to be you and to do what you do.

So, what is going on if, most of the time, you don't feel like that? Know anyone with that problem? I do.

That is what the rest of this book is about.

2. THE CYCLE OF A THREAT RESPONSE

What You Will Learn

Evolution has given us a series of sequential responses to threat. When these are working well, everything flows nicely. Our bodies and our brains are in sync and we can deal appropriately with anything that it is going on around us and within us. But something has happened to interrupt this flow. Becoming human has given us great advantages over the animals, but it has also led to a malfunction at the heart of the way that we respond to threat. To understand why we need to understand the mechanics of a threat response and how being human has messed it up.

Mary And Her Perfect Job

Mary works in an office mainly staffed by women. She loves her colleagues and her work at a charity that supports the disadvantaged, delivering aid to some of the most challenging environments on Earth. Being there gives her a sense of meaning and makes her happy. She thought she would stay there forever, but she finds herself staring at her computer screen, re-reading the resignation letter she has just written. She feels lost. How did she get here?

Nine months ago, Ann joined her team. She was smart and successful but didn't really understand the work Mary was doing on their communications strategy. This didn't seem to matter. Ann was super friendly and the team often socialised together after work. Ann went out of her way to connect with Mary, and Mary quickly came to regard Ann, like many of her co-workers, as a friend. She felt safe with Ann and trusted her. This was, frankly, a relief, since she had been worried about this new appointment and how it would change the niche that she had carved out for herself.

Then, odd things started to happen. The established relationships Mary had with her superiors began to show signs of strain. Ideas she would confidently put forward were stalling. Relationships with her colleagues she felt at ease with started to be more difficult. Everything seemed to be all smiles and business as usual on the surface, but something had changed. She began to feel unsettled. Before, she'd lie in bed on Sunday night and look forward to coming into work, but now found herself worried about what the next day would bring. Mary's sleep was suffering; she woke up not rested, but stressed and she'd bring this uneasy feeling into work with her.

She couldn't tell if she was making these problems happen because she felt less well in herself, or if something else was really going on. It was impossible to make sense of it.

Until one day, out of the blue, Ann interrupted Mary's presentation in a meeting to criticise both the detail of what she was proposing and also the overall point of doing it in the first place. This was a shock. In previous private meetings, Ann had been supportive. Mary was shocked. Instead of contradicting Ann, she kept quiet, accepting that her plan might need rethinking.

From then on, all of Mary's joy, spontaneity and creativity, which had been the hallmark of her working success previously, seemed to ebb away. She no longer felt confident, or excited to share ideas with her colleagues. She would simply trot out mediocre solutions which she hoped would not be criticised. She started to dread work and her relationship with Ann became submissive. She felt powerless and dominated.

Mary's friends and family urged her to take action. They said she should confront Ann, or her bosses. They pointed out how she had grown her role from nothing and had added so much with all her previous energy and great ideas to a rather conventional organisation. She had an easy case to argue, but Mary just couldn't do it. She felt so shut down. Before long, all she could think about was leaving; it seemed the only way to solve the problem.

So, she spends her morning at work composing her resignation letter. As she reads the words she's written, she can't believe that in a few short weeks she had gone from loving her job so much to only being comforted by the thought of leaving it. She's baffled, exhausted, confused and heartbroken. As she stares at her screen, silent tears roll down her cheeks. What is she going to do next?

If only she understood how the nervous system worked. Then it might have been obvious.

What Goes Up Must Come Down

We all know that when you run on a treadmill in the gym, your heart rate goes up and when you stop, your heart rate comes back down. But it's not just your heart rate that can fluctuate in your body. Many systems in our bodies have these characteristics.

There are set points for these systems, like my resting heart rate, and the body then varies around them as it responds to specific activities or circumstances. Another example is body temperature. This fluctuates every twenty-four hours as we sleep and wake up.

There are lots more examples of the same pattern, such as the endocrine system, blood pressure and so on. But all you need to know right now is that after something changes, it is supposed to go back to something we can think of as normal. So, if you've ever been on a treadmill, got off again and stopped huffing and puffing, then you already know what this is. In medicine this is called homeostasis (which is just Greek for 'the same place').

The body's response to threat acts in just the same way. It goes up when we perceive a threat, and then it goes down once the threat has been avoided, returning to that magical place of homeostasis. A bit like this drawing below.

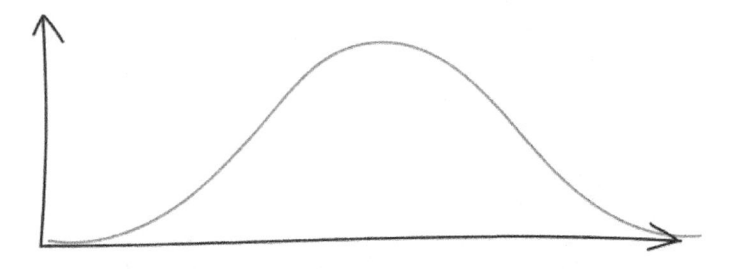

Along the bottom of the graph, we are measuring time. So, from left to right is our journey of responding to a threat. This might be a fleeting moment, or a few minutes. The difference between running and resting is what is measured up the left-hand side of this graph. You could think of it as the body's threat response, allowing you to start to deal with a threat. Clinicians might call this 'activation in the sympathetic nervous system', which is just a fancy name for our accelerator.

Typically, in the animal kingdom, the threat either eats you or you get away quite quickly. And once it's over, it's over. Have you ever watched an animal documentary showing a herd of gazelles being chased by lions? Once one or two have been caught, the rest of the herd very quickly go back to grazing. Just a short while ago, they were running for their lives, but now they are back to how they were before. It turns out gazelles are pretty cool customers.

Peter Levine's pioneering work in this field has shown that, like the gazelle, we have evolved to follow this simple pattern in our own biological accelerator. We accelerate to respond to a threat, and then, when the threat is over, we stop accelerating, but it takes a while to recover back to homeostasis, or 'normal'.

In the same way that the accelerator causes a car to speed up (and not using it allows the car to slow down), our nervous system speeds up in response to threat, and then slows down when that threat is over, returning to its original set point. Only we don't call activation in our nervous system speed; we call it charge. We charge it up in response to threat, and then discharge it once we are safe again. Like in this picture.

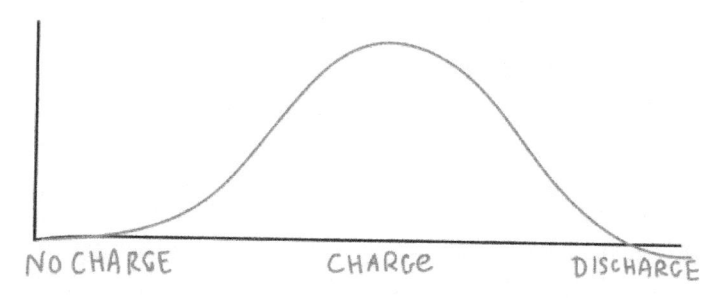

[Graph showing a bell curve with x-axis labeled: NO CHARGE, CHARGE, DISCHARGE]

You've probably gone to catch a train with what you thought was time to spare, and then suddenly thought you've lost or forgotten your ticket. Know that feeling? Most likely, you shifted all of your attention to looking for the ticket and emptied your pockets or bag in a panic, but then when you found your ticket and the threat was immediately gone, you gradually calmed down. You stopped speeding up the moment you found your ticket, but it still took a while to recover back to how you had been before. To put it more scientifically, your system charged up in response to threat, and then discharged when it was gone.

Overwhelm

If that was the whole story of the nervous system, then there'd be no point to this book. Unfortunately, things get more complicated. What happens if the threat keeps coming and you don't get away? Or you still can't find your ticket and you see the ticket inspector approaching? You can't keep accelerating forever. Just how a car has a top speed, there's a limit to how charged up the body can become, and, at that point, something different happens.

When the body is overwhelmed by its own response to a threat, it hits a sort of red line that it simply cannot go beyond. This is a problem because the threat is still there, but the part of this graph above the red line is no longer possible to get to.

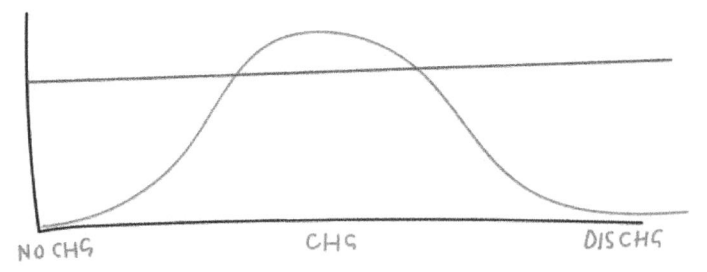

NO CHG   CHG   DISCHG

So, to continue to respond to the threat, a new response to that threat is needed. Do you remember the stack of pancakes from our introduction to evolution, the layers of evolved responses to threat? If fight or flight isn't working, then where are we going to go to next? We go back in time and evolution to something we developed in our bodies even earlier than accelerating. We freeze.

The freeze response is the earliest evolved response to threat. It runs deep in our human bodies. In a mammal or a reptile (or a jawless fish, remember?) it looks exactly like what it says it is; the animal will become completely still. But humans are more sophisticated. We have a range of ways of freezing, from being completely inert, to going to a different place in our heads.

People who have been physically attacked often say that, in the moment, they left their bodies and it was as if they were watching it happen. For most of us, it's a response that activates when we don't think we can run or fight any further, or when a threat is simply overwhelming.

This is what Mary did in the meeting when Ann

confronted her. She had no idea how to respond to Ann's sudden, unexpected attack. Just like any mammal, she could have walked out (flight) or argued back (fight), but she didn't feel able to survive either of these strategies. Walking out would have been unprofessional, but the idea of arguing with Ann felt too dangerous. The mammal in her had no choice but to freeze.

Now, this was a choice made by her mammal brain, not her human brain. It happened in her biology, not because she made a decision. It is a hardwired, automatic response that has been developing over the last five hundred million years in our human bodies. That's much, much older than our thinking brain.

We already know that activation goes up as we respond to the threat, and then comes down again once the threat is gone (assuming we don't get eaten). We can now see that if this activation crosses the red line, then in the middle of this cycle, we need to take a break. This is like hitting the pause button on a movie. Everything just stops, and then, when it is safe again, it all starts up again in exactly the same place, carrying on as it would have if it had not stopped at all. You might say it looks like this.

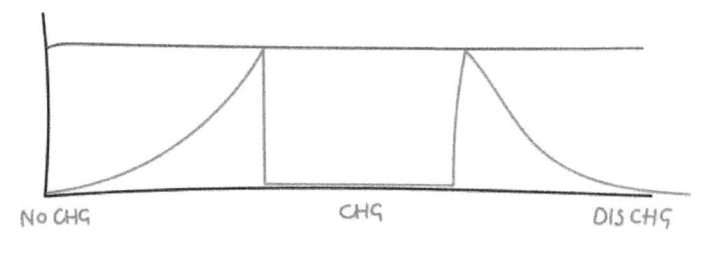

NO CHG   CHG   DIS CHG

Storing Up Trouble

During her fateful meeting with Ann, Mary ends up half way through this diagram, going from left to right. She is in the well of the freeze. That's why she doesn't do anything. If she were a gazelle out on the African savannah, things would be very similar.

When a lion chases a gazelle to kill it for food, the gazelle's job is to run away and to survive. The chase begins, and the gazelle's threat response activates, so the accelerator starts to go up. The lion gets closer and the gazelle runs harder. As the lion gets even closer, the gazelle might add a bit of fight to its flight, kicking up its hind legs into the air behind it.

But it gets caught. At this point, it freezes. It might be tempting to think that this playing dead is a cunning act, but it's actually the hard-wired biological processes of going through the gears according to the history of evolution: fight and flight has been exhausted so the next layer kicks in.

This process and order is built into the very core of our physical brain-body biology. There is nothing that we can do to change it.

Whether we are a gazelle lying on the grass or Mary speechless in a meeting, we will freeze when we reach this point of overwhelm. We may even stop breathing momentarily. We certainly aren't going to risk speaking. We were full of the potential for responses because our system had been fully charged up, and yet we do and say nothing. We don't move a muscle, but we are very far away from being relaxed.

But that means that there is something not quite right about the graph above.

So far, we have understood that as the accelerator

comes on, the system becomes more charged and as it comes off, the system starts discharging. But when we freeze, everything stops moving, even though there is still lots of charge in the system. It's a bit like having all the brakes on a car while the engine is running flat out; the car may no longer move, but it is anything other than still.

What happens next can come as a big surprise to many people.

Discharge

Go to www.theinvisiblelion.com and watch the Discharge Video. It's only twenty seconds long. If you do it right now then all of this will make so much more sense.

In the video, we see a gazelle caught by a cheetah, lying on the ground inert, frozen. The cheetah is starting to try to eat it. But a gorilla comes into view, maybe helping, maybe even competing for the prey. The cheetah is chased away. As the cheetah gets far enough away, the gazelle shifts its state from frozen back to a more charged-up threat response. It starts to shiver and shake back into life, reversing the freeze of its fight and flight energy. Very soon, it is leaping up from the floor and running for its life. Watch closely and you can see that it even kicks its hind legs out while it runs, because this is exactly what it would have been doing when it froze.

This was one of Peter Levine's breakthrough observations. It turns out that freezing when the lion starts to eat it can almost accidentally lead to the gazelle's survival. Lions sometimes drag dead (or nearly dead) animals away for their pride or for eating later and can also be interrupted or distracted after the kill. And once the gazelle appears to be dead, the lion's own nervous system changes and it focuses on other problems. This distraction provides the gazelle with an opportunity to recover to a less threatened state, and then to escape.

All of the energy which was originally mobilised for fight or flight remained dormant in the gazelle, ready to explode into life again when the coast is clear. It is like the wires are re-connected when the coast is clear again. You have paused your movie just at the most climatic action scene to answer the door, been kidnapped by aliens and come back twenty years later to the same living room, with the same movie on pause. Press play and it will burst into life, picking up where it left off.

So, the diagram for survival after an overwhelming threat needs to combine both the pause in activation and the charge in the system, which this activation has stored up. So, it looks more like this.

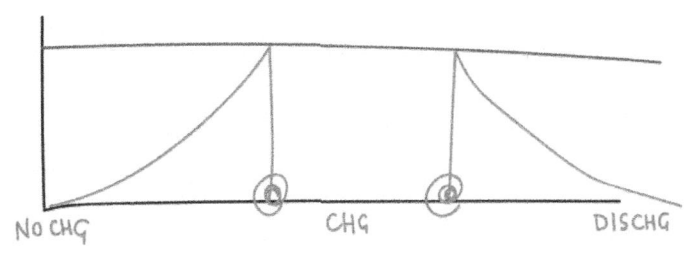

NO CHG   CHG   DISCHG

The new blue circles at the bottom of the well of freeze represent the activation charged-up in the system. It is this frozen blue blob of energy which, in the video when the gazelle gets up, has exploded back into life and takes off exactly where it started. The gazelle is back to fighting and running, discharging the energy it stored up in its system when it froze.

What's important here is that something happened to trigger the gazelle from its inert, frozen state into an immediately aggressive state of fight and flight. The difference? Its environment got safer. The cheetah went far enough away that it was no longer an immediate threat.

Safety

When it comes to understanding our own nervous system, it is really important to remember that safety can be the trigger for discharge, which can look exactly the same as a response to threat. Because it is! It is the unfinished response to the original threat.

This is so important, I'm going to say it again: when the situation became less dangerous, the gazelle stopped pretending to be dead and became itself a dangerous running maniac.

I can't emphasise enough how important this is to understand. Dwell a moment on it and take it in.

When things got better, the gazelle seemed to go from docile to deranged.

Another way to relate to this as a human is: sometimes, when things get better, I seem to get worse for no obvious reason.

Does that remind you of anyone?

Eric And Intimacy

Eric didn't have a great childhood, by all accounts. Yes, he and his two older brothers were physically looked after and got a decent education, but things weren't very comfortable at home.

THE CYCLE OF A THREAT RESPONSE

Eric's father left when he was quite young, and he didn't have much of a relationship with him as he grew up. His mother had a problem with alcohol; she wasn't a stereotypical alcoholic single mother who got angry or had a series of relationships with abusive men. She was, in fact, extremely docile. Fragile, even.

Eric was successful enough at school, although he lived in the shadow of his brothers, both of whom excelled at sports; so, despite being less academic than Eric, they were admired much more by his peers. He had a difficult relationship with his brothers. They were close to each other and he looked up to them in the absence of a father figure at home. But they were competitive with their younger brother and he often felt they were unkind. He craved their help, but they would put him down and he found that living with this kind of social bullying, day in and day out, made it hard to stay optimistic about life.

Eric would say that he was close to his mother, though. Or rather, that she was very close to him. The truth was she clung to him and became tearful or weepy if he wasn't able to give her the time she needed. Her drinking was a constant backdrop to their domestic set-up. She would become more and more needy as the evening wore on and he dreaded her late-night outpourings. Instead of sleeping or studying, he would end up counselling his own mother as she rehashed for the umpteenth time how difficult her life had become.

Eric cared and he loved her, but she exhausted him. Caught between the sadness of his mother and the aggression of his brothers, he trod a narrow path through his teen years.

Eric wasn't great with girls; he was shy, geeky and spotty. His few experiences with women left him feeling scared and inadequate in a way he couldn't easily understand or explain. But everything changed when he went away to college to study engineering. Maybe because he was away from home, or out from under the shadow of his brothers, he felt a new lease of life, particularly socially.

Early in his first year of college, he met Suzanna. She was shy like him, but had a wild side, and they hung out together at the alcohol-fuelled Freshers' parties. He found these parties overwhelming, but he liked the way that Suzanna seemed to gravitate towards him when she wasn't busy causing trouble elsewhere. Pretty soon, he realised that he was in love with her.

If she hadn't taken the lead, he might have never done anything about it. But with Suzanna he experienced the kind of connection, excitement and companionship he'd been missing. They had a whirlwind romance, staying up all night talking, missing lectures to camp out by the lakes, going to parties together and feeling the security of being there as a couple. And then there was the sex.

Eric would have said that he was happy. He was finally making friends more easily and his studies were excellent. Life now made sense.

Except for his temper. At first, it was just the odd tantrum that seemed to come out at the weirdest times. Like when he and Suzanna were curled up in bed, watching TV after an idyllic weekend. Suddenly, as if out of nowhere, he was raging about Suzanna changing the TV channel without asking him. He really didn't care that much about what he was watching, he knew, but he was furious with her anyway. And he had no idea why.

Gradually, things got worse. Eric often got angry without really knowing why. There was nothing in particular annoying him, but he would get upset nonetheless. Suzanna, initially blindsided, kept her reactions to a minimum (we could say she froze), but gradually she became more and more upset by these incidents. She started to fight back. But she didn't do it with words.

Eric noticed that she was becoming less engaged with him. Something had changed. He didn't feel so connected to her. Oddly, although he didn't like the situation, he noticed that he had become calmer. The temper tantrums lessened. But Suzanna interpreted this as Eric being happier without her, so she was doubly upset. Things came to a head one summer evening at a campfire party with their friends.

They had spent an idyllic day outdoors, relaxing, laughing, drinking. It felt like the old days. Eric had finished his assignment for the term and he was at peace with himself. Being with Suzanna at that moment felt timeless to him, like it had always been that way and would always be. He wanted the moment to last forever. As the evening wore on and the sun went down, everyone became gradually more drunk and things got a bit blurred. And then out of nowhere, Eric found himself arguing with Suzanna. Afterwards, he couldn't even really remember why.

He accused her of overwhelming him and putting too much pressure on their relationship. But as he heard himself say the words, even he didn't really believe them. He just felt an overwhelming need for distance. Wound up and drunk, he eventually pushed her away, aggressively. She stumbled and fell, hard. Everyone turned and stared while Suzanna's friends ushered her away, distraught. On the one hand, Eric felt relieved and calmer. But he was also devastated and ashamed. Soon after, Suzanna transferred to a different college.

Eric thought that all relationships were like this. His future ones frequently were. He came to the conclusion that the only way to be happy in a relationship was to be with a woman who was very independent, yet he yearned for closeness. This yo-yo approach to intimacy stayed with him his whole life. He never did solve the problem of why his relationships never made it past the honeymoon phase. And he never really found happiness. It baffled him indefinitely.

If he'd known about the lion and the gazelle, maybe he'd have got it.

The Complete Threat Cycle

I'm going to summarise all of this in one diagram. First of all, I'm going to reduce the video to a storyboard of a lion meeting a gazelle. Here is a gazelle drinking from the watering hole.

Now a lion turns up, and the gazelle runs for its life.

The lion catches the gazelle and is about to eat it. The gazelle freezes.

Somehow, the lion is distracted, and the gazelle is safe enough to unfreeze. It runs off, kicking its heels.

The gazelle discharges its nervous system and ends up back where it started, both in its nervous system and literally back at the watering hole.

So, putting it all together, we have, from left to right,

a gazelle at the watering hole with a relaxed nervous system; a lion arrives and the gazelle is activated into fight or flight; the lion catches the gazelle and is about to eat it, so the gazelle goes over the red line and freezes; the lion wanders off and the gazelle survives, which triggers the discharge of its stored up activation; the gazelle returns to rest and goes back to the watering hole. The whole thing can be over in a minute or two.

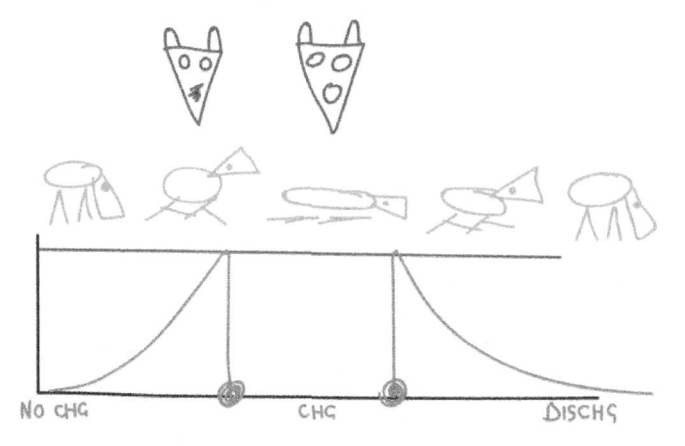

This story has a happy ending. The gazelle survives, all of its energy is discharged as it runs away for the second time, fighting off a lion which is no longer there. Minutes later, it's back at the watering hole, eating and drinking with its buddies. You could watch this happening in the wild every day of the week.

This has been happening all over the planet for millions of years.

The gazelle's nervous system returns to its original resting point, and it's as if this terrifying, death-defying chase had never happened. Biologically it is history; done and dusted. If it has a memory, the story might remain there, but its body returns to a healthy resting set-point of no activation in its system. The biological cycle of the threat response is over. It is complete. It is in the past.

But humans, as you may or may not have noticed, don't seem to work like this. Let's look at why.

The Dawn of Self-Awareness

Planet Earth has trundled along, pretty consistently, for millions of years. If you were to visit Earth, say, fifty million years ago, and then come back a million years later, nothing much would have changed. But, in the last five thousand years or so, very significant changes have happened.

And all because of humans.

So, what is it that's so different about humans?

One answer is that we think and talk about ourselves in a way that other species don't seem to do (I'm doing it right now). This ability to reflect on ourselves has had huge consequences for our planet. And it's because of your nervous system.

We are going to add some self-awareness into the story of the lion and the gazelle and see what happens. We can make the gazelle human. You, even. I'm going to represent this on our trusty diagram by drawing boxes of self-awareness around each stage of the gazelle's drama with the lion, like the frames of a movie story-board.

We know this story from the outside, looking in. Now we are going to imagine that we are the gazelle, and through the miracle of self-awareness, we can see our own story as if we were observing it rather than just living it.

There are five frames in this story-board, each of them happening in turn. It looks something like this.

THE CYCLE OF A THREAT RESPONSE

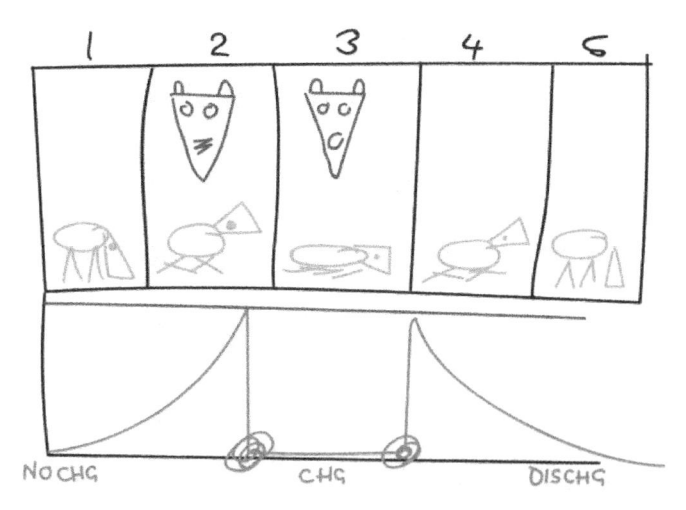

Now we can start to see what a nervous system threat cycle looks like in a human being. Our bodies and our biology go through these five stages automatically, just like the gazelle's (because, remember, the threat response is hardwired in us from millions of years of evolution), but our mind observes these five stages as if it was entirely separate to the body that is running them.

This is because we have three brains. Remember? Our reptile and mammal brains are still running much the same as they would have done a million years ago. And our newer human brain is now watching, gathering information and trying to make sense of it.

Our human brain, our great evolutionary advantage, is really not much more than a super-computer that tries to link cause and effect, trying to change the future into something we actually want. That's why we are obsessed with logic; we want things to make sense. None of us like it when we can't understand what's going on because it robs us of our one, unique evolutionary advantage.

We are not the fastest or the strongest species on Earth, but we certainly are the deadliest. Why? Because we can connect cause to effect and understand why what is happening is happening; which means that we can choose the outcomes we want and have a pretty good chance of making them happen.

So with that in mind, can you see the problem with the story above? One of the five boxes doesn't make any sense and that's a big drama for the human's thinking mind.

Interrupting The Threat Cycle

Let's investigate:

Box 1	There's no lion and the gazelle is relaxing at the watering hole. That makes sense.
Box 2	A lion appears over the horizon. The gazelle runs for its life. This also makes sense.
Box 3	The lion is about to eat the gazelle and the gazelle drops into a dead faint as if paralysed. Well, maybe that's less obvious, but we kind of get it.
Box 4	There is no lion anywhere to be seen, but the gazelle is running and fighting for its life. Does that make sense?
Box 5	There's no lion. The gazelle is relaxing at the watering hole. That makes sense.

Can you see the problem? Box 4 doesn't make any sense at all. Why would the gazelle run away from nothing? By reading this book we can understand it because looking in from the outside we can see the whole story and we also now know a lot about the nervous system. But just imagine you only turned up for box 4 of the story.

You're wandering through the African savannah and suddenly you see a gazelle running like mad, kicking its hind legs, freaking out. You look around, immediately alert to find the cause of this behaviour, but there's nothing. Just a peaceful plateau of docile animals. This gazelle is going to seem pretty crazy to you.

Is this ringing any bells? Maybe you know that person? Maybe you are that person? Has anyone ever said to you that you were over-reacting? And on the one hand, could you kind of see their point, but on the other hand, it felt like the only sane reaction to be having at the time?

This is what was going on for Eric. He had frozen so many of his reactions to life while he was growing up. He needed to rely on his mother to take care of him, but she was herself somewhat of a threat. He didn't feel relaxed with her, and sometimes she would completely overwhelm him. What was he going to do, from the age of four or six or eight? Fight her off? Move to a new town? No. So he froze. And all that frozen energy was stored up in his system, waiting for an opportunity to be released.

That opportunity came with Suzanna. His nervous system was finally able to move out of the loop of boxes one to three. He found something that felt safe, unthreatening. The lion, as it were, had moved on. That's why he was able to complete his unfinished stress cycles; it just wasn't very pretty. That intense argument that came out of nowhere? It actually came from the frozen activation charged up in his system, popping up and saying hello. His body wanted relief from holding on to all of that unfinished business. It wanted to heal.

The problem was that these automatic processes were not understood by Eric, or Suzanne, or their friends. And there are few things we humans are more threatened by than not understanding something. That's why people run away from street magic. When we can't connect cause and effect, we think reality has gone haywire, and we get scared. After all, in that moment, we have lost our greatest evolutionary advantage and that makes us vulnerable.

A New Threat

So, box 4 contains a major problem for the human biology. Just as the nervous system starts to feel safe (maybe for the first time in ages) and just as it starts the important and often powerful biological process of discharging some of that stored-up activation, the very act of doing so creates a huge amount of fear and threat to the humans watching it. One of which is you!

So, when you transition from box 3 (freeze) to box 4 (discharge), which is your only path back to box 5 (rest), you are interrupted by your own self-awareness of the process. You can't understand what is going on and so you become threatened by your own efforts to release this stored-up activation from an earlier threat. Congratulations; you have just created with your thinking brain a new threat, just as an old threat was trying to complete its own unfinished business. And we know what happens when we encounter a new threat, don't we?

THE CYCLE OF A THREAT RESPONSE

That's when the Erics of this world get stuck in a perpetual loop of safety and threat, and the nervous system becomes locked into a swirling vortex of unfinished business, uncomfortably going nowhere, never completing its discharge or getting back to its normal set point with no activation charged up in the system.

This changes the diagram. We no longer have a smooth continuation of our response to threat. Our efforts to discharge the energy that has exploded back into our biology in box 4 are frustrated by the equally strong force that is our human mind telling us not to do it, because it's bonkers. And being bonkers is a threat. These two very powerful opposing forces result in a hugely strained biology in the body, with two parts of our brains wrestling against themselves, but going nowhere.

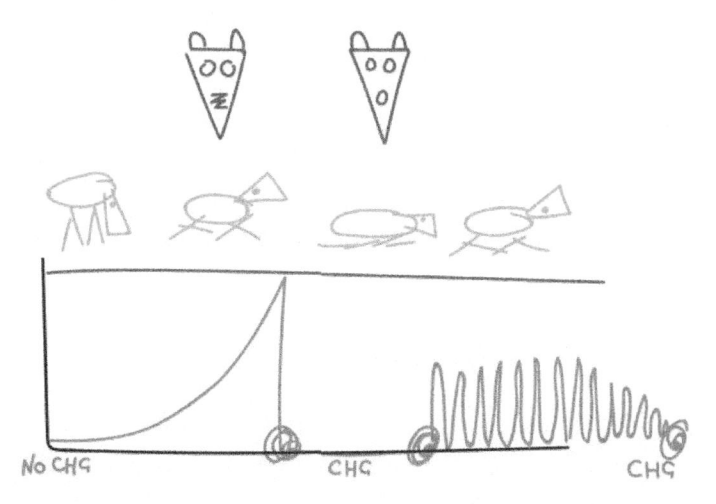

If you look closely at this new diagram, you will see that the blue line never gets back up as far as the red line, so it can't get back out of its frozen well. As soon as the frozen activation starts to be released, before it can even get back to full flow, it is shut down by another part of the brain. This goes on in an excruciating tug-of-war until, eventually, all the energy subsides. But it has not been discharged. It has just been forced back into its box. There has been no opportunity for it to get up over the red line and organically discharge back to its normal resting state.

Instead, it is forced back into the well of frozen activation. Nothing has been completed or achieved other than a very uncomfortable few minutes, hours, days or even weeks, depending on the severity of the reaction.

Have you ever had the experience of feeling like someone or something has rented space in your brain? You keep looping the same thought over and over again? And then, days later, you wonder why? Well, this is what was happening.

So, the end of the graph changes from being a completed point of discharge, to somewhere exactly the same as the big blue blobs in the middle of the graph. The whole process is back where it started the moment you first froze ready to round again, and again, and again. Going nowhere, painfully and slowly. It is stuck in a loop.

No Rest For The Wicked

Obviously, this is counter-productive. The body stays where it was in the middle of the diagram, never getting back to the resting point from where it started. The process of trying to discharge was also quite unpleasant, yet unproductive.

So, ironically it is not only bad experiences which

trigger our strong reactions to threat. Safety can be just as problematic when it follows unfinished responses to an earlier threat. Whether it's a longed-for relationship, or when we make some money, or buy a house, or move to a new town or get a better job, whatever it is that makes our bodies feel like there is no longer any immediate danger can let loose our biological triggers for discharging all of that frozen activation.

This then also feels all wrong, totally counter-intuitive, unwelcome and, therefore, also threatening. So, we shut it down and go back to square one (or box 3, actually). And so it goes on.

But it doesn't have to do so indefinitely. Safety is a great opportunity for healing, but only if you really understand what is happening.

And that is exactly what this book is for.

3. A THREAT RESPONSE INTERRUPTED

What You Will Learn

We know how self-awareness can interrupt a threat cycle and undo millions of years of careful evolution in our responses to threat. But so what? We are going to look at what happens to the overall experience of being human when this flaw in the system emerges. After all, we experience threat over and over again in our lifetimes, in different ways, and with different emphases at different ages. This has many consequences, some of which you will already be painfully familiar with.

Dysregulation

I'm not very keen on jargon. However, I want you to learn at least one new word to help you to talk about the consequences of your unfinished responses to threat. It is going to be a lot easier to say that a nervous system is 'dysregulated' than 'a nervous system which is charged up from its incomplete responses to earlier threats'. But what does dysregulated really mean? To answer that we need to build a slightly more complex model of how our responses to threat build over time, one after another.

In everything we have looked at so far, we have considered the process of responding to just one single threat from a starting point of a healthy nervous system. Let's look at it again, but this time, instead of starting with a perfect nervous system (which, for most of us, is a bit unrealistic), we are going to start with the nervous system we had at the end of the last chapter. It still has a charge in it from our first encounter with the lion.

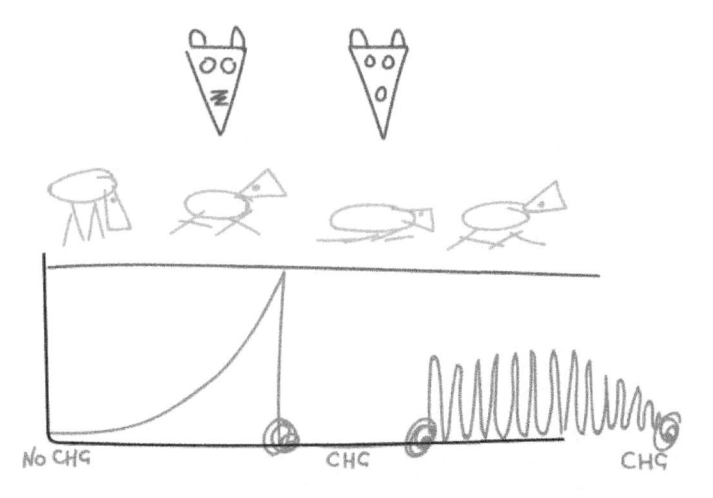

So, what do you think happens when another lion comes into view? We already have a lot of unfinished business with the first lion. This incomplete response to the first lion is now also going to be triggered by the

A THREAT RESPONSE INTERRUPTED

second lion. This changes how the threat cycle starts.

The smooth blue line, which would be a gradual activation in response to a threat, is no longer so smooth. It jumps up more quickly in an exaggerated response. We are adding together my normal response to a new lion on the horizon with the activation from my unfinished response to when the first lion was about to eat me. So, I'm now responding to the second lion on the horizon as if I'm about to be eaten by the first lion (remind you of anyone?). As a result, you might see me start to run wildly for my life, when, in fact, I should really be just starting to jog away, saving my energy in case things get worse.

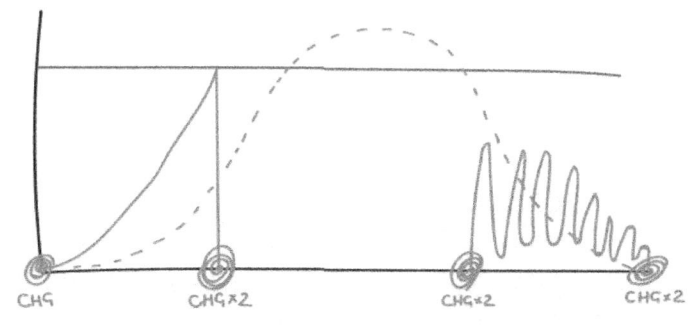

But that's not the only problem. Because I am reacting more quickly, I will reach my red line (where the freeze response kicks in) much more quickly too. So, when the other healthy gazelles are really starting to make a run for it, I'm now already overwhelmed. Once again, I freeze, but too soon this time which actually makes the situation more dangerous than it needed to be.

Now even more energy has been stored up in my nervous system from two encounters with a lion. If I am lucky enough to survive this second lion, I have the energy from the threats of two lions in my system, which now both need to be discharged. I have even more unfinished business to deal with.

So, sometime later, when things have calmed down, I will need to have an even greater discharge of energy than the first time. My human brain watches this discharge, which looks like running and fighting with a lion I can't see, and it freaks out even more because it makes even less sense now. And so, I stuff it all back down again.

I now have two-lions-worth of fight and flight energy stuck in my system. What do you think happens when the third lion appears?

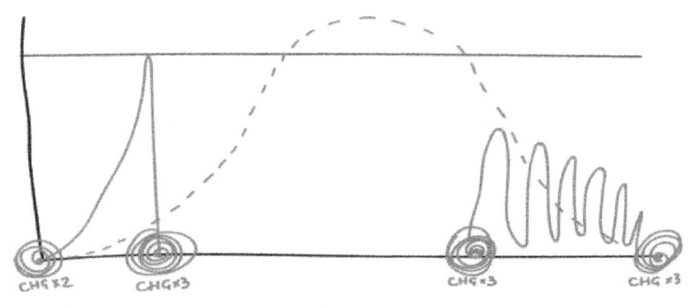

Or the hundredth? Or the ten thousandth?

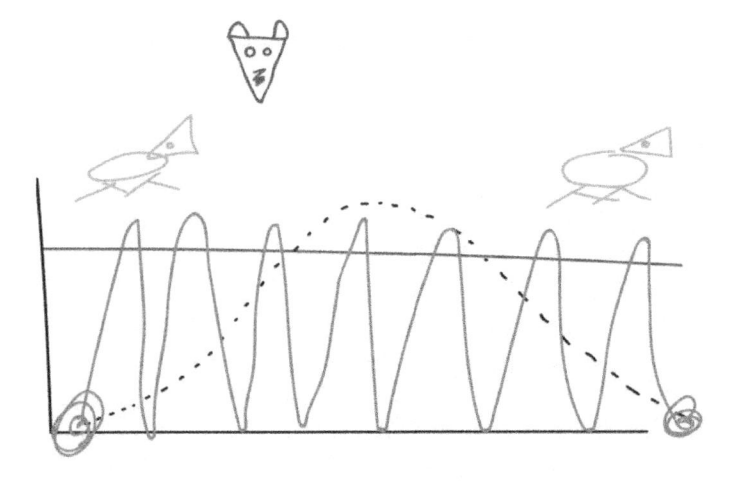

Once our nervous system is dysregulated, we can no longer smoothly respond to any threat. Instead, we immediately spike in our threat response, regardless of the level of threat. Then, exhausted or overwhelmed, we crash into a frozen state far too soon for the actual level of threat we face. Then we might spike again. Then crash. And so on. We have gone from a smooth analogue response, to threat to an on-off digital response to threat.

We've seen elements of this in Mary's and Eric's stories. You've probably experienced it yourself, so you will know that it doesn't help us to manage threat very well. Worse, it doesn't allow us to discharge our earlier unfinished responses to threat either.

It can feel like we are running all the time, whether there's a lion to threaten us or not. And, as a result, we have little capacity to react appropriately to any real threat when it happens.

This is dysregulation. We are either on or off all the time. There is no flow, no regulation. It's exhausting.

Broken Biology

Dysregulation is not the way were are meant to be, so, to keep going in this malfunctioning state, the body has to change too. The first consequence is that the brain becomes at war with itself to keep dysregulation going. The mammal and reptile brains are trying to do what they've been doing successfully for millions of years. But the self-aware, thinking, human brain is screaming "no" and getting in the way.

When the balance of the nervous system has been lost like this, the brain is in conflict. It goes from the diagram on the left to the one on the right. And, as you might already know, this is a shift from something which feels natural and organic, to something which feels uncomfortable and unnatural.

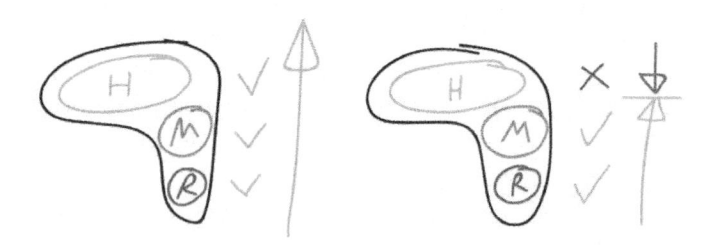

You may not be the first person to have noticed this. One of mankind's earliest and best-known stories arguably tells the same tale; the first one in the Bible.

I'm thinking about the story when Adam ate the apple from the tree of knowledge, and then everything went wrong. In that moment, Adam and Eve went from being in a perfect organic flow with nature, to being cast out of Eden into a world which was much harder to bear; they started fighting, their children killed each other, their relationship with the natural world of food and animals became strained. The rest of the book of Genesis is basically about how much we all then suffered as a result.

Dawn Of Dysregulation

At some point on this planet, say a million years ago, there were no self-aware species. No mammal was having thoughts like 'what's the point of life?', or 'do my friends like me?', or 'why am I reading this crazy book?'. Today, that is happening all the time, all over the planet. So, between then and now, some animal, or some person, must have had the first ever conscious thought.

This was the moment when the first organism became self-aware. Before that moment, in over five billion years of Earth, this had never happened. After that moment, it happened more and more. What were the consequences?

A dysregulated nervous system, of course!

It is the self-aware thinking human mind that interrupts box 4 and leads to the failure to discharge all of the energy stored up from the overwhelm of an earlier threat. This leads to a broken biology and an everyday experience which is no longer in the organic flow of life.

But more than that, it makes us difficult to live with, destructive towards each other and our environment, and actually changes the way our brains grow. In that one moment of gaining self-awareness, we started a chain-reaction that has led us away from our natural biological selves and made being human (and being humans together) much, much harder.

It has been a disaster. A fall from grace, if you like. An exit from Eden. In the story, the fig leaf becomes the symbol of all of this. What better metaphor could you have for becoming self-aware? The Garden of Eden is biological balance. And the fall from grace is dysregulation. Whether you tell the story from the point of view of the anatomy or mythology, all the same consequences follow.

Reality Shifts

Something else peculiar happens around box 4 when we can't discharge our reaction to a threat. You know how we don't really like it when we can't understand what is going on? We have another way, which you might recognise, of coping with that.

Imagine you are Eric and you start to feel really upset and angry for what seems like no reason, because, on the surface, everything is fine. What are you going to do with this information? At this point, you are effectively this gazelle in Box 4, running from nothing. For the human brain, this doesn't make sense. There seem to be two ways to solve the problem.

First, we could stop the reaction. Bury it. I think we are all familiar with this strategy. We boss ourselves around, telling ourselves not to be so crazy. Sometimes, it works. Some people can exercise a lot of control over themselves. For others, the eruptions of frozen energy continue even when we tell ourselves not to be so silly, the threat isn't there, and we should be happy rather than freaking out.

In that case, there's only one other solution if we don't want to think we are going crazy.

We have to invent a lion.

A lion that is not immediately obvious.

You might say, an invisible lion.

We have to add a new detail to our diagram of a dysregulated nervous system. Our threat response is now not only incomplete, but it is also delusional.

A THREAT RESPONSE INTERRUPTED

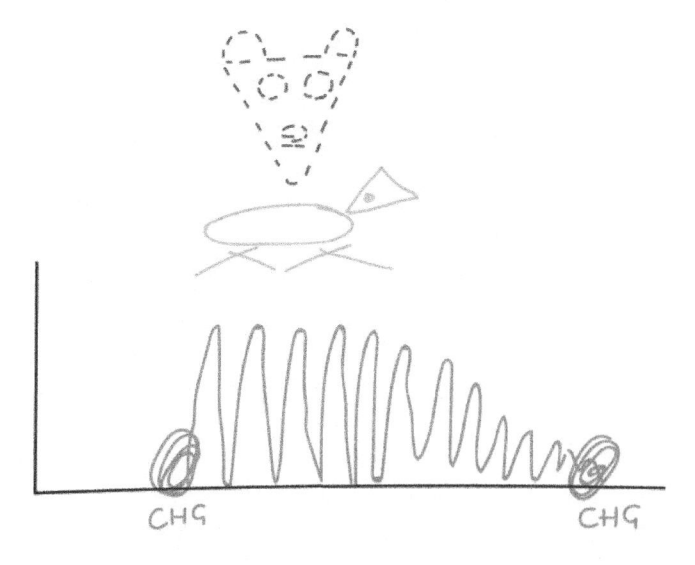

This makes far more sense to our logic-loving human brain. After all, if we are having an experience in our bodies that looks a lot like running from a threat, then there must be a threat to run from. Nothing could be more obvious. So, we make up a threat. We've all done it. And we've all had it done to us.

Sometimes, it's that thing where you have a really nice colleague at work, and, for some irrational reason, you hate them. Or it might be that you, like Eric, believe that your partner is causing you distress, which is out of scale with what they are really doing. This kind of thing happens frequently in families. We can often feel safe around our family members, but, paradoxically, that doesn't stop us from acting out and telling ourselves it's because everyone is ganging up on us.

We know from Eric's story that feeling safer can temporarily make us feel threatened. And then we have to find someone to blame. We all have so much unfinished business in our nervous systems that, as soon as things improve, we start to feel like they are getting worse and that we are under attack. And logic dictates that if we are under attack, then someone must be attacking us.

This kind of shifting of our reality to suit our nervous systems is the basis for all manner of disagreements and conflict between ourselves and others. Our bodies are time-travelling, reacting to something that happened before, while our minds are busy trying to make sense of that in the present. See how confusing that could be?

So, we have to reinvent the threats of an earlier time in the here and now, in the room, in the office, in the home, in the family, so that we can feel sane.

Internal And External Threat

This brings up another very important difference between us and the gazelles, another consequence of self-awareness; how we experience threat. Threat isn't necessarily about just a physical threat, like a car crash or an unfortunate encounter with a lion. It is also about how I experience a threat and how I talk to myself about that in my thinking, human brain.

In our story of the lion and the gazelle, we look at what can threaten a mammal. Typically, that would be being hunted by a stronger mammal. But humans have something other mammals don't appear to have; we have a constant conversation going on with ourselves in our brains. We have successfully reduced the threats to ourselves from other mammals using the science, weapons and technology created by our excellent human brains, but, at the same time, we have increased the threat to ourselves from ourselves. We now threaten ourselves with our thoughts.

Consider our reaction to noticing ourselves discharge fight-and-flight energy when we can't see any obvious threat to run away from. We observe our so-called 'overreaction' or 'irrational behaviour' and we have a thought about it. That thought scares us, and so it becomes a new threat for ourselves. We have just threatened ourselves by thinking that we might be going crazy. This threat is created internally, but its effects are just as real on the nervous system as from a lion.

Just try it out. Start telling yourself that you are going to be fired tomorrow, or that your boyfriend is going to leave you, or that your mother loves your siblings more than you, and see how your body reacts. You might notice that your biology changes. Maybe you feel more tense, or heavy, lethargic or blank. You will have succeeded in using your mind to threaten yourself, and your nervous system will react. See how pervasive it is?

This is why cognitive behavioural therapy, or CBT, has become such a popular treatment in the psychology world. It's a technique that helps people get a grip on some of the thoughts and actions we create for ourselves which then threaten us.

People who practice it notice that when they are able to think less threatening thoughts, they then have less severe symptoms of their problems. The practice is helping people with dysregulated nervous systems and training them to trigger those systems less by their own thinking. This is very useful.

But when you understand the story of the lion and the gazelle, as you now do, you can probably see that

CBT is a way of reducing symptoms from a much more significant underlying problem. It is not, therefore, a cure itself; rather, it's a strategy for reducing the symptoms of the problem. For many people the world over, it's a great start, but it should not be done at the expense of techniques which can help to get the nervous system back into regulation.

PTSD

I know I said I would not talk about stress or trauma in this book, but just for a moment I am going to break this rule. The reason I don't talk about them much is because they are frequently misunderstood. Here, I am going to tell you what they actually are.

Being in some degree of danger and then feeling overwhelmed can happen to anyone, even a gazelle with a very nicely functioning nervous system. In a dysregulated system, it can happen very easily. In mental health, this is often referred to as a trauma. This experience of going over the red line is what defines a trauma. Therefore, a trauma is defined by what happens in the body, not the event in the outside world.

Events like a car crash, or combat in war, are often given as examples of trauma. After all, these are extreme threats, so it makes sense to us that the nervous system would hit the red line pretty fast. Whatever the cause, there is a lot of work left to do when this happens. Once you've gone over the red line, the unfinished responses to the threat will need to be discharged later. If not, you have a problem.

This problem is often called Post Traumatic Stress Disorder, or PTSD.

Now that we know what we know, it is easy to

pinpoint what PTSD is in terms of how the nervous system works. PT (the Post Traumatic element) refers to the effect of going over the red line and then freezing. You can see exactly where that occurs on our favourite diagram.

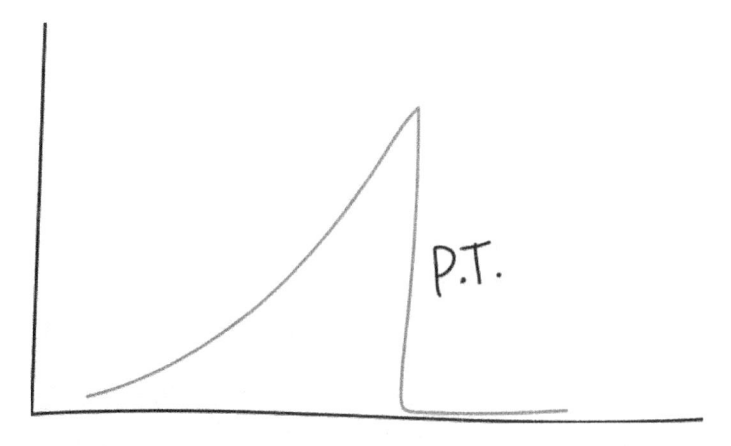

The second two letters, SD (Stress Disorder), refer to the effect of not being able to discharge this stored energy, resulting in a dysregulated nervous system.

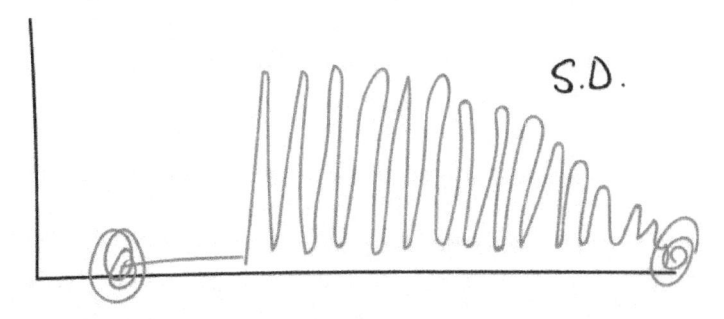

Remember, the nervous system can also be triggered by much smaller threats than a car crash or war when they happen to an already dysregulated nervous system. The response can be much the same as it would be to a bigger threat, even if the cause is very different. The result, though, feels the same.

This is why trauma, stress and PTSD can't only be defined by events like a car crash or war. It could be triggered by anything.

PTSD In Everyday Life

Imagine someone has taken your lunch from the work fridge, and you are absolutely distraught. To make this into something that doesn't drive you completely crazy, you might tell yourself that whoever did it is a terrible person, the worst of the worst. This makes the scale of your reaction seem more like a reasonable response. And that's why sometimes, we need to invent an invisible lion to make our responses feel proportionate and, frankly, to make ourselves feel more sane.

This kind of reaction is not usually called PTSD, although we can now see that once you accept the biological definition above it actually is! If the problem persists or is severe enough, you might end up getting a professional opinion from a psychologist or a doctor who might want to give it a label, something like Generalised Anxiety Disorder or even Borderline Personality Disorder, or Narcissism, or OCD.

We could map any of these disorders onto this story of the nervous system. But, as I found during my own stay in my psychiatric hospital, names and labels aren't all that useful. To me, it feels more useful to say that a person has a dysregulated nervous system, and then to look at how this crippled state of biology is interacting with the circumstances in their life.

PTSD from a single incident, such as a car crash, especially when it happens to an adult, often resolves itself. For people recovering from a car crash, it seems that about a third recover quickly, a third in a few months after a period of nightmares and flashbacks and a third don't recover at all. In nervous system terms, this is like saying that the first third allow their mammal systems to discharge the activated energy quickly, the second third takes more time and notice more symptoms of trying to complete this threat cycle, whereas the final third just can't do it at all. This last group probably already started with a more dysregulated nervous system before the car crash, so it is much harder for their systems to succeed with the organic process of healing.

For this dysregulated group, there are usually other problems, too. The nervous system is a very powerful, fundamental part of our anatomy. It connects our brain to our movement in almost every conceivable way. It affects our heart-beat, how our blood vessels contract or expand, what we tell our limbs to do, which hormones we excrete, when we breathe and numerous other vital functions. It is fundamental. When it is dysregulated, so is the body itself.

After a single-incident problem in adult life, like a car crash, we can recover. But what if we have a car crash every day? Even worse is if this happens to us when we are very young. The brain is still furiously growing from birth to about three years of age and it continues to develop significantly until the age of about twenty-five. During this time, if the nervous system is fundamentally dysregulated, the brain will actually grow differently. This leads to a problem which psychologists or doctors might call developmental trauma.

With developmental trauma, the physical brain is

actually changed by the history of our experiences of threat, growing away from what it was supposed to become. Our biography quite literally becomes our biology. So, a dysregulated nervous system can even change who we are.

Born Threatened

Threat is relative. When we are very small, we are often more threatened by the same mammal than we would be when we are fully grown. Think about a toddler with a small dog, for instance. They might be alarmed when a puppy comes sniffing around for treats, whereas the adult just laughs. Threat is all about scale and what is survivable. For a young child to go hungry can feel like a life-threatening situation if she has no way of providing her own food. For an adult, feeling peckish is just another problem to solve. Therefore, for children, the same world is a more threatening place than for adults.

We're all familiar with the old Freudian cliché that people's problems started in childhood, and this might be truer than we think. First of all, everyone's story starts in childhood. That's a given. But we also experienced more threat in childhood than some might imagine.

And to make matters worse, babies are actually born not ready to manage their own nervous systems yet. They need mothers to help them regulate. This can make them look like they are dysregulated, even though they don't yet have any baggage. We all know how babies can become inconsolable and need soothing, learning to regulate their own nervous systems, just like they eventually learn to walk and talk. That's why early caregiver bonds are so important when it comes to managing the amount of threat that babies accumulate in their nervous systems.

So, in understanding the story of the nervous system, we understand that childhood is a very fragile time. But some people would argue that therapists place too much emphasis on the childhood, and that it should just be left behind. It might surprise you to hear that I couldn't agree more.

There is nothing of any importance in the past; if it is really in the past. The only thing that matters is to what degree your earlier experiences have not yet been completed in your nervous system and are, therefore, still present today. A goal of therapy should be to finish these experiences so that they can be left behind in the past and stop endlessly looping in the nervous system today. Then a new sense of regulation can happen, new relationships can be formed and the brain can even grow differently.

Ancient And Modern

When you understand the story of the nervous system, it makes sense that practices like mindfulness have emerged in recent years as an important healthcare and wellness technique. We also talk about things like yoga, tai chi and meditation in the same vein. These practices have even become accepted into mainstream medicine and are now hugely popular.

It was the same way about five thousand years ago too. About five hundred years ago, the Age of Enlightenment started to sweep away such silliness as superstition, religion and spiritual practice. Science took over. And, ironically, these days, the science of anatomy and neurobiology seems to have brought us back around to where we were about five thousand years ago. But why?

The answer lies in the battle for our brains. Remember this diagram?

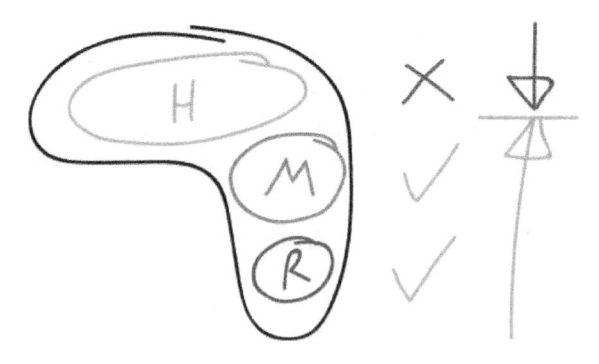

The problem here is the power of the thinking, human brain. If we could turn that off and let the mammal and reptile brains do their thing, then we could discharge our unfinished business from incomplete threat cycles, and then we would heal. After all, that's what mammals have been doing for hundreds of millions of years. We can do it too; it's hardwired into our bodies. The only thing that stops us is the thinking, human brain.

If only we could turn it off, then two helpful things would happen. First, we would stop generating new threats with our thoughts, and second, we would leave the reptile and mammal brain-body system alone to do its thing. That would result in us discharging activation from our frozen system and, over the long-term, restoring us to regulation. Then even our brains could regrow as they were meant to.

No surprise, then, that both of these effects are observed in meditation from way back when right up to the present day. From the earliest Sanskrit texts on meditation, there are descriptions of tremors and heat accumulating in skilled meditators.

This is discharge.

And, from the most modern brain scans, we can see that the brain has something called 'plasticity' which means that it can keep growing and healing itself up to the age of about ninety-five. It just needs a chance to do so, and guess what has been observed to facilitate that?

Those ancient yogis knew a thing or two, didn't they? They knew that if you can just get the thinking, human brain out of the way, the body does the rest and dysregulation can be reversed.

They knew it five thousand years ago. And now, science is just catching up. The rest of this book is about what it has missed, so far, and how to apply it.

PART TWO

WHAT THE LION FEELS LIKE

REVIEW OF PART ONE

Animals have evolved to be able to handle threat. If they hadn't, they would've died and become extinct. This means that responses to threat are very fundamental and biological for all species, including humans.

We also know that there are different stages to the response to threat. In really basic terms, we could call these the human, mammal and reptile responses. These are social engagement (human), fight or flight (mammal) and freeze (reptile). A well-functioning brain and body will move through these stages if the threat escalates, and back again if the threat is survived.

You'll be pretty familiar by now with the first diagram below, which shows a normal response to threat. And remember the one below that? This is a more complex version of the same thing, passing through a stage of freeze because the threat response hit the red line, but they end up in the same place.

THE INVISIBLE LION

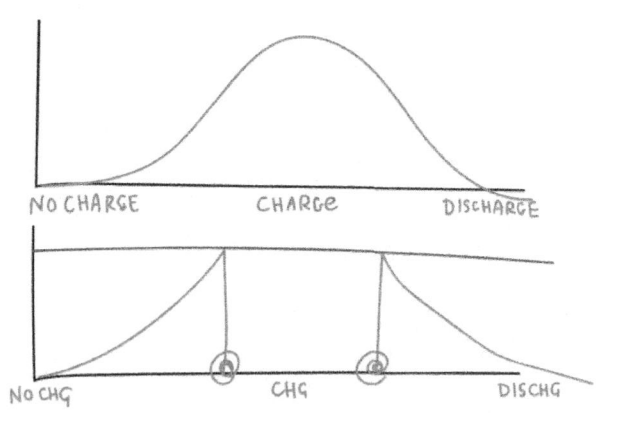

So far, so straightforward, for hundreds of millions of years.

But, then, the human mind gets involved. The human mind is self-aware, so when it observes itself running away from no lion, this causes all sorts of problems. The healthy discharge of energy is interrupted by the internal idea of a threat, created as a result of not understanding what's going on.

Additionally, we may be tempted to invent an invisible lion to make us feel less uncomfortable with this awkward combination of our self-awareness and biology. Not surprisingly, this confuses both the body and the mind.

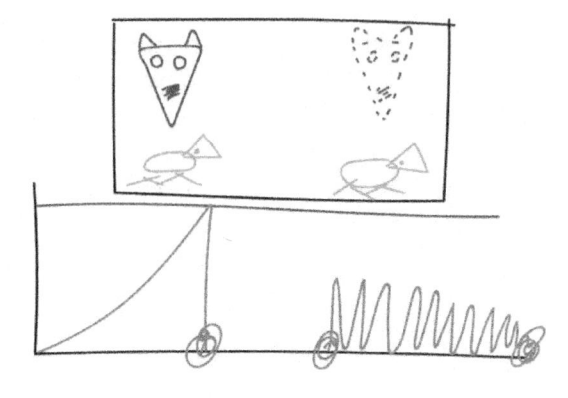

The end result is an unfinished response to threat, which leaves frozen activation energy stored-up in the body. This causes a distortion of the next response to threat. Doing this a few hundred or thousand times over leads to dysregulation.

A dysregulated nervous system responds to threat very differently to the ideal one we first looked at. It swings up and down inaccurately, and that makes for an ineffective response to threat.

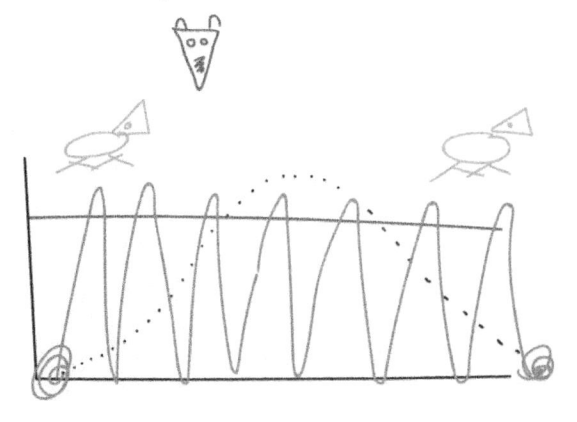

Meanwhile, the brain fights itself for control, the thinking, human brain at odds with the mammal and reptile brains.

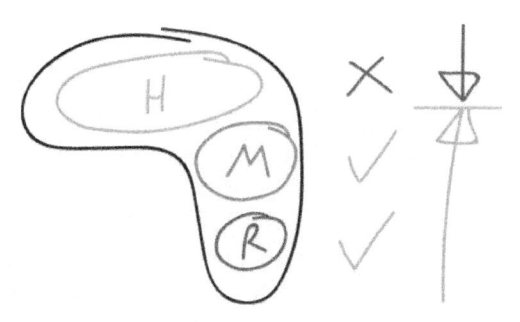

This causes many, many problems for humans.

4. HEALTH PROBLEMS IN THE BODY

What You Will Learn

We now know what dysregulation is and why it happens. But so what? What does this really mean for us in our daily lives? The first areas we are going to look at is something which has fascinated almost every corner of every culture ever seen on this planet; our health. It turns out that there is a lot more to healthcare than just the successes of our modern medical system, and much of what is not yet treated very well can be helped by understanding this story of the nervous system.

Dysregulation Is Unhealthy Biochemistry

Dysregulation fundamentally changes the body's biochemistry. This isn't necessarily a profound statement. After all, everything changes the body's chemistry. If I eat a sandwich, my body has a chemical reaction to it. If I eat cyanide, my body also has a chemical reaction to it. The outcomes of each, though, are very different.

In general, the body is chemically changing all of the time. Some of these changes are in response to things we do or eat, some of them because of things that happen in our environment (like the appearance of a lion), and some of them as a result of fairly routine things like sleep.

These changes happen around a set point (remember homeostasis?), like your body temperature going slightly up and down around a normal body temperature, or your digestion getting mobilised to take care of a sandwich and then going back to rest.

Some biochemical changes, however, are not always reversed. Think about gaining weight, for example. As a middle-aged man, I definitely think about this from time to time. Something has happened in my body which has created what looks like a change, and which is not going back to normal on its own. If I want to do something about that, I have to change my biochemical processes; I could change what I put in my body, or what I do with my body, or both. This will cause a different biochemistry in my body, which changes my weight.

A dysregulated nervous system is a change to the body (and I'm including the brain as part of the body) and can be the kind of change, like gaining weight, that goes in one direction and stays there. These changes to our once perfectly balanced biochemistry show up in many ways. In general, we refer to them as health problems.

Health, however, is a very broad topic. Throughout the history of mankind, there has been a keen focus from all recorded cultures on health: how to find and maintain good health, and how to avoid and treat poor health. However, different cultures, at different times, have looked at health in different ways. Historically, there have been three different domains of healthcare that have been separately investigated by these different cultures; mind, body and spirit.

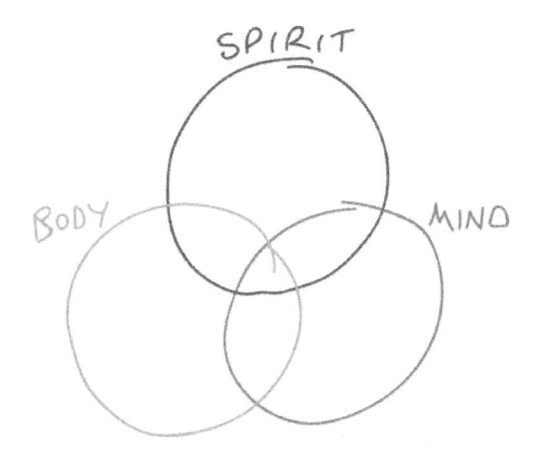

Diagram: three overlapping circles labelled SPIRIT, BODY, and MIND.

If you think about this chronologically, it seems that we started out with the idea of health being related to spirit, or to God or to religion. A very long time ago, if you had a health problem you would go to a priest, or a medicine man. There was a belief that your health problems related to trouble with the gods, or something you had done, linking behaviour, religion and health together. Remedies might have been prayer or meditation, or something even stranger, like making an animal sacrifice; practices that we'd now call superstition.

Then, along came science. It arrived in different ways, at different times, but we generally now see it as a consequence of the Age of Enlightenment from about 1500 AD. Health became all about knowledge and logic, and far less about superstition. That's when medicine as we know it began in earnest. Now it was all about the body, so, instead of talking about your moral failure when you got ill, we talked about your high blood pressure.

Medicine viewed the body as a machine, measuring the activity of this machine and suggesting ways to intervene in it. Over time, technology, like the X-ray or MRI machines, underpinned major medical advances that helped us do this better. We became able to get accurate pictures of the real problem, literally, rather than guessing.

Then, just over a hundred years ago, some health problems were suggested to be a problem not of the body, but of the mind. Freud is often credited with pioneering this viewpoint. He was just a family doctor in Vienna, trying to help people with often baffling, nonsensical physical symptoms, like an arm that suddenly could not move for no obvious organic reason. He started to think that these problems might not be in the body at all, but, in fact, be in something we were calling the mind. His idea was that the body had converted these problems from the mind into problems in the body; he called it conversion hysteria.

Since then, we have developed a habit of talking about mental health as well as physical health. And for many people in many cultures, we still talk about health in the context of possible spiritual problems, such as the wind disease of meditating Tibetan monks. So, if mind, body and spirit are the three lenses through which we tend to look at health, let's see what dysregulation does to each of them.

Medically Unexplained Symptoms

I'm not a doctor, so I'm not going to pretend that I understand all of the huge volume of work which is physical medicine. But I do understand, from being a patient, that medicine and its treatments are not failsafe. And so do doctors. One of the biggest frustrations for our conventional health services is the amount of time they have to spend on problems that don't suggest an obvious cause and don't get any better with treatment.

In the United Kingdom it is estimated that of one in four of the problems brought to a physician, the doctor will not find an obvious explanation. Medical tests for any causes of the symptoms come back normal, but the symptoms persist. These are called 'medically unexplained symptoms'.

Here are some of the medically unexplained symptoms listed on the Royal College of Psychiatrists' website in the United Kingdom.

Pains in the Muscles or Joints
Back Pain
Headaches
Tiredness
Feeling Faint
Chest Pain
Heart Palpitations
Stomach Problems; Pain, Feeling Bloated
Diarrhoea and Constipation
Collapsing
Fits
Breathlessness
Weakness

Paralysis
Numbness
Tingling
Rapid Heartbeat and Palpitations
Chest Tightness and Breathlessness
Dizziness, Faintness and Feeling Light Headed
Feeling Strange Or 'Spaced Out'
Shakiness and Tremor
Indigestion, Feeling Sick, Diarrhoea
Dry Mouth
Tightness in The Throat
Numbness and Tingling
Headache, Muscle Tension and Neck Stiffness
Sweating and Feeling Hot or Cold
Loss of Appetite
Loss of Weight
Low Energy
Tiredness
General Aches and Pains
Irritable Bowel Syndrome
Fibromyalgia
Non-Epileptic Attack Disorder
Somatisation Disorder and Somatoform Disorder
Dissociative Disorder
Health Anxiety
Body Dysmorphic Disorder

This is just one list, drawn from one page on one website about medically unexplained symptoms. You can imagine what a huge burden this is on people who suffer from these problems and for the health services that are trying to treat them.

Interestingly, the one refrain that seems to pop up when doctors talk about these various medically unexplained symptoms is the repeated use of the word 'stress'. As you know, I avoid using the word 'stress', because I believe it's not very well understood. However, now that we know the story of the nervous system, we can be more articulate.

When doctors talk about stress, they are talking about one of two things. Either it's the threat in your environment right now, like being unemployed or having your husband leave you. Or it's your unfinished responses to earlier threats in your life that are hanging around inside your nervous system. And probably if things are bad it is going to be a combination of the two.

Unfinished Business

When we look at things in terms of the nervous system, it's not a huge leap to suggest that if you have unfinished business stored somewhere inside your nervous system, this is going to create a biochemical change in your body. When the impulse of very strong energy, like the mammalian fight-or-flight response, freezes in your body, it is obviously a biochemical change because your body has gone from moving to not moving, at the very least. However, it would be very hard to say exactly what it might do to what bit of your biochemistry in every individual case; impossible even. But what sort of things might it do?

Imagine you are swinging your fist to punch someone, then suddenly, a ninja warrior leaps into your path, catching your fist in mid-air, holding it stock-still. How does your fist feel now? How does your arm feel? What about your shoulders and neck? Your back? In fact, how is your whole body? Chances are, it is tense.

Maybe even stuck, off-balance, frustrated, full of movement, yet going nowhere. It might even hurt. How would you release all of these sensations? You would need the ninja to let go. Then your arm could complete its punching action (even though your opponent was long gone) and everything would release. You might end up a bit breathless and feeling a bit silly, but you'd recover soon enough.

Interrupting the nervous system's response to threat is a bit like this. That stuck state of being held by a ninja, of not going anywhere and yet being full of activation we often call stress. But this is not a very good description of what's actually happening. If your doctor wanted to be really accurate, she might say, 'You have at least one incomplete response to an earlier threat and this is affecting the biochemistry of your nervous system. This has all sorts of consequences for your nervous system, your muscles, your hormones, your energy levels and even your sense of reality. We can probably understand most of your medically unexplained symptoms this way'.

Imagine you spend your whole life like that person throwing a punch that gets caught in mid-air by the ninja. I invite you to go to that place; feel the frozen punch in your body. Now take that body into daily life. Go to work with that body. Hang out with your friends with that body. Go to sleep with that body. Try to have relationships with that same body. How does it feel? Go through that list of medically unexplained symptoms and ask yourself intuitively if any of these symptoms make sense in someone going about their daily life with a body full of frozen response. You might just find they do.

This is not stress. It is dysregulation. We do fine

with stressors or threats when we have a regulated nervous system. After all, the whole point of the nervous system is to respond to danger with a threat cycle and help us healthily to survive the threat, returning, again healthily, to where we started out. We've spent hundreds of millions of years perfecting our response to stress. Stress is not the problem. It's our broken response to stress that changed our biochemistry and lead to health problems in our bodies.

So, dysregulation has the capacity to make us physically unwell when seen through the lens of the idea of physical health. It changes our bodies in ways that are difficult to evaluate and explain with the normal tests of physical medicine.

There are libraries filled with books that will try to give you an alternative to the modern idea of physical healthcare for the body. I'm not going to try to repeat them or to compete with them here, but they may all be trying to explain to you different ways of coping with a body affected by dysregulation.

Often, when conventional medicine is defeated, there is a temptation for doctors to suggest that maybe the problem is in fact 'in the mind'. If those doctors' tests say the problem is not in the body, does this mean there's something wrong with the mind?

People suffering from things like Myalgic Encephalomyelitis (or ME) and fibromyalgia, often have to push back against the idea that these syndromes might, in fact, be psychiatric disorders. They can feel trivialised by doctors suggesting that it's in the mind, but what does that even mean? After all, what is a mind?

5. HEALTH PROBLEMS IN THE MIND

What You Will Learn

The story of the nervous system can give us a new and exciting insight into the problems of the body and the mind, particularly the ones which up to now appear to be difficult to explain. This includes everything labelled as medically unexplained symptoms in physical healthcare, and we will see that almost everything labelled as mental healthcare is, in fact, also a medically unexplained symptom.

So, there is a huge advantage to understanding dysregulation. It appears to have a powerful effect on our bodies, which, in turn can have severe consequences for what we have decided to call our minds. This has led to a lot of smoke and mirrors about what mental health problems and behavioural health problems, like addictions, really are. The story of the nervous system gives us a better view.

Mentally Unexplained Symptoms

The entire discipline of mental healthcare is one of dealing with a medically unexplained symptom. When we looked at problems in the body, we saw that medically unexplained symptoms are a handy label for anything that doesn't seem to have an obvious cause, once doctors have run their normal tests. These tests look for physical clues as to why a malfunction has occurred, like the presence of a virus, for example.

In mental health, the whole thing is unexplained. In fact, you could say that the concept of mental health is something which we have come to rely on as a place to go when physical health doesn't know what to do. Just think about someone who is screaming. If they'd just hit a nail through their thumb, we wouldn't think they have a mental health problem. We'd think they have a nail in their thumb and the screaming is a normal reaction. But if we can't find a nail in a thumb, we think they're seriously disturbed.

But what if they had a nail in their thumb last year, and they've only just got around to reacting to it? Well, we'd still think they're bonkers, of course. It would be diagnosed as a mental health problem. Recognise this story? This is the story of the invisible lion.

Jennifer Part One

Jennifer is one of those people who most of us would instinctively feel safe with. She had done really well at school and her friends would say she was both kind and good company. From the outside, it would really be hard to see why anything would go wrong with her life. Sure, like most people, her family was a bit messed up. Her parents were divorced, but remained active in her life. Her older brother was a bit dark in his outlook and moods, and her eldest sister had dropped out of school to live in a commune. But, overall it seemed like Jennifer had the best possible version of an ordinarily messy middle-class life.

In her twenties, Jennifer found being an adult quite challenging, even though she was good at it. She wondered whether life was just like that for everyone. She had an interesting job as a human-rights paralegal, but it was emotionally draining. She never had a problem finding men to date, but, somehow, there was always a drama. Her social life was full, yet more and more she found herself saying no to things and wanting to isolate herself from the world. Then she started to have digestion problems.

At first, she thought these health problems might have been hormonal, perhaps due to her monthly cycle, but her periods were becoming more intermittent. She began to feel anxious about eating because of these random fits of discomfort and, sometimes, had even more severe digestive pains. She went to her doctor, who arranged for all sorts of tests to be done. Nothing conclusive came out of them and, eventually, Jennifer was told that she had Irritable Bowel Syndrome. She was relieved to have a diagnosis at last, but, as time went on, she found that her diagnosis wasn't as useful as she had hoped.

The treatment seemed to be mainly about adapting her diet and lifestyle, and one of the suggested causes was stress. She could work on her diet, but her lifestyle and the stress associated with it was hard to address. What was she supposed to do? Give up work and run away to a commune like her sister? She would find it even more stressful to be unemployed and uprooted. On the other hand, work was hard and it often felt like her so social life was more of a chore than a pleasure. Recently, she hadn't even wanted to think about boyfriends; her so-called relationship was still torturing her.

Things did not improve, so a friend suggested that Jennifer saw a therapist. The therapist was a psychologist and, after some exploratory questions, suggested that Jennifer was overly anxious. Jennifer thought this was stating the obvious somewhat, but the question was, what to do about it? The therapist asked whether she had ever considered taking antidepressants. Jennifer was surprised; she wasn't depressed. And she didn't like the idea of medication because she didn't think that she was that bad. In some ways, seeing the therapist had actually made her feel worse, and, as a result, Jennifer wondered if she was losing her mind. That thought made her feel worse, especially when her Irritable Bowel Syndrome kicked in.

History Of Mental Health

The history of this thing we call mental health is a somewhat troubling one. The process of it becoming an organised, legitimised area of healthcare is full of smoke and mirrors.

In 1952, the American Psychiatric Association published a book called the Diagnostic and Statistical Manual of Mental Disorders, or DSM for short. It was intended to give clinicians a common language for diagnosing mental disorders, and it's still used today, in its fifth edition, DSM 5. To the outside observer, some of what they came up with may have sounded a little absurd. For example, if you were generally very anxious, they'd call it Generalised Anxiety Disorder. A bit literal, to say the least. But to understand it properly, you have to know the context.

Freud effectively invented mental health as a way to explain the unexplained. At the time, he took problems with the body that could not be diagnosed with the model of physical medicine and created a new problem to explain it; a problem with the mind. This trend continued, and, fifty years later, doctors were saying all sorts of things about the mind to try to reformulate problems that couldn't easily be explained, like tiredness, pain, and even hysteria. Inevitably, they would get into a bit of a muddle, using different words and made-up phrases to explain the unexplainable. The American Psychiatric Association thought that it would be better if everyone used the same language. So, they kind of made it up.

One of the original DSM authors has gone on record to say as much, and it is easy to see why. What else could they do? Their job was to make a medical model out of all of the things which doctors were dumping outside of the existing model of physical health. As a result, we now have a thing called 'mental health', which is concerned with the health of the mind. But where in the body is the mind, exactly? Ask a doctor to autopsy a mind, and see how far that gets you.

Terms like Generalised Anxiety Disorder, along with the five hundred or so other disorders in today's DSM 5 are really not much more than a way to say back to the patient what she has just told the doctor. If I say that I'm really depressed, and you tell me I have a Depressive Disorder, then I haven't learned very much. By contrast, when I visit a physical doctor because I have a pain in my heel, I might learn that I have an inflamed tendon after some basic movement tests. I don't get told that I have Painful Heel Disorder.

All so-called mental health symptoms happen inside your body. Your brain is in your body. If you are tired and crying, it's happening in your body. Even though the *DSM* is little more than a way of organising our language on the subject of mental health, it has been allowed to become equivalent to a doctor's diagnosis. It is a warehouse of words used to hide the fact that we don't yet know what is going wrong with that person's body.

Explanations Not Observations

There is a better way.

When you include the story of the nervous system in your view of healthcare as a whole, everything in the area we call mental health has a different context. The original goal of medicine was to provide a mechanistic explanation for the working of the body. And our story of the nervous system already does this rather beautifully. It also explains (not describes, but explains) almost everything listed as a diagnosis in DSM 5. Really.

There is a gulf of difference between observing something and explaining it. If you were to stand and watch ducks fly south for the winter and count them, it would tell you that a large number of ducks fly south on a given date. You could then do the same thing again and again, and eventually label it as Ducks Flying South Disorder. This is observation. It tells you that ducks do fly south in the winter. Broadly speaking, the science of psychology is about making such observations and then telling us what we can expect next from what we've observed before.

Or you can really get to know what is going on inside a duck. You can discover that the duck's physical body requires warmth to survive, and therefore, it seems likely that the duck might have to move to a warmer place as winter sets in. From this, you can actually predict what ducks are going to do and explain why they are doing it when they do it. This is an explanation, not an observation. Then, when your observations fit your prediction, your theory about how ducks work looks good. In the rest of this book, you will see that nervous system theory predicts a lot of what has actually been observed, but not yet explained in mental health studies. It looks good.

The story of the nervous system is an explanation, not an observation. It is a bit like a chain of falling dominoes. It starts with dysregulation, then, as each domino hits the next, lots of changes happen in the body and the brain as a consequence. These changes have further consequences for our thoughts, feelings, reality, choices and relationships, and so on and so on. But each of them is broadly predictable from the one that comes before, once you understand how the nervous system works.

Diagnoses Not Capital Letters

A good diagnosis tells you what's causing the problem. Then you can fix it. For example, saying that your boat has a hole in the hull is a diagnosis that ultimately helps you avoid sinking. Saying you're suffering from Water in Hold Disorder is less helpful because it tells you that you need to get water out of the hold, but not why. If you go to the doctor with a sore foot and he says you have Sore Foot Disorder, then that's not very useful. If he tells you you have a thorn in your foot, then you can take it out. What we want is the cause, not a rephrasing of the problem.

Doctors and psychiatrists do, of course, have a range of treatments that they can apply to the conditions diagnosed in DSM 5. One of the most common treatments is medication. This makes perfect sense when you think of mental health as a sub-set of health in the medical model; after all, doctors are used to finding out what is wrong with us, and then using either drugs or surgery to fix it. Both have also been used in mental health.

The problem is that drugs can be very good at treating symptoms, but not necessarily at addressing the cause of these symptoms. This is like standing under the last domino in the chain and holding it up. Sure, that takes care of the fallen domino, but the whole chain is still pressing down on it from the other side. So, you have to use an awful lot of energy to keep it upright.

This is a bit like the experience of many people who take antidepressants and similar psychoactive drugs. Often, they feel better in some ways, but don't like the experience overall because they don't feel themselves. It doesn't feel like a cure, more like a respite. It isn't a cure. It has not fixed the cause of the symptoms. The drug has just masked the appearance of the symptoms.

Drugs can be very useful. Anti-depressants saved my life because they made me well enough to get treatment. But the drug was not the cure. For that, I had to work on my nervous system.

(By the way, it is important to note that there are also problems which can happen to the physical structure of the brain, independent of the nervous system, such as perhaps Alzheimer's and Parkinson's disease. These will also get thrown into the category of mental health, just because the organ they occur in is above the neck and we have some kind of idea that the brain and this thing we call 'a mind' are the same.)

Addiction And Dysregulation In Daily Life

The global value of just the coffee and alcohol industries between them show how much we rely on outside chemicals to keep our nervous systems in balance. Drugs and alcohol are the perfect substances for moving our nervous systems up and down. They are in effect just chemical brakes and accelerators. Most people use them from time to time. Or a lot.

I once was asked to deliver a lecture on the nervous system at a friend's addiction clinic. I shared much of what I have shared with you here in Part One. The audience seemed really interested in what I had to say. But afterwards, my friend said it had been a disaster. His clients took away the idea that if only they could heal their nervous system, then they could take as much drugs as they liked. I obviously failed to make it clear that a well-regulated nervous system doesn't need or want drugs. They become unnecessary.

But we don't appear to have a planet of organically regulated nervous systems. I could even argue that every great industry on Earth is simply selling nervous system regulation to a species with an epidemic of dysregulation. Make a list; drugs, alcohol, sex, shopping, smart phones, holidays, and so on. These are the things which can regulate us when we can't do it for ourselves.

The way we use food is another way we regulate the nervous system, and it's quite effective at slowing us down from an out-of-control threat response. Think of it like this: if you were running from a lion, would you stop for a hamburger? Of course not. Therefore, if you're eating a hamburger, your body will tell you that you are not running from a lion. This is a big relief to someone who always feels like they are running from an invisible lion.

But it is not just substances that regulate us. Behaviour gets out of whack too. Social anxiety is an interesting one to relate to the nervous system. If the nervous system is already running at a high level of threat while you're at home in your bed, it is completely normal not to want more threat. In theory, the presence of people helps us to feel safer, calmer, more regulated. In practice though, those people can also be seen as a threat. If, on balance, your experience (probably from childhood) is that people are a threat, then socialising just creates more threat. This is never welcome to an already dysregulated nervous system.

Most of the diagnoses listed in DSM 5 can be explained (not just described, but explained) by the story of the nervous system. Let's take a few common ones and see if this idea holds up.

DSM 5 Diagnosis	Nervous System Explanation
Alcohol/Substance Abuse	Moves the nervous system up and down
Alcohol/Substance Dependence	Moves the nervous system up and down
Anxiety Disorders	Threat response over-activated
Adult Attention Deficit/Hyper-activity Disorder (ADHD/ADD)	No one sits still or learns when they are being chased by a lion
Bipolar Disorder	Swings between over-activated and crashing into under-activation

Major Depressive Episode	Nervous system has crashed through over-activation
Hypomanic Episode	Extreme activation
Manic Episode	Extreme activation
Depression	Nervous system has crashed through over-activation
Eating Disorders	Introducing food to the gut regulates the nervous system
Generalized Anxiety Disorder	Threat response over-activated
Obsessive-Compulsive Disorder	The invisible lion feels so real is must be in the room somewhere
Opioid Use Disorder Symptoms	Moves the nervous system up and down
Panic Disorder	Threat response over-activated
Postpartum Depression	Nervous system has crashed through over-activation
Posttraumatic Stress Disorder (PTSD)	Dysregulation
Schizophrenia	Possibly a genuine brain health problem
Social Anxiety Phobia	Threat response over-activated by the threat of people

Disorders which say we are too up or too down also fit into the nervous system story easily. The same goes for disorders like Bipolar Disorder, which mix the two.

Dysregulated Not Disordered

This is just a toe in the water of the DSM and the world of mental health in general. The main point I want to get across is that the advent of the concept of mental health was a reaction by doctors to a problem which physical medicine could not explain. It is a whole medically unexplained symptom class of its own. Just as the nervous system story can help with medically unexplained symptoms in physical medicine so it can help with the whole medically unexplained symptom class of mental health in general (not everything, but most of it).

If you can't get enough of the DSM 5, here are my top ten for silliness from over five hundred of their diagnoses. Do they really tell you anything at all? See if you can deconstruct them for yourselves through the lens of the story of the nervous system.

My favourite is Restless Leg Syndrome, which, personally, I would love to see renamed as Running Away from an Invisible Lion Disorder!

    Nightmare Disorder
    Restless Legs Syndrome
    Conduct Disorder
    Separation Anxiety Disorder
    Antisocial Personality Disorder
    Obsessive-Compulsive Personality Disorder
    Acute Stress Disorder
    Bereavement
    Pain Disorder
    Panic Attack

I mean none of this as a criticism of the hard work that went into creating the DSM in the last seventy years. It's a brilliant piece of observation, which has a very important and valid place in healthcare. It just isn't equivalent to a medical diagnosis if by that you mean an explanation. And if someone claims it is, then that, in my view, is smoke and mirrors.

6. HEALTH PROBLEMS IN OUR BEHAVIOUR

What You Will Learn

The third sphere of healthcare that we talk about is the rather ambiguously named realm of the spirit. But what could that possibly mean in relation to our modern ideas of health? It turns out that there is a way to make it mean quite a lot, without being too woolly, if we look at the long tradition of spiritual programs concentrating on individuals' behaviour as a path to feeling better.

Coincidently the nervous system is also greatly affected by behaviour. How we behave is an indicator of our own dysregulation and therefore, conversely, actions we take to alter our behaviour can change our experience of dysregulation. This is important because if we are to get to the point of healing our nervous system through discharging our unfinished business left over in it from earlier experiences of threat, then this is only possible if we are strong enough to get back over our red line during these experiences. This requires some stability in the nervous system itself. Regulating our behaviour can regulate our nervous system, bringing us enough stability for the ancient and modern practices which will then help us to discharge and therefore heal.

Spirit of Recovery

Before we had the notions of western medicine or medically unexplained symptoms or mental health, humans still had just as many problems with their nervous systems. These symptoms were understood differently then and they still are in different parts of the world.

The original area of healthcare was often considered to be a religious problem, or, what some people might call, a spiritual problem. Way back then, people would go to the priest or the medicine man when they had what we would now call a physical health or mental health problem, but that would not typically be how the problem would be assessed by the spiritual master. This would lead to some quite different questions from those we expect from a modern doctor.

For instance, the spiritual master's diagnosis of health of an ordinary mortal like you and me would most likely start with an enquiry about our behaviour. In a Catholic confessional, you must confess your sins, a list of things you have done or thought. A Buddhist master might ask you what you have been chasing after (or avoiding) to cause your mind and body such disquiet. A Muslim cleric might enquire about your prayer habits and observance of the rule of law. An orthodox Jew similarly has many rules to follow; most of them are things you must or must not do. So, doing becomes an act of healthcare. It has always been at the heart of what we might call spiritual health.

There is a basic human urge to appeal to some kind of greater power to restore us when we are suffering. Often, we have channelled that urge through men and women who seem to have a hotline to that higher intelligence. And what answers do they give us?

Generally, it is in the form of a set of instructions to do this or do that or do the other. And usually it is something so basic and down-to-earth that it seems unrelated to this lofty idea of a supernatural intelligence that can just fix everything in a flash.

Why? What is it that these mystics think they know that is so baffling to the rest of us?

By now, perhaps, you will guess that, it is the story of the nervous system!

Our behaviour is hardwired to be determined by our nervous system. That is actually what our nervous system does; it tells our bodies what to do. So, dysregulation in our nervous system means dysregulation in our behaviour. Remembering that all biological systems go both ways, it must, therefore, be true that regulating our behaviour regulates our nervous system.

This might help to explain why historically spiritual advice was always telling us what to do. It is to try to regulate our nervous system, the key to a healthy body, mind and therefore, presumably, spirit.

Jennifer Part Two

While Jennifer was worrying about her Irritable Bowel

Syndrome and her therapist's suggestion that she might need medication, other problems were also coming to the surface. The so-called boyfriend situation was not good. She was stuck in this on-off thing she had with Mike. He would fluctuate between being completely into her, and then just dropping off the radar.

At first, she saw this as a challenge. But then there were times when she really needed someone, like when she was unwell, and he just didn't seem to be around. There were other times when he was more present, like when he wanted her to join him on a holiday with his friends from college, but those were the times that she seemed to find some reason to avoid him. He would complain that she was out of control. She would have to agree that she was rather emotional, but she'd always assumed that this was just part of her charm. Her aloofness was cute when she was a teenager, but now it seemed to hold her back.

As she observed her friends settling down and her colleagues appearing to handle cases more easily at work than she seemed to, Jennifer worried whether or not she was really okay.

Jennifer wasn't used to showing vulnerability. With her friends, she'd always seemed to be the one who had everything sorted. But she desperately needed a friend now. She asked her best friend Katy if she thought there was anything wrong with her. But Katy reassured Jennifer, reminding her that she had always been a larger-than-life character, and that this was part of her attraction. Sure, she sometimes over-reacted, or failed to notice what was going on for other people, but, Katy said, she was entertaining and well-liked.

Katy thinks Mike is great. She actually thinks that Jennifer doesn't give him enough of a chance. She has a totally different take on their relationship, though; Katy wonders if Mike's hot-and-cold behaviour is down to the fact that he wants more and Jennifer doesn't see it.

Jennifer is baffled. It seems that her role in life is to be the one who entertains everyone else. Her therapist says she has anxiety and wants to medicate her. Her boyfriend wants to leave her, but doesn't seem able to stay away. And her gut is revolting, literally. How is this a good life? Jennifer was always supposed to be the one that everyone else wanted to be. She is going to be thirty this summer and there's nothing about being her for another thirty years that she is looking forward to. What has gone wrong?

Reactivity

Our behaviour is run by our nervous system. We can't shout at our boyfriend unless the nervous system tells our lungs and voice-box to move in the way that creates a shout. We are hardwired.

Looking at our behaviour offers us a window into the functioning of our nervous systems. One of the big clues in Jennifer's story is that Katy says, in a light-hearted way, that Jennifer overreacts to things (her therapist, in more clinical language, might even have said she is reactive). But what is she reacting to?

We now know that reactivity builds up in our nervous system if we have not finished reacting to a previous threat. There's a good chance this will affect our behaviour. In fact, overreacting is perhaps the most obvious sign that something is not quite balanced or regulated. Overreacting is actually just time-travelling; you are reacting late to something else. But it doesn't feel like that at the time. Has anyone ever said to you, "Hey, you're overreacting"? Did it help? I'm willing to bet that your response probably wasn't, "Oh yes, you're absolutely right. Thanks so much for pointing that out."

We tend to disagree with any suggestion that we're overreacting. And we disagree because our bodies are in charge. They're telling us exactly how much reaction is required. And since our bodies evolved before our thinking did, we tend to be very invested in what they are telling us. If we feel like we need to run, or to fight, then there is a lion, and that's that. Our body's reaction is how we know that the lion is real. But to everyone else though, the lion is invisible.

This creates a distorted relationship with our environment and our behaviour. Just as we can overreact, we can also underreact. The trickiest thing is to respond just right. Not too much and not too little; it's the Goldilocks model of human behaviour.

Perhaps all of those spiritual and religious sets of instructions were actually there to try to steer us more towards this perfectly balanced Goldilocks path of behaviour. Perhaps they even encourage us to fake it 'til we make it.

Unfortunately, most of us either don't want to do this, or simply can't do it. Generally, we are utterly sold on our invisible lion being real and view our own behaviour as perfectly normal. It's the other people who are therefore crazy.

Baggage

In my workshops, I developed a simple visual aid on a whiteboard for understanding this problem. It starts with a graphical representation of you (or me). It's rough and ready but go with me here. It's simple enough that anyone can draw it. This is what you look like. This is the raw material.

Recognise yourself? This is a dysregulated nervous system. The red mess in the middle is you. And me. And pretty much everybody you'll ever meet. The squiggly lines represent the unfinished business in your nervous system. It's the frozen activation stored in your nervous system, not yet discharged. I like to call it 'baggage'.

Love or hate the word, it's fairly common language to talk about baggage. We are all aware that we're carrying stuff around with us from earlier in our lives. We'd love to leave our baggage behind, but somehow we seem to be attached to it. We move to different towns, cities, countries even, in the hope of starting again, but our baggage always comes with us. It's part of us. It is woven into the fabric of our nervous systems and will always be everywhere that we are. It is our history, happening right now.

Baggage on its own doesn't really seem to be that much of a problem for our behaviour, per se. We can carry it around and it sits there, a bit heavy perhaps, giving us health problems maybe, but generally dormant moment to moment. Until it gets stirred up.

Life happens. Stuff happens. People happen. All kinds of influences and information come into the view of our nervous systems. It affects us and we react to it. Sometimes we overreact to it. However, until there is something to react to, we might not look any different to someone else with no baggage, no matter how much of it we are carrying.

Triggers

Everyone who has any baggage knows that sometimes we are calm and sometimes we are going bonkers. There's a difference between having a reaction and not. Something has happened to make that change. I like to call this a 'trigger'. The widespread use of this term shows there is an intuitive understanding of the nervous system that shows up in our language. We understand that, among all the events and influences in life, there are some things that get to us and other things which do not.

Have you ever found yourself saying, "So-and-so just really pushes my buttons"? Often, we mean this as a negative comment on the other person, but, actually, we are talking about ourselves; they are my buttons. We are disclosing our baggage and talking about our own dysregulation. We just didn't know it at the time.

So, now I can add to my diagram of my dysregulated nervous system a trigger, something coming at me, directed towards my baggage.

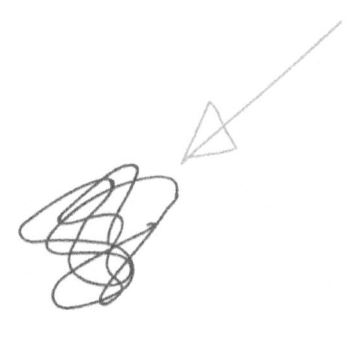

The green arrow is life happening. It might be an obvious threat, like someone shouting at me, or it could be something more subtle, like thinking I'm going to get fired for no obvious reason. It could be a real external threat like a lion, or something I have generated inside of me, like a thought.

It doesn't really matter what the trigger is, but it is important to grasp the idea that it is real, regardless of how dysregulated we are. In fact, a useful way to understand how real triggers are is to think about how they might affect a perfectly regulated nervous system. I think we can agree that a real lion should worry everyone. In the diagram above, the size of the green arrow is an indication of how severe the real threat is, independent of it hitting anyone's nervous system and baggage. Let's say this one is maybe a 3 out of 10, which we can write as 3/10.

So, a real trigger arrives at my real baggage. What would you expect to happen next? A real reaction of some kind, I guess. But what sort of reaction?

Let's say the trigger is someone pushing in front of you in a queue (it's happened to all of us). What kinds of reactions have you had to that in your life? What have you observed when it's happened to others? Generally, we tend to react in three different ways to such a trigger:

One, we might do nothing. Especially if you're British. Well, that is, we might say nothing. On the inside we are doing double, triple cartwheels. But we smile a frozen, polite smile and do nothing. If there were a reaction scale, this is a 0/10 reaction.

Two, we might get very angry and shout or even push at the person who has, in our view, so despicably wronged us. These are the kinds of reactions that end up going viral on the internet. It seemed normal to the person doing it at the time, but completely over-the-top to almost everyone else watching it. This is a 9/10 reaction.

Or, three, we might just lean over and politely say that actually there is a line behind us and we would be grateful if the person could join it there. This option doesn't leave us with much angst and it doesn't end up on YouTube. Its outcome is uncertain, but it does seem like a reasonable reaction to a slightly annoying situation. It is, perhaps, a 3/10 reaction to a 3/10 trigger.

I like to call this reaction, amazingly, a reaction. I told you I try to keep it simple. So, we have baggage from our dysregulated nervous system. Triggers are real. And reactions are the result.

In the example I gave above, there are three kinds of reactions. These can be represented in three different versions of my diagram of a dysregulated nervous system.

Under-Reaction

Here's our terribly British 0/10. There is no reaction at all. But there is still a lot going on, and it's contained within that black box, which keeps anything from escaping.

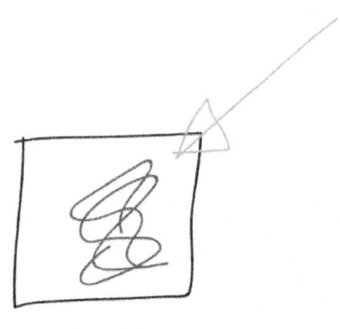

From the outside, this person might seem completely calm. But inside, they are anything but calm. I think we've probably all been there; we get triggered, but we are afraid to show it, because (and perhaps quite rightly) we are worried that we will explode.

The problem with having delayed reactions to earlier threats, via our baggage, is that the timing of the reactions won't always be ideal. Think back to our three-part brains; they don't all want the same things. The mammal might want to have a very strong reaction to some terrible trigger (like your boss' offensive language), but the human brain thinks that this would be a bad idea because throwing a tantrum in the meeting room might be bad for your career (and your thinking, human brain, to be fair, has put a lot of work, thought and planning into this career). So, your brain ends up in conflict. When you let reason win out over the biology of the body, things are stored up that need to be finished later.

This was the very beginning of the story of the nervous system and how self-awareness led to dysregulation, remember?

It takes a lot of energy to suppress these reactions of ours, and we can get very stuck as a result. This energy has to go somewhere. We have to reabsorb it back into our bodies and into our nervous systems. This changes our biochemistry and can end up being called a health problem.

Might this explain Jennifer's difficulties? She chose to work in human rights. This suggests that she has a passion for justice, which might be a reaction to her childhood. Nothing so extraordinary happened in her family, but as the youngest child of divorced parents, it would be understandable if she now has baggage around people being vulnerable through no fault of their own. She might even have been attracted to her career to try to work through this baggage. But, of course, the flipside of that choice is that her work would then have lots of triggers. It is possible that Jennifer is getting lot of triggers in her life and is unable to manage her reactions.

Stephen Porges' Polyvagal Theory explains that when the nervous system goes into an under-reaction, it can affect the body below the diaphragm. This is also where lots of mysterious digestive disorders are experienced. So, it is possible that suppressed reactions in Jennifer's nervous system from her baggage are affecting her body below her diaphragm. Maybe her doctor is partially right that stress is causing her Irritable Bowel Syndrome, but it might be more accurate to say that her under-reaction to her baggage being triggered is changing the biochemistry of her stomach.

Over-Reaction

As a worker in a law firm, it wouldn't be appropriate for Jennifer to explode at work in response to the triggers she experiences there, but if she did, what would that look like? Well, this is our YouTube star.

Here is a 9/10 reaction. The trigger has hit (or activated) the baggage and the combination of trigger, plus all of those stored-up unfinished reactions in the baggage, creates a pretty large reaction.

This makes perfect sense. Even the maths adds up; you might have a 6/10 stored away in your baggage; add in a 3/10 trigger; put them together, and the result is 9/10, and possible YouTube notoriety.

This is also why if you are the one having the reaction, it feels so reasonable at the time. And this is what makes the invisible lion so real for us. Okay, there might not be a real lion in the room and the trigger is only a 3/10, but the body is registering a reaction of 9/10, and nothing feels more real than the body's reaction.

When this happens to us, and someone tries to tell us that we are overreacting, it can feel like that person is trying to con us. They're trying to deny that the lion is really there. We know the lion is there because we can feel our reaction to it. This person telling us it isn't there is denying our reality. Or is it? It can be very hard to know. Occasionally, we look back on situations and agree that we went over the top. But, at the time it seemed perfectly reasonable.

A good example is with emails and messages. Ever sent one in the heat of the moment and then, maybe a week or a month, even a year later, read it back and thought, "What on earth was wrong with me"? Chances are, you were triggered. At the time, you would have one hundred percent believed that this trigger merited such a strong reaction. But, later on, when you're calm and not experiencing the trigger anymore, but now just observing it, you have a different reaction. When our baggage is not involved, we can see the trigger for what it is; maybe a 3/10 and not the 9/10 we were so convinced of.

It can be very confusing, dispiriting even, to lose the idea that our sense of reality is always perfectly accurate, but it is also the path to sanity and to health. This over-reaction was also happening to Jennifer. In other areas of her life, where she felt more at liberty to have her strong reactions as she felt them, she was able to be more expressive. As she grew up, there were more and more triggers in her personal life. Mike would come and go and she would experience this as abandonment, then pressure.

When Mike wanted more, that was a trigger. When he retreated to lick his wounds, that was a trigger too. As a result, she came to see him as very unreliable, although her friends saw things a little differently.

Jennifer's reactivity (which had been branded as a charming, theatrical trait in her childhood) was making her behaviour difficult to live with. Again, the triggers were real (Mike really did come and go) and her baggage was understandable coming from a divorced home, but these over-reactions were not helpful for keeping relationships in her life healthy and easy. What might have worked better?

Goldilocks Reaction

There is a Goldilocks solution, the path of a nicely regulated nervous system. It looks a bit different. You'll see straight away that there is no baggage for the trigger to hit. As a result, a 3/10 trigger results in a 3/10 reaction.

This feels right. It's obvious. In this scenario, no one has to stuff anything down inside and nothing crazy is happening. This is the reaction of someone simply solving a problem. This person gets on with life. They get on with themselves. They probably get on with other people, too.

Maybe we should say that this is not a reaction at all, but just a response. When you are not reacting from all your baggage, one way or the other, you are just responding. Nothing else needs adding to that story to make it make sense. That's what we are all yearning for, both to feel sane and to get stuff done.

Reptile Mammal and Human

Here's what all of this looks like from the outside. Imagine you know nothing of the story of the nervous system and that you've never heard of dysregulation or triggers or baggage or reactions. You're just wandering through life, and you meet these kinds of people.

These are people who seem shut down, people who appear to over-react and people who seem fairly reasonable. And anyone can be any of these three different people at different times.

When we are not triggered by threat, we just deal with life as it comes (the ideal, Goldilocks-approved nervous system). When we experience considerable threat, including when our baggage is set off by a trigger, we become highly activated in our threat-response, which looks a lot like fight-or-flight energy. When we are overwhelmed by threat (maybe when our reaction from a trigger hitting our baggage is too great), we shut down in a freeze response. This corresponds to the three main responses to threat from evolution which we learned about in Part One of this book; the social engagement system, fight-and-flight, and freeze

The problem is that when you meet someone, you can't see their baggage. All you see are these behaviours. So, if you don't know the story of the nervous system, it can be very confusing. People then tend to ascribe these different behaviours to aspects of personality, and make judgements about what kind of a person they're dealing with. They might take one, or a series of responses, like the ones above, and define an individual by them. In this way, people can end up wholly identified by their nervous system responses.

And this is a mistake, because nervous systems can change.

It seems fairly obvious that we would like our nervous systems to look like this diagram all of the time.

However, the reality for most people is that, too often, we get stuck in rather uncomfortable states, like these ones instead.

So, what would it take to transform one into the other? How could we get to the ideal diagram from the other two?

If you look at the diagrams, you'll see that there are only two ways to do that. One is to remove all the baggage and, if that's not possible, the other would be to do something about the reactions.

And that's it. It's really quite straightforward.

Managing Triggers

If we start with the basic reality that we have baggage, then one way to never experience the problem of over-reacting or under-reacting to that baggage is to not have any triggers at all. Is that realistic? For some, maybe. It's perhaps no coincidence that mystics of old would go up a mountain and meditate in a cave for twenty-five years, emerging in some state of perfected bliss. And no wonder! They were successfully avoiding the world and all its triggers while probably also doing something to discharge their baggage, which eventually then re-wired their brains. Job done.

You, however, may not have access to a handy mountain cave and a spare twenty-five years, so we'd better find another way.

Of course, it's unreasonable to expect to eliminate all triggers from your life, but we could certainly think about how to reduce them and what effect this would have on your nervous system. Remember the original reaction diagram, when we saw a 3/10 trigger resulting in a 9/10 reaction? It looks like this.

HEALTH PROBLEMS IN OUR BEHAVIOUR

What we actually want is a 3/10 reaction for that 3/10 threat. How could we get from there to there? If we want the reaction to be only 3/10 and not 9/10, then we could try reducing the impact of the trigger in the first place, so it doesn't feel so big. If we draw this on our diagram, it might look like this.

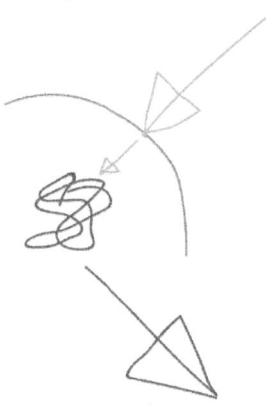

Now, we've put something in the way of the trigger to reduce its impact. It's a bit like a Star Trek shield. You can see that the missile is incoming, so you put up something to make it hurt less. If this was possible for our nervous systems, then the result looks quite promising; the trigger could go down from a 3/10 to a 1/10, and, as a result, our reaction will be less too, maybe a 6/10, which is a big improvement. There's still work to do to get to a Goldilocks 3/10, but we are on the right path.

But what could this blue shield actually be in real life?

Let's go back to Jennifer for an example. She was overwhelmed at work, quite possibly from seeing the vulnerability of her clients every day and the impact on her own sense of vulnerability as a child. She was also overreacting to Mike, as he seemed to come and go in her life. Both of these were triggers. At work she would freeze, (which is really just her response to a potential over-reaction) and at home she would lose it, which, in turn, seemed to trigger Mike to run away and everything would start to go wrong again.

What she needed in each context was to have smaller reactions, so that both might be more manageable and less damaging. The first step would have been to have lessened the triggers.

Jennifer Part Three

As Jennifer became more aware of what was really going on for her, she asked to mix up her caseload a bit so that she was put on some less difficult or less upsetting cases. She even linked her Irritable Bowel Syndrome to the shutdown that her feelings of overwhelm was creating, explaining to her manager why she needed to find some more balance in the emotional load of her work. And it worked! The result was less wear and tear on her nervous system. Gradually, over a couple of weeks, she noticed that she felt a bit brighter when she woke in the morning. She was sharper in the day and the lurking sense of dread she'd been feeling as she approached her caseload lifted. She was careful with her diet, took some exercise, started sleeping better, and slowly she noticed that the symptoms that had been so difficult to manage were getting less frequent and less troublesome. It wasn't that she was completely free, but she felt like she had restored some sense of control over what was going on in her body. She didn't just feel like life was happening to her anymore; it felt more like a collaboration between the world and her own sense of what she could bear.

With Mike, she now felt able to set up some necessary structure around their relationship. She explained to him how difficult she was finding his coming and going and asked him to limit their interactions to Thursday through Sunday. It felt really artificial at first; ignoring his messages during the week or not making plans with him when she would normally have jumped at the chance. But, quite quickly, she noticed a difference. She would still react to the smallest bump in the road or disagreement, but she knew that during the rest of her week she would have time away from these triggers to calm down. This made her feel less panicked.

Occasionally, she also saw glimpses of these incidents as if she was outside the couple, looking in. When that happened, she could see clearly that Mike was a frightened, vulnerable person too, not just someone who was doing something bad to her. She wasn't ready to share this insight with him yet, but it was shocking to her to feel like a different person in the same situation. As a result, she felt a deeper sense of empathy and connection to Mike. She wasn't even sure if she liked it, but it was at least different. And that felt like progress.

Managing Boundaries

In both situations, at work and at home, Jennifer was dialling down the triggers in her life. She did this by doing something that's talked about a lot in pop psychology, but which (in my experience, at least) has never really been explained very accurately. This was the blue line in the graph that formed a shield between her nervous system and the outside world. It lets some things in and keeps others out. This is often called a 'boundary'.

The term boundary has a long history in behavioural health. Boundaries are frequently suggested as necessary for someone recovering from addictive problems, damaging relationships or mental health problems. It seems obvious, in a way, that by controlling your environment, you can gain some control over yourself. But there is a catch to this grand plan. If you don't understand why you need to do it, it can go wrong.

Boundaries are not something which you impose on others, or on the world at large. They are protective measures you take for yourself. This important difference emerges when boundaries go wrong, because boundaries are not failsafe.

For example, if Jennifer tells Mike not to contact her during the week and he does it anyway, what should she do then? She may well be tempted to shout at Mike and accuse him of not respecting her boundaries and even try to get him to change his behaviour. The danger here is that she's lost the whole point of what she's trying to do in the first place. She loses her own regulation by trying to get Mike to do what Jennifer needs him to do. This is the wrong way round.

The whole point of a boundary is that I do it for myself. I manage my boundaries; no one else. First, I notice what is a specific trigger for me. Then I come up with a plan to reduce the intensity of that trigger. And, finally, I have to manage that plan for myself.

If I delegate managing that plan to someone else,

often someone who themselves can actually be a trigger, then I am totally missing the point. If Mike is not collaborating with Jennifer and adhering to the boundary she has imposed, then she has to do something about it, like turn off her phone or not respond to him. And when she does, something magical happens.

When we take responsibility for protecting our nervous system, we start to live in the world in a different way. Life no longer just happens to us. We get to have a say in how that happens and, therefore, how we feel.

There is nothing in life that feels as wonderful as a well-regulated nervous system. Everything we think we are trying to do in life, everything we want, everything we try to get, is really just a strategy to try to have that regulated nervous system. The more directly we start to do this for ourselves, the sooner we will become happier.

In Part Four of this book, I'll talk in detail about how to do this. For now, it is enough to take onboard that working with boundaries has just three steps:

1. I get to know what is a trigger for me
2. I try to put a boundary in place to reduce this trigger
3. If it doesn't work, I keep trying (note that it's me who keeps trying, no-one else)

It is never somebody else's problem if it is not working. I am the only person who can manage my own nervous system, and if I have to move to the moon to do that, so be it! It will be worth it.

Managing Reactions

Let's say we have done our best to reduce the triggers in our life. That's great, but we are still going to have some that get through. These are going to hit our baggage, and the result is going to be some reasonably large reactions.

When I've joked about those 9/10 reactions ending up on YouTube, it's because we have all been there, to some extent. Something that seems entirely appropriate and normal to us at the time, looks absolutely crazy to others.

So, when it comes to managing our reactions, we're aiming to turn a scenario like the diagram on the left into one that looks more like the diagram on the right. We may have tried our best with the triggers, but we could only do so much. So, now we are dealing with the aftermath of the trigger hitting the baggage. How could we transition from the one on the left to the one on the right?

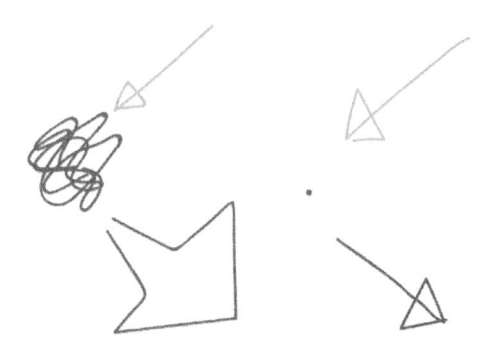

In a way, what we are asking is (a) how do I want to behave and (b) how on earth can I make myself do that when that's not how I am feeling. These tricky questions have plagued people for centuries. Every society on Earth has come up with different answers, often encapsulated in an established system of orderly behaviour. In some places they might call it 'culture', in others 'manners', in yet another 'rules'. These systems can vary wildly from place to place, but within any given place, they are remarkably consistent.

We kind of just know what is acceptable and what isn't. Growing up in England, seeing two people shout at each other in the street looked like a sign that something quite scary was happening. But one day I was on the streets of Cairo and was astonished to see two people shouting at each other, then two minutes later laughing and embracing. That was more normal there.

Wherever you are, there are unwritten rules of conduct. Step outside of those rules and that's when things get difficult, threatening or even dangerous. So, the idea of having some kind of control over our reactions is even embedded in our societies. It turns out that this can also be a very good idea for the nervous system. Throughout time we have lived in communities that tended to have lots of dos and don'ts. Rules have regulated us.

Managing Ourselves

So, we clearly have choices, even when we are having a strong reaction. But it might feel, at the time, that these choices are not within our control. For example, our reaction may be so strong that we shut down, almost involuntarily.

This is not ideal. We need to have some reactions to life around us. If we just clam up, we can't say what we need to say and do what we need to do. This is what happened to Jennifer at work, and the end result was that her nervous system became so shut down that her digestion started to malfunction. Her fear, of course, was that if she didn't clam up, she would explode, and that wouldn't have been appropriate at the office.

Even the problem of being frozen is actually a problem of not knowing how to handle a really strong reaction. But, if we could transform any 9/10 reaction to a 3/10 reaction, then we would never need to clam up or explode ever again. Imagine that.

Assuming our boundaries have failed and we have already lost the battle against the trigger and our baggage, we are left with only one possible way to deal with the inevitable, resulting reaction. We can call this containment. It looks like this.

It's not easy. The idea is that you can catch the full force of your explosive reaction and reduce the effect of it on the world outside of your own body without completely shutting it down. Now, this might sound impossible, or even pointless, but it is actually a very important part of healing your own dysregulated nervous system.

I am putting a barrier up between myself and the outside world. It is not a wall. It is not a box. It is a porous barrier that allows some of my energy out, but not all of it. Maybe in the diagram above my reaction is still a 9/10, but I hold on to most of it. So, what you see is a 3/10 reaction. Just right!

Containment is a filter on your behaviour. It can be very hard to do and that's why we benefit greatly from practicing it. Like a soldier, you should practice it when you're not under fire. That way, you might remember what to do when you are. You will get plenty of opportunity to do that in Part Four of this book.

Managing Reality

The big question, though, is what happens to the missing 6/10 from that reaction if I've gone down from 9/10 to 3/10? The answer, unfortunately, is that it rattles around in me. I can't dump it out onto everyone else, so now I have to feel it myself. And that's extremely difficult and often unpleasant to do; and something that might feel unfamiliar. After all, when we're angry, it is so much easier to yell, "You're an arsehole", than to say, "I am very upset".

When we explode onto others, we act as if our reactions are perfectly matched to our triggers. If I am having a 9/10 reaction, then it is so much less painful for me to make sense of this by saying that you are a 9/10 arsehole. That way, it all makes sense, without me having to have any baggage.

Before you heard the story of the nervous system, you didn't officially know this, but you will be familiar with wanting to feel that the pain is not coming from the inside. We like to invest in the reality that the pain has been done to us. "Without you, I'd be fine". "You are the problem". Ever had those thoughts?

In fact, most of the time, for most of us, the opposite is true. I'm the problem. Not because I'm bad or rude or flawed or difficult, but because I'm dysregulated. Our nervous systems have too much baggage in them. And, generally speaking, that's absolutely no one's fault other than evolution's.

Maybe you could not complete your response to an earlier threat at the time, and nobody subsequently helped you to do it. You can't be blamed for being a mammal and following a hundred million years of hardwired biochemistry. Yet we don't want to accept this. We still don't want to be the problem, even if we can forgive ourselves for it by understanding a bit of neurobiology. Because even if it makes sense, it still really, really hurts.

When I want to yell at someone, I want to yell at them, not at me. I don't want to hold onto most of that energy and feel how uncomfortable that is. I don't want to know that it comes from me and my unfinished past. The last thing any of us want is to actually be the hand-grenade; we want to be able to pick it up and throw it away. But look what happens if we don't.

Coming Full Circle

When we practice boundaries and containment, something magical happens. Those borders that we drew to fend off the triggers and hold in our reactions actually join up, and we start to look and feel rather differently. If we were really on our game, we might get to be something like this.

HEALTH PROBLEMS IN OUR BEHAVIOUR

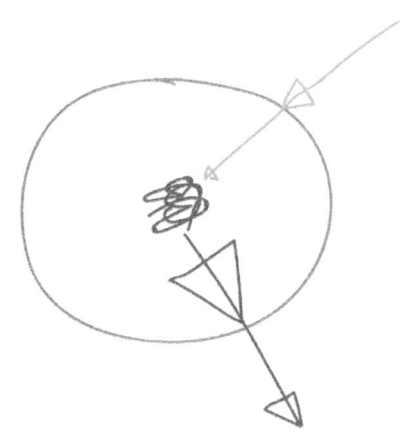

The barriers of boundaries and containment have created a circle. We now hold all our baggage inside a protective bubble. This shield presents boundaries to our triggers and provides containment to our reactions. You now understand what is going on in there, but if we were just passing by, how would this person look? If you could practice boundaries and containment, how would you look?

Imagine zooming out from this picture, away from the bubble, so that it gets further and further away, becoming smaller and smaller. Nothing has changed, other than you can't see everything that is happening in there. Keep going, and it would look like this.

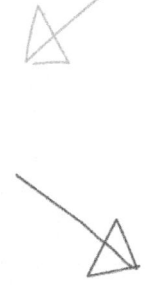

It's magic. Remarkably, it has become the embodiment of a perfectly regulated nervous system.

There is no way to tell a person with no baggage from someone who is successfully managing boundaries and containment. They are not going to feel the same on the inside (because, remember, a lot of energy is still rattling around in this system), but they are going to look the same. If the goal is to start to try to manage my own regulation, this is a very important step because, in order to discharge the unfinished business in my nervous system, I need to be able to hold my nervous system stable enough to get back over the red line and out the other side.

Often, when we have been very dysregulated for a very long time, we lack this kind of stability. In nervous system treatment, stabilisation is the first phase, before any discharge can be worked on (sometimes called processing). Boundaries and containment contribute greatly towards stabilisation. From here, real change can start to happen, and the baggage can start to be reduced.

Fake It Until You Make It

So, how could we do this in practice? Let's consider what it would look like if Jennifer did this successfully and see what happens when she starts to apply containment in her life.

You can't do this if you are frozen. If you are the kind of person who isolates and never speaks up, then this is going to be very difficult, and you will need other ways to access your nervous system to get going. That's why we treat people in community at the clinic so that they have to stay in relationship. In Jennifer's case, therefore, she would not be able to do this at work, yet. But she needs to start in a place where she is somewhat out of control. Welcome back, Mike.

There is one, very simple way to practice containment. If you follow this rule of thumb, you can never, ever go wrong. But it is maddeningly hard to do. Ready for it?

The rule is to never, ever, say the word "you". Told you it was tricky.

Containment is not about closing everything down. It is about speaking up, but within limits. We will explore this in the context of relationships more in Parts Three and Four of this book, but, for now, let's get a preview of Jennifer's progress in containment with her reactions to Mike.

The goal is to give Mike a window into that bubble at the heart of her reactions, zooming into that diagram, not out from it. This means simply describing or explaining this three-stage process of trigger-baggage-reaction. And all without saying "you"!

So, when Mike overwhelms Jennifer with what she sees as his incessant demands for her time and attention, she might notice what is going on for her just before she shouts at him and catch it in time. This is her opportunity to explain her reaction, rather than just to have it. Maybe she even breaks it down into those three parts for him:

During our phone call on Sunday, I felt like I have to give more time and attention to our relationship than I am able to. This is a trigger for me.

I have a lot of baggage around this because my mother was very needy, with no husband, and she worried about my older siblings. It felt like I had to support her, not the other way around.

My reaction was to get very angry. I wanted to run away or yell. I felt really out of control and uncomfortable. I hate that feeling.

Obviously, this is not easy to do. It was quite hard for me just to write it, so imagine doing this when you are already feeling out of control. However, it is a skill which is well worth trying to learn, and, in Part Four, of this book I'll show you how you can do that. For now, though, it is important to notice that however dysregulated your nervous system is, there are ways to recover some semblance of normality quite quickly. You can move from the diagram below on the left, to the diagram below on the right, just by using boundaries and containment.

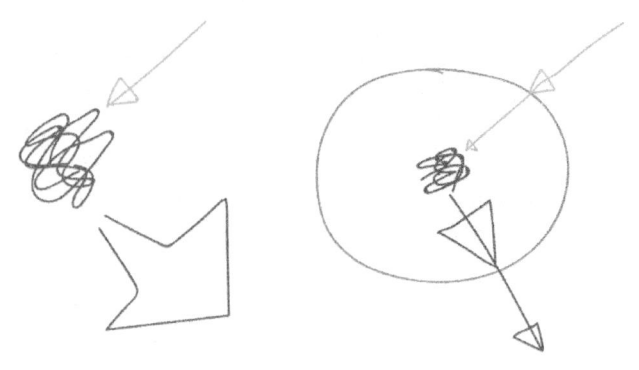

When we succeed in doing this for our nervous systems with boundaries and containment, we set up some profound new conditions for healing, which mimic the earliest needs we had in life.

Holding Space

We were born looking like we were dysregulated. Infants are overwhelmed by themselves, let alone everything else. In fact, we are not psychologically born until we are three years old, because it takes that long for our brains to fully grow. So, we need some protection until then. We need something, or someone, to hold us, much like in the diagram of a nice bubble above.

We can't do this for ourselves when we are a baby. We don't have boundaries or containment. Someone needs to do all of this work for us, to protect us. Our mother (or other primary caregiver) holds our nervous system when we are young. It is similar to being held in a physical womb, but this is a psychological holding formed by this relationship. This acts on our biology in a direct, physical way, but it is not about being physically held in the literal sense. This kind of holding is done in another way.

We tend to have an intuitive sense of what this is. We certainly know it when we don't get it. Jennifer, for example, might say that her boss did not hold her at work, so she was getting overwhelmed and it made her ill. She also might say that Mike did not hold her in her relationship, so his comings and goings meant that she never felt safe. The idea of being held has everything to do with feeling safe, and I think that we can now see that this metaphor of holding is actually someone else doing the boundary and containment work for us, just like we all do for babies.

As we grow up, it seems that we start out with the opportunity to have this done for us by our first caregivers. Then, later on, in childhood or adult life, we either learn to do this for ourselves, or we have to rely on other adults in our environment to help by doing it for us.

When we start to practice boundaries and

containment, we are setting up this very powerful transition to being able to practice regulation for ourselves and not to have to get others to do it for us. When a mother successfully and reliably regulates a baby, eventually, the baby starts to learn how to do it for themselves. Sometimes we say that the baby internalises this attachment with the mother and starts to mimic it. In the same way, as adults, we can actually mother ourselves by creating this nice, holding space of the bubble of boundaries and containment. If we do, something wonderful starts to happen.

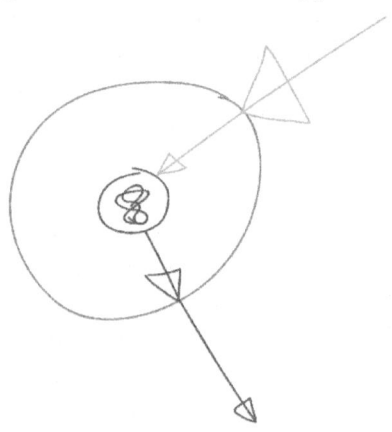

As we hold the space for ourselves of the blue bubble in this diagram, we start to make room for another internal set of holding to emerge. This is exactly like the baby beginning to copy the mother. The mother is the blue bubble. By holding that external safe space, she makes room for the baby to create its own internal bubble as it gets older. This is the smaller circle around the baggage.

In that nice safe bubble, the nervous system becomes more regulated in its responses to threat, without being overwhelmed and creating too much baggage. That's how, with an ideal childhood, a baby turns into an adult that looks like this.

Stowing Baggage Restoring Regulation

When babies and children grow up in an environment that regulates them, they are able to develop regulated nervous systems and become adults who get on easily with life. A good childhood leads to better outcomes in later life. This story of the nervous system explains exactly why. But what if you had an imperfect childhood? All is not lost. Because this also tells you what to do if your childhood was not the greatest. Until now, a troubled childhood has often been seen as a life sentence. If things went wrong, you were stuck with the nervous system consequences for life. However, we now know that this is not necessarily the case.

As we can see from the diagrams above, if we can rebuild an external holding space of boundaries and containment, then we can also slowly rebuild our internal holding space for our nervous system, learning to become more robust and more regulated. From this safe space, we can then start to deal with the baggage properly. The nervous system gets stronger and is then stable enough to begin to discharge its frozen activation.

There are now a number of body-referencing psychologies which specifically help with this problem in the nervous system (like Peter Levine's Somatic Experiencing and Pat Ogden's Sensorimotor Psychotherapy, and others listed in the Further Reading section at the back of this book). They may use different words for some of this story, but the jargon doesn't matter. The key to any treatment is this two-stage process of restoring regulation in your nervous system; stabilisation and then discharge. Once this starts to happen, then it is even possible for the brain to start re-growing parts of it that did not develop ideally during childhood, which is sometimes called 'integration'.

In my opinion, this is also exactly what all these ancient methods of spiritual practice were intuitively doing too. They had rules and regulations which were trying to set up a holding space in which nervous systems could be held. And they had nervous-system referencing practices, like yoga and meditation, which would allow the nervous system to discharge. Putting the two together restores regulation.

At the clinic, we set up our residents to live by this method. It is a residential home where people would stay for months in an environment with boundaries and containment, so the combination of holding in the community and expert treatment targeting the nervous system is very powerful. Our residents have group meetings to explore their behaviour and individual sessions to work on their nervous systems.

We have had people come to us who had been unable to get well in many of the normal ways associated with healthcare for the mind or the body. Where psychiatric hospitals, therapy, medication, even surgery had failed, they would start to heal significantly with these powerful methods.

Getting Help

Like anything powerful, it also has the risk of being explosive. Look what happens if things go wrong. If we fail with our boundaries or containment, there is backlash. The blue bubble is like a soap bubble; if you put one hole in it, then the whole thing pops.

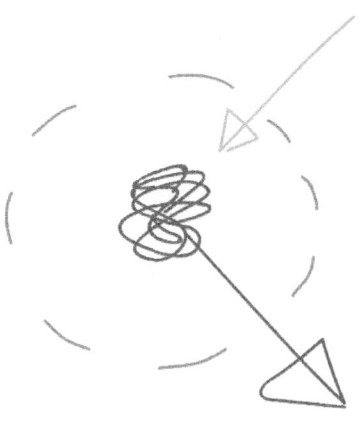

Usually, if I lose my boundaries, I lose my containment, too, and vice-versa. This is, I suppose, obvious. If I let someone shout at me for too long, I'm likely to start shouting back. Then, once I start shouting, it is very hard for me to notice when a trigger is now getting too much for me, too. So, this is not an easy path. Once my bubble pops, I am vulnerable again. If I am working on my baggage when this happens, then this is going to hurt. I'm probably already feeling both vulnerable and raw.

Restoring the nervous system to optimal regulation takes a real desire to get there and discipline to practice. Practitioners of all kind can help, from somatic psychotherapists to tai chi masters. Groups help, from group therapy, to 12-step meetings. Friends, family and even nature can help. And it is worth it. Bessel van der Kolk's book, the Body Keeps the Score, is a great compendium of what works for whom. You can find the details in the Further Resources section of this book.

I know from my own experience that to have a biology inside of me that feels safe is utterly transformational. My whole experience of life shifts from an awareness of threat, to an openness to the possible goodness of life, but it takes work. And instructions (like this book). And it can be completely annoying; having people telling you what to do or how to do it is annoying.

However, the intention of those original spiritual and community leaders thousands of years ago may just have been as simple as trying to help people to restore their dysregulated nervous systems, long before there was any real science, healthcare or education to help them in these other ways. So, once you understand the story of the nervous system, it's not really that annoying after all.

Dysregulation Squared

I hope that by now it is clear that the nervous system in a human mammal is a fragile thing and that there are ways in which we have tried to help ourselves to cope with that for thousands of years. The consequence of the story of the nervous system seems to be exactly what we see in real life. We have all sorts of problems which we have come to talk about as problems in our minds, bodies and behaviour. All of this is a result of a dysregulated nervous system. It's messy.

So far, we have looked at the problems of one nervous system trying to regulate itself. We've looked at the ways in which we might be able to help ourselves do this better, and we've seen how difficult and sometimes unsuccessful it can be. On our own, we can fall down, pick ourselves up, reset and try again. But that is a model of a world of one. This is only the beginning of the problem, the very tip of the dysregulation iceberg. I'm afraid it gets much worse.

What happens when more than one person is doing this? Even if you look at two people at a time, the downside of dysregulation is going to be chaos squared. In the real world, no one is doing this alone. That's where life really gets interesting and where we will most easily recognise the powerful effects of a nervous system in everyday life: when we look at multiple nervous systems together.

PART THREE

WHAT THE LION LOOKS LIKE

REVIEW OF PARTS ONE AND TWO

Let's look at what we have learned so far about the nervous system.

We know that it gets dysregulated after many incidences of not completing its responses to a threat.

This results in us having two problems, which we often think are unrelated. The first one is that our bodies then start to have a different biology that we sometimes call physical health problems.

The second is that our behaviour changes. We start to live in a different reality, where an imaginary lion is present. We need this lion to make sense of our new biology, instead of thinking that we're going crazy. This then changes our reactions to the world and ourselves.

Each of these problems cause what we then sometimes call mental health problems; if I'm anxious, or shouting, or drinking, it all goes in the same box.

This fits with how we have historically looked at health in different ways, at different times, in different societies, through three different lenses, and is often called mind, body and spirit.

We can explain physical health problems that seem to have no obvious cause (medically unexplained symptoms) and most mental health problems, all of which have no obvious organic cause.

We have diagrams to represent these problems. This is the picture of our threat cycle, resulting in dysregulation and an imaginary lion living with us all the time.

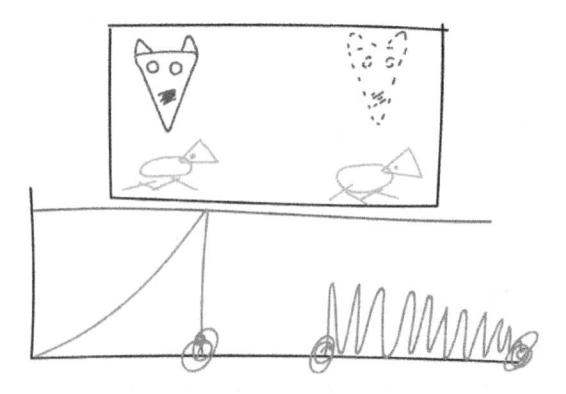

We can also model a dysregulated nervous system attempting to function in the real world, where its baggage meets triggers. Our behaviour shows up naturally in the consequences, which we call our reactions.

These resulting reactions can be turned into something resembling a well-regulated nervous system by using boundaries and containment. And we noted that this is also how organised forms of healing (which have sometimes in the past been called spiritual paths) encourage people to behave.

This makes sense, given the importance of regulating and stabilising the nervous system before trying to heal it. When it goes well, we go from one of these patterns of behaviour to this one.

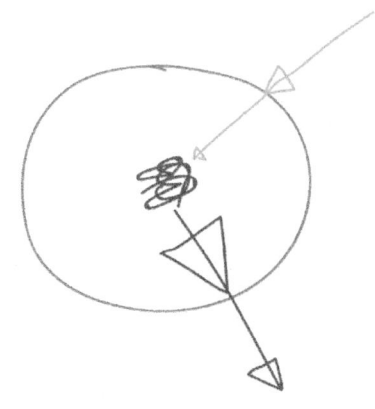

This makes it possible to begin the deeper work of healing the nervous system by discharging its baggage to get it to here.

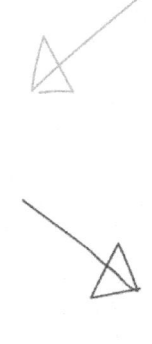

7. WHEN NERVOUS SYSTEMS MEET

What You Will Learn

When any one person interacts with another, a relationship happens. These relationships sit on a spectrum from the transient, like a barista you buy your coffee from, the functional, like work colleagues, the social, like acquaintances, to the significant and intimate, like close friends, family or partners. Each of these are materially influenced and can even be defined by the forces of regulation or dysregulation in the nervous system on each side of that relationship.

If you take our basic premise that people are either over-reacting, under-reacting or getting it just right, it turns out that you can have six different kinds of relationships between two people. And getting to the one you really want is less difficult than you think because now you know the story of the nervous system.

Dysregulated Together

As we have seen, our reactions to things are not always ideally matched to the reality that they are reacting to. But they may be the perfect reaction to something that has happened before. The potential to react in this way has been stored in our baggage. This can then be set off at any time by a trigger.

Sometimes, our reactions are so intense that we try not to show them at all, and that's when we have an under-reaction, which looks like no reaction at all. Neither of these over-reactions or under-reactions fit the trigger. They are too much or too little. Only the Goldilocks nervous system, which is perfectly regulated, gets it just right. This gives us, roughly speaking, three kinds of reaction: under-reaction, over-reaction and just right.

So, we now know what the invisible lion feels like, and this is very familiar from our own experiences of ourselves; from health problems to behavioural problems, to just the general experience of how chaotic it feels to try to live a normal life. But what does it look like when we meet it in others?

Imagine these people meeting each other. I'm going to characterise each of these reaction styles as a separate person, although we know that someone can behave like any of these people at different times. Generally though, some people tend to be more like one of them than the other. We've probably all accused someone of being closed or shut down, or liable to overreact, or even easy going. That doesn't mean that they're like that all the time; we just like to describe people generally by their most common ways of behaving. If we take that as a starting point, we can see where it leads.

So, we have three kinds of people, like balls of three colours. How many different combinations of coloured balls could you create if you were asked to put two of them together? The answer is six. And remember, these could be any relationships, friends, family, someone you met on a bus, colleagues or a lover. Here they are.

1. Over-reaction with Over-reaction

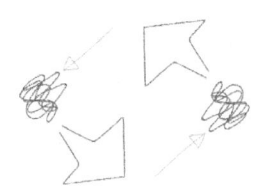

2. Under-reaction with Under-reaction

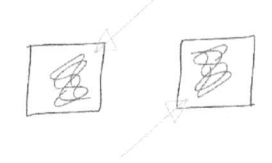

3. Over-reaction with Under-reaction

4. Goldilocks with Over-reaction

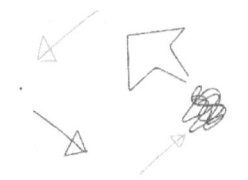

5. Goldilocks with Under-reaction 6. Goldilocks with Goldilocks

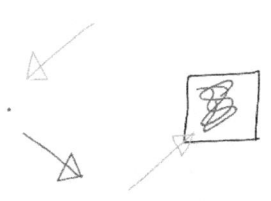

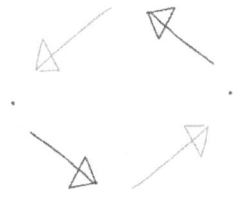

Each of these pairings is going to have different dynamics. Let's look at them in turn and see if we can find anything familiar. To do this, we are going to take each diagram and imagine that it comes to life in real time. Two different things then happen.

Firstly, the triggers hit the baggage and create reactions, which then become the next person's trigger. And so on.

Secondly, when two people (or two nervous systems) come into contact with each other, there is the possibility for each of them to move closer together, or farther apart.

When you imagine these two different ways for one of these diagrams to come to life, something interesting starts to happen.

Over-Reaction In A Relationship With An Over-Reaction

I think it's clear what is going to happen here. If we animate this cycle, the triggers get bigger and bigger as the reactions from one person become the next person's trigger. So, it blows up very quickly. And if we allow these two people to move, they will fly apart from each other quite soon.

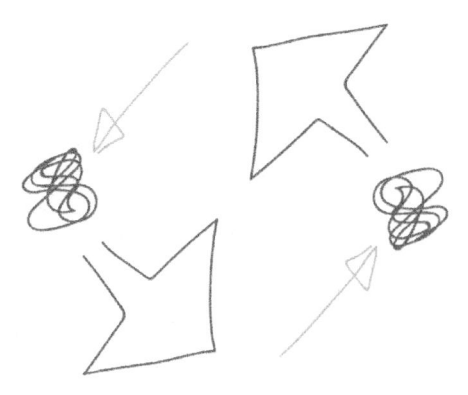

We've all either known relationships like this or been in them. They tend not to survive very long in a normal setting, like the workplace, but there are two special circumstances where they do because of the desire to hold the relationship together, whatever the cost.

Usually, this is because of family ties and something we call 'being in love'. Relatives and lovers will go through these cycles many times, even if they are aware of how badly their interactions typically end. There can be so much need and hope bound up in these special relationships that giving up on them becomes virtually impossible.

Maybe that is a good thing. Families are important, and their relationships can be very nurturing. But, these kinds of explosive relationships can also be very damaging. At their most extreme, they may result in violence. Crucially, they also don't help either individual to start to heal their nervous systems. With these constant explosions, there is no sense of safety to support the discharge of the baggage. It just isn't possible when so many new threats are being experienced.

If relationships like this can't be avoided, then they

can at least be helped by putting some extra space between the people in it. This can help them be in this cycle less often and for a shorter time. This relationship can only become less damaging in the long-term if each party gets to grips with their baggage. The first step towards this is boundaries and containment, but that may be hard to achieve without some help.

Under-Reaction In A Relationship With An Under-Reaction

By contrast, these two people are as docile as they come. Nothing moves at all.

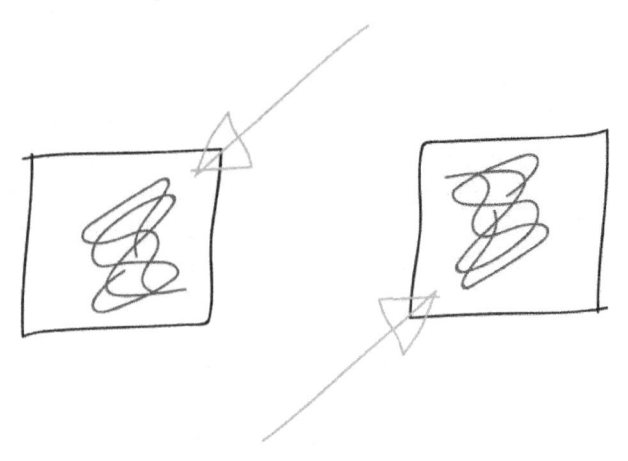

There is very little connection in this model; both people are so checked out of communicating with each other that you wonder why they are together in the first place. But, in some relationships, like colleagues at work, you can see that it might suit their circumstances perfectly to be so cautious and measured in how they interact.

While this relationship is not damaging, it is not nurturing, either. There is no healing here. Instead, it looks a lot like life on pause. At some point, each of these people needs to feel safe enough to start expressing their reactions, rather than holding onto them. But that's going to be very hard to do unless they find someone who feels a little more nurturing to be with, or who feels safer to be nurtured by them. They might drift apart and come back together again, but it feels like there is no dynamic here anyway.

People can hide out in this kind of zombie state for a very long time. Some might even say that most of us are, to one extent or another, living this kind of life or stuck in this kind of relationship. It is not always obvious. We don't have to look like zombies to be sleepwalking through life.

Gabriella Part One

Gabriella was the kind of person that others just wanted to be around. Attractive, energetic and smart, she brought any room to life. Everyone either wanted to be her or to be with her. And she was the last person you'd expect to have problems in relationships. Surely she could have anyone she wanted?

And yet her experience was so different. She came from an ordinary family. Her father was a policeman who had worked hard and provided well for his family. She had an older sister who had always been a bit severe. Her mother was clearly a problem though, having suffered with episodes of something that had been labelled bipolar disorder for all of Gabby's life.

It was at its worst after her sister was born and the girls had grown up around the fluctuations of their mother's condition. Generally, they dealt with it well, with humour even. It was almost like it was another member of the family; so much so, that when they were young, their father would talk about mummy's friend who could come to visit. During these times, Gabby's mother was hard to reach. Sometimes she would stare out of the window for what seemed like hours. Occasionally, her father had to come home from work. Family and friends would help out too. They muddled through. It was the only family Gabby and her sister ever knew, and, so the only upbringing they had; to them it was normal. And after all, no one died, the family was together and they lacked for nothing materially. This was a good life really.

Gabby's twenties were a whirlwind. She got a break in marketing and was irrepressible, becoming successful, very young. She was always at the centre of glamorous people and events. She had a string of enviable lovers. This worked well for her, as long as the party was in full swing. She noticed, though, that when life was more ordinary, something was definitely missing. If she was ill, for example, no one was there to make her soup and look after her in her pyjamas. These were not the kind of relationships she had.

She drifted away from her sister, and, to a certain extent, from her parents. Gabby's sister still lived with them, and although the thought of living at home as an adult filled Gabby with horror, sometimes she also felt a pang of jealousy about her sister still being there. She particularly felt that her father was now very focused on her sister, and although she was glad he was there for her, she somehow felt abandoned by both of them. Her mother, meanwhile, was becoming a stranger in her life. She didn't reach out to Gabby, and this pattern of disengagement continued until it became the norm. Very occasionally, Gabby noticed that she felt furious with her mother, but this quickly gave way to the family story about her mother's illness and the need to be compassionate about that. Anyway, Gabby was doing well. She had the perfect life. Her family's difficulties were behind her.

Gabby was successful in PR because she could make other people feel happy. She'd learned to do that for her father as a child, stuffing her reactions into that black box so that she can perform. Her whole life had been an act. Perhaps every work relationship she ever had was exactly like this one above. Everyone was pretending and so no one was connecting.

In the place of any nurturing relationships, superficiality ran riot. Gabby's life was always about finding the next lifestyle high, the next boyfriend, the next party, the next pay-check. All of these things might be great fun, and no one would blame her for enjoying them, but it was not a life lived with relationships, it was a life lived instead of them. And this included her relationship with her father, which then showed up later in her relationships with men.

She was pretending to have a great relationship with her father. In fact, they were both acting out the under-reaction with under-reaction dynamic above. He was trying to keep it together by hiding his reactions from the whole family and she was learning to do the same. That's why they drifted apart in adult life; the relationship lacked connection. Gabby was aware, at the edges of this experience, of the occasional flashes of anger, resentment and abandonment she felt towards him. These momentary experiences confused her. That wasn't how she was with her father, was it?

So, this dynamic is more common that we might first guess. In subtle ways, it might be how we survive most of our relationships at home, work and play. But eventually you have to ask the question, is this enough? How much does it cost you to hide out like this? In the end, arguably, it would cost Gabby everything.

Under-Reaction In A Relationship With An Over-Reaction

In this dynamic, the excess reaction created by the first person's baggage is getting dumped into the second person's black box, and staying there along with all of that person's own reactions. This is going to create an awful lot of overwhelm in that second person's nervous system.

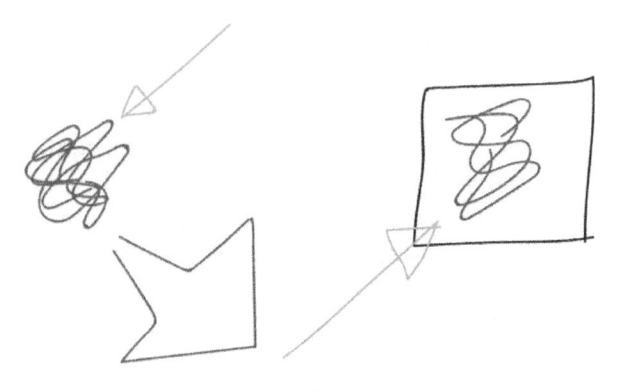

The basic problem with an under-reaction is that it gives you less activation than you need to provide yourself with a normal level of safety, and that's how people end up staying in abusive relationships.

Remember that the nervous system's purpose is to regulate how we respond to threat? If we don't respond at all, we can't keep ourselves safe from threat. If we are in an interaction with someone who is threatening, and we are stuck in under-reaction then we have no power to change that interaction and we end up at the mercy of the other person.

This kind of relationship can cause a lot of harm to both parties. The out-of-control person with the over-reaction doesn't benefit from this relationship either.

No one is pushing back on that over-reaction, so they are learning nothing about how to start to regulate their own nervous systems. It's a messy situation with no winners.

Think about how these two would move in relation to each other. You would hope that the more vulnerable one would move away to safety. But the problem with under-reaction is that movement is constrained. When we hear stories of women being abused in domestic relationships, we wonder why they don't just get away. This is why. It is the shut-down, vulnerable nature of these people that makes them available to abuse in the first place, and then keeps them trapped there in their immobilised nervous systems.

In the end, it is likely that the under-reaction side of this relationship may become ill in one way or another. There is so much unprocessed material being stored up in that body and it becomes unsustainable. When there is no access to discharging the unfinished reactions to earlier threats, the body absorbs a lot, and this changes its bio-physiology. This might even end up looking like the kind of medically unexplained symptoms we thought about in Part Two.

But it is not always that obvious.

Gabriella Part Two

Just when everything seemed to be going so well, Gabby fell in love! David was a catch. She'd had attractive boyfriends before, but this was different. She felt like something of what she had been missing her whole life was put right with him. He was really there for her. He got her. Nothing ever seemed to be too much for him. He always took time to put her first, despite his incredibly high-pressured job. He seemed, well, perfect.

Gabby started to calm down her social life a little and spend more time with David, going to events with his friends, supporting his work. She liked how that felt. It gave her the sense that they were becoming a team. She even spent a holiday weekend with his family, who seemed refreshingly normal, despite all being extraordinarily high-achievers. Life was good, finally! She had a glimpse of where her future might be going a million miles away from where she grew up.

When David wanted to meet Gabby's family, she was hesitant. She wondered how much he would judge her once he met her low-achieving sister and her entirely unpredictable mother. She also felt weird about her father. She couldn't say why, but thinking of her father and David in the same room made her feel angry, sulky even, like a nightmare teenager. She wanted to avoid it, but she and David started to row about her reluctance to let him meet her family. David seemed to resent not being included in her life, but she thought she was protecting him. She didn't know if he could handle the kind of life she had grown up with.

But there was something more. She felt in control when she went into David's world. She could immerse herself in it, and then withdraw. What would happen if he met her family and it all went well? How would she handle that? For the first time since they met, she realised that although her initial focus had been on evaluating David and trying to make sure he liked her, she was now much more nervous about what would happen if he did! She'd never had a boyfriend before who stuck around in that way, and now she was feeling suffocated, claustrophobic even. She reacted by going back to type. She became Gabby the marketing girl.

She went on a charm offensive with David, planning his favourite things, being gracious and fun with his family and friends. At the same time, she started to actively manage her own *life in a much more strategic way. She organised social occasions with her own friends and included David and his friends. This made her feel much more in control than if he just hung out with her friends on his own. And she invited her family to town. She booked them a hotel and planned out the whole weekend, scheduling the whole thing perfectly and including David in everything. It worked. Nothing went wrong. David wasn't rowing with her anymore. She wasn't overwhelmed.*

But she felt terrible.

In this story, Gabby has taken over and everyone else is going along with it like deer in the headlights. She is the one having an over-reaction, and David is doing the under-reaction. Gabby has become out of control. She has transitioned from the under-reacting state she gets into with her father, which is progress, and is now over-reacting, because she feels safer with David than with her father.

In fact, David was an opportunity to heal the under-reaction to under-reaction dynamic she had with her father. If they had both been able to recognise this and work on it, then David could have acted as a kind of a safe proxy, allowing her to do this relationship all over again, but, this time, to have her reactions in a safer way.

However, neither of them understood the nervous system, and so Gabby started to take over to manage how unmanageable her own reactions were becoming. She did this with so much charm that everyone around her is just shutting down as she steamrollers through. But no one is happy. There is no love, no joy, no connection. And, bafflingly, although she gets everything she wants, she ends up miserable.

Goldilocks In Relationship With An Over-Reaction

In the diagram below of a regulated nervous system on the left and a dysregulated nervous system on the right, the person on the left has a normal reaction to a trigger. This then becomes the trigger for the person on the right, which then creates a much larger reaction.

As before, the triggers and reactions will start to get bigger and bigger in this circle if the two people stay together, although this will now happen less quickly than if both nervous systems were dysregulated. Each time you go around the loop, the over-reaction from one side escalates the situation. Eventually, even a well-regulated nervous system is overwhelmed.

At this point, the well-regulated nervous system would start to move away in order to stay regulated.

So, if the person on the left moves to the left, to get away from the overwhelm from the person on the right, how do you think the person on the right would respond to that? They start to chase after them of course. After all, it's no fun having an over-reaction on your own. In fact, over-reactors typically need someone else to project their reaction onto, otherwise they have to feel all that unpleasant activation on their own. They need an emotional dustbin.

So, the better regulated person leaves, with the out-of-control person pursuing them. Does that remind you of anything? You can see this relationship all over social media, for instance. One person will make a reasonable point about anything from global warming, to which is the best biscuit to have with a cup of tea, and someone else will go completely bonkers. The first person then calmly restates their point and leaves the conversation. The out of control person typically then gets the last word in, with escalating rage, insults and capital letters.

Anonymous exchanges are good illustrations of this because they are uninhibited by real-life contact. In our daily lives, a similar dynamic exists in our relationships. They might be less extreme, but the pattern is the same. You could say that Gabby had a relationship like this with her mother when her mother was out of control. She would try to keep things on an even keel, but then just got out of there as soon as she could. When this dynamic repeats over and over again, the person who is trying to get some distance might end up staying away for good.

This is often how families get estranged or how romantic relationships end. People want to stay connected for all sorts of reasons, but they just can't take the over-reactions anymore. Eventually, they fade away or give up.

And the person on the left might, in fact, be an imposter; someone with a dysregulated nervous system who's just good at boundaries and containment, so they look like someone who gets it just right. This might be harder for them than it looks because in order to stay that way, they might have had to move away from this relationship which was too overwhelming.

It is understandable, but this is an opportunity missed. The less well-regulated person could learn a lot and feel safer if they were able to stay in this relationship, but, to do that, they would have to modify their behaviour. This is where boundaries and containment come to the rescue.

Goldilocks In Relationship With An Under-Reaction

The person on the right is so overwhelmed by themselves that they are frozen. They have no reactions at all. What do you think would happen next in this scenario in real life?

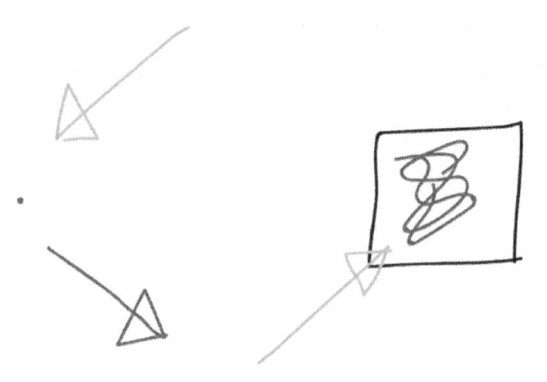

Not much. Whatever the person on the left puts into the situation, they get nothing back. It probably isn't a very exciting relationship for either side. There is no drama or fuss, nothing is getting broken in the kitchen, but, equally, there is no connection.

It seems obvious that something has to pass from one side to another for there to be any kind of connection. When someone is shut down and they only show an under-reaction, it can be really hard to feel connected to them. So, where does this relationship go next? The person on the right is too frozen to move in either direction, right or left. Probably the well-regulated person initially moves towards them, seeking some kind of response or interaction, but the black box will not let anything out, so, in the end, if this continues, the person on the left probably just drifts away.

When this happens in a family or romantic relationship, it is usually a long, drawn-out dying of something that was once there. With no glue between these two people anymore, the relationship evaporates. You might recognise this dynamic in your life. This is how I would picture Gabby's relationship with her sister, who was so shut down from her early childhood that she was never really available for Gabby to connect to. This continued in adult life, and, eventually, Gabby just drifted away. No fireworks. No defining moment when the relationship was over. It just drifted into no man's land.

People report marriages like this. One side of the couple says that the other is uncommunicative. They might feel it as rejection, like they are not worth talking to. But if they don't know about the story of the nervous system, they don't know it's actually quite the opposite; this is a sign that nothing can be done or said because there is so much that needs to be done or said that the nervous system shuts down in overwhelm.

The passivity, the silence, the evasion can all be interpreted as a cry for help from inside the walls of that lonely black box.

And it is very lonely in there. You can see that

above. There is nothing emerging to connect with anyone else. There is no tether to hold this person safely in place. This closed-down under-reacting person might easily end up alone, and, in part, this might be a relief, but they are left with their baggage and no one to help them with the process of healing it.

These kinds of relationships are often characterised by sadness, rather than the anger of more explosive ones. In the end, people just can't reach each other, which is the opposite of what they need to recover. If only they could open up a bit without exploding. What would that look like?

Goldilocks In Relationship With Goldilocks

Now, that is just right! Imagine a world where every reaction to every trigger was perfectly balanced. This is not an artificial world, but one where there is no baggage and people are free to interact in a way which makes perfect sense to their immediate environment at any given time. How they find the world is how they treat it.

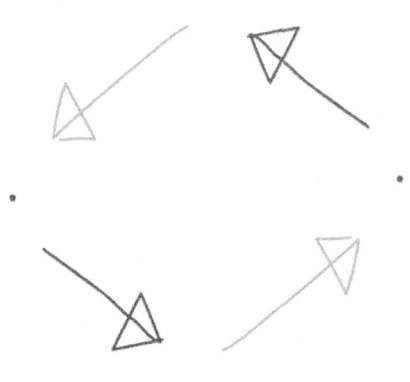

I don't know about you, but I feel instantly more relaxed, just looking at the diagram above. This is the world we all want to live in. As we have seen in Part Two, we can start to make that happen for ourselves and for others with boundaries and containment; it is possible to fake it until you make it. We can choose to begin that journey today. It might look like this.

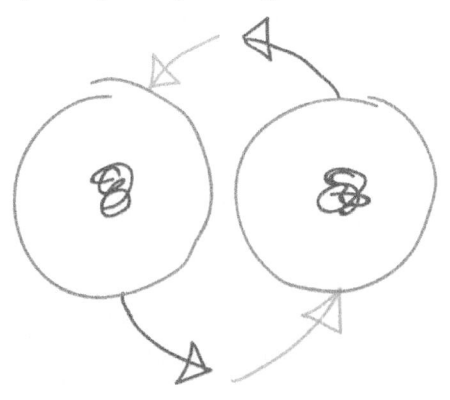

These two people have dysregulated nervous systems but by using boundaries and containment, they are simulating the behaviour of people with no baggage. In Part Four of this book, I'm going to explain how to do this. Both of these people might have been in the previous two types of relationship, where someone was over-reacting or under-reacting, but, by changing their management of their nervous systems, perhaps even just a little, they have been able to move into relationships that seem to be perfect, at least on the outside. It takes a lot of work on the inside, but the rewards are worth it.

When people can come together in safe, manageable relationships like this, they have the potential to hold each other in a way which allows their nervous systems to settle and to heal.

How do you see the two people above moving relative to each other? They have the space and regulation to wobble gently back and forth. They can occupy adjacent space together, and it seems to be easy. Coming and going is no problem. It is safe to be close and also safe to move a little further away. If you have ever had a really great housemate, I think this is the kind of relationship you may have had. It's easy to talk through problems together, and you can come and go without triggers and reactions. Either there is no baggage, or you just don't set each other off.

Gabriella Part Three

During that weekend when she choreographed David meeting her family, Gabriella's father had asked her what was wrong. She resented the question. Her mother had been on good form; she'd been a little distant, but not frozen, which was a great relief, so that wasn't the problem. Gabby's relationship with her sister was still difficult. She would occasionally experience flashes of anger when it seemed to her that her sister was being pathetic, but Gabby stage-managed herself beautifully. And everything had gone exactly as planned. So, when her father asked her what was wrong, she was blindsided. Nothing. Her life was perfect. David was perfect. The weekend was perfect. He had no right to know that she was dying inside. It was none of his business.

Three weeks after her family had come to visit, David invited Gabby to go away with him for a romantic weekend at a beautiful hotel. She asked him what the special occasion was, and he said that he wanted to talk to her. All her friends speculated that he was going to ask her to marry him. She, of course, told them they were crazy, but a part of her could see it coming too. She was thrilled, but also terrified. She wanted him to want to propose, but she didn't want to deal with the pressure of answering the question. She gave herself a pep-talk to just be open to what might happen. She knew that this was the right thing at the right time in her life. It all just made sense. She needed to play her part.

The weekend started fabulously. Gabby and David had a wonderful time together, and it seemed like in a moment, it was already Saturday evening. Gabby sensed something in the air and felt butterflies in her stomach. She couldn't bear the tension, so, over drinks, she asked David what it was he wanted to talk about. He looked nervous, a bit uncomfortable. She was composed and told him just to take his time and not be scared. Relieved, he said that he'd been thinking a lot about their relationship and he felt that things were going too fast.

He wanted to go back to how things were before. He thought that maybe he had been wrong to push her to introduce him to her family and he wanted to apologise. He could tell that she hadn't been happy that weekend and he felt it was better to just concentrate on what they did best, which was having fun and not taking things too seriously, like on this weekend break.

Gabby was gobsmacked. Even though she hadn't really wanted David to ask her to marry him, Gabby certainly didn't want him to not want to marry her. The relationship soon fell apart. David didn't like the person Gabby now became: angry, resentful, demanding. That wasn't the Gabby he had met. And so he moved on quickly to the next party girl. Gabby was left devastated. Guess what she did next? She threw herself back into work. Once again, she excelled at everything. She made all her clients and friends feel special. She thrived. But inside she was dying.

This is what she had been doing her whole life. This was why she was so angry with her father and distant from her mother and sister. She had been keeping them happy by burying her pain. That was the only way she could cope. She now made a fabulous living using those skills, always making everyone else feel good about themselves. She sold it so well. But no one was ever there for her.

Gabby had a series of increasingly disastrous relationships in her thirties and forties, each time with men who were more and more charming, and harder and harder to pin down. She told herself she longed for something different, but she always went for the same man. She never married or had children. Her mother then died and this was a tipping point for Gabby. She gave up everything she knew and moved home to live with her father and sister, to look after them. Her sister's mental health by this point was not good, and her father was lost without her mother.

When she looked back on her life, Gabby would say that these years she spent at home with her father were the happiest of her life. But they were also the opposite of what everyone else thought was her life. How could this make any sense? The most perfect girl they all knew ended up alone, unattached and childless, nursing her ailing father. No one could make any sense of it at all. But they didn't know the story of the nervous system.

Maybe Gabby started with a Goldilocks relationship with David? When we fall in love, there's a flood of new chemicals in our system that change all of our biological pathways. The nervous system is just a hardwired biochemical mechanism, so, if you put new chemicals in, you will get a different result. The biology of falling in love actually lowers our reactivity so that our baggage doesn't fire off in the same way as normal.

This explains what people describe as the honeymoon period of new romantic relationships; nothing is a problem and everything is good, just like a Goldilocks relationship. But, eventually, the chemicals wear off and the cracks begin to show. David had started to feel the triggers of being excluded from Gabby's family. This seemed to press his buttons, and, from there, everything began to go sideways.

Who We Chose

It seems that we have a canny, unconscious knack of finding people, places and things that trigger our baggage in the way which we least want. And it is not just in love. Over time, we can learn about our baggage and try to hide from experiences that trigger it, but it usually doesn't work. People often end up having the same relationships over and over again, at work, at home and with their families, and especially in love.

Perhaps this is because I always have the same baggage, so my experiences feel the same with any different person, but it could also be that we are all exceptionally talented at sniffing out the triggers we need to try to activate our baggage so that we can heal it.

Whichever one the problem is (and it is probably a bit of both), it is incredibly frustrating! We can go round and round in circles with either the same person or new people, who are basically the same person in disguise, and this plays out in all kinds of ways in every possible setting of our lives. Basically, if there is another nervous system there, this is what's going to happen.

People leave relationships, jobs, towns, even countries, and find that they end up back where they started. They could give up, but that's not the way forward. The holy grail of relationships is to try to offer the Goldilocks relationship above, regardless of how difficult it is to do so. Not an over-reaction. Not an under-reaction. Practicing boundaries and containment to see if you can do something differently.

You could do that right now, in the next minute, with someone in your life. Just pick up the phone and send a text without using the word "you".

The people in a Goldilocks to Goldilocks relationship might in fact be highly dysregulated, but they are working to manage that, and, therefore, successfully managing to be in relationship. Anyone can improve the quality of their relationships in any area of their lives at any time, just by understanding that the perfect relationship doesn't exist for most people unless they are willing to be a partner in creating it. People are learning to manage their own dysregulated nervous systems in relationship every day, and doing a great job of it.

It is hard work, but having better relationships is always, always possible. I will explain in more detail in Part Four of this book, and you can practice it every day, now that you know the story of the nervous system.

8. HOW NERVOUS SYSTEMS FORM ATTACHMENTS

What You Will Learn

So far, we have built a model of the way people behave with each other and seen how these dynamics are both caused by dysregulation in the nervous system and can impact on another person's dysregulated nervous system. If this model is correct, then these patterns should show up in real life. Of course, lots of work has already been done to try to explain why people are the way they are. If our story of the nervous system is correct, then it should show up in all of these pre-existing theories.

In the next three chapters we will examine this suggestion to see if it works, starting with attachment; the relationships between mothers and their babies.

Understanding attachment

Attachment is the term given to a very special situation, when one nervous system is a baby or a child and the other nervous system in this relationship is their primary caregiver. We can build this model of behaviour just like we did with the pairings of two nervous systems earlier in this chapter, but, this time, one of the people in the diagram is always going to appear to be dysregulated.

Babies have a narrow range of being able to regulate their own nervous systems. As they grow they increase their capacity to be more regulated, but while they are learning to do this they often need someone's help to regulate. When things are going well, we do this naturally for children. For example, it is innate to parenting to soothe a baby. We hold it or swaddle it, sing, rock and coo until it is calm again.

Each of these activities is a mechanical intervention which settles the baby's nervous system. Touch, sound and movement are all hardwired into the nervous system and you can effectively hack this part of the body by using these methods. We still do it as adults; most of us can say that after a massage we feel calmer, or that we use music to feel more balanced, or that we feel better after a good dance.

A new-born may exist outside of the womb, but psychologically, it is not born yet. The time between physical birth and psychological birth is a very important and vulnerable time. This is when we learn from our mothers to regulate our nervous systems. Without that first step, it is going to be very hard to find regulation in later life. That's why this period, typically thought to be from birth to about three years of age, is given special consideration when discussing human relationships. And that is the study of attachment that has been going for well over fifty years. Dan Seigel has done some very compelling work on it recently through the lens of neurobiology and anatomy.

Attachment Styles

We can use our models of relationships from the earlier sections to look at the different kinds of dynamics that might occur between baby and mother. The word mother here is used as a shorthand for the baby's closest caregiver, which usually is its actual mother. Mothers are set up to do this job really well because they have a biological connection to the baby from the first moments of life. However, fathers and other relatives of any gender, even unrelated carers, have all been observed to do it well enough to allow the baby to learn to regulate for itself.

So, let's start with the baby. This nervous system is vulnerable and not yet able to fully regulate itself. So, although it has no baggage it can look a lot like a dysregulated adult. It currently has no boundaries, no containment, nor the capacity to choose to do either of these things. It needs a parent to take care of this need. In an ideal world, the parent would be well-regulated, and the dynamic would look like this.

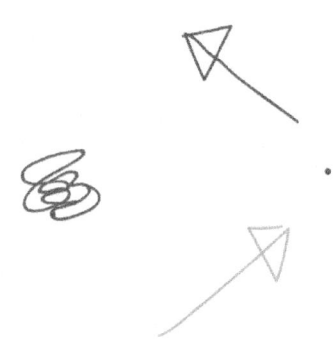

With this model of a parenting relationship, our unregulated new born would begin to build the internal experience of regulation by experiencing the adult's regulation in relation to its own distress. Over time, this is mimicked so that the growing child starts to be able to regulate on their own. This is how the child gets to learn how to manage its own experience in relation to the world during its first few years of life. It allows the two of them to grow into a nicely regulated relationship, which will turn out to be the ideal dynamic below.

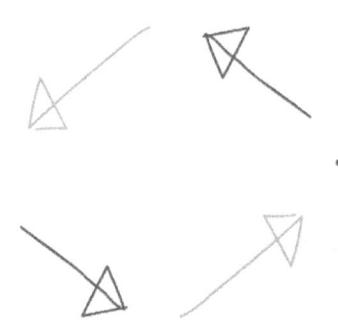

This is called secure attachment. The child is secure and grows up to have secure attachments in adult life and, therefore, better relationships. Not just romantic relationships; by and large, all of their relationships stand a good chance of being secure and functioning well. Family, friends and colleagues will all benefit from this person being able to bring a well-regulated nervous system to the messy business of getting along with other humans.

But that's not the end of the story. If you look at the first diagram of the baby and the mother, I wonder if you can guess how many other types of attachment there are. If the baby on the left is always the same, how could the other side of the diagram vary? Who are the other types of people we could put in there as caregivers and what would that look like? Well, as we know, there are two other nervous system types to throw into the mix. And, as it happens, there are two more common types of attachment, resistant and avoidant.

Resistant Attachment

Let's look at the dynamic with an over-reaction from a caregiver.

Can you imagine how this works out for the baby? If most of the care they receive is like this, then they will be constantly overwhelmed by the unfinished business in their mother's baggage. The baby isn't going to feel safe and they are not going to learn to regulate their own nervous systems from this person. In fact, they are likely to find it hard to manage this relationship at all. It's far from ideal.

This child forms what is known as a 'resistant attachment', characterised by outbursts of anger and ambivalence. The anger will probably get more obvious as they get older, because the bigger and stronger they are, the safer it is to fight instead of to freeze. This could explain the so-called terrible twos.

Avoidant Attachment

But what if the mother was in an under-reaction instead? Certainly, things would be quite different, but still not okay with this dynamic.

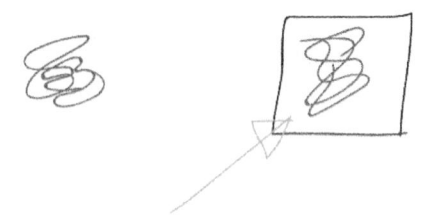

This baby is going to struggle to maintain a satisfying, nourishing connection with this mother. There isn't interaction or emotional response coming back to the baby to teach it how to regulate its own nervous system. This baby is going to be underwhelmed, rather than overwhelmed. Over time, this child will not be learning how to stay regulated in a relationship.

On the surface, it may seem like this is less

threatening at least less than the over-reacting caregiver relationship, but unfortunately the neglect in this relationship is likely to be equally bad at helping the child to grow its own well-regulated nervous system. Instead, it will be disengaged and mimic the behaviour of this primary caregiver in its early relationships and go on to have an 'avoidant attachment' style.

Attachment Research

During the initial work done on attachment theory back in the 1950s, researchers began to see that children who did not appear to have secure attachment separated into two different types. When they put them in a stressful situation by removing the parent temporarily, one of these types was characterised by outbursts when their parent returned to the room. The other type acted distant and indifferent. Does this remind you of anyone? Both sets of children were experiencing the threat of not having their caregiver around. They had the same trigger, but one type was having an over-reaction and the other an under-reaction.

When researchers looked at how these children's home lives were generally functioning, it seemed that the children who experienced an over-reaction in the home would grow up to have the kind of nervous system that overreacted when they experienced threat, whereas those who experienced distance and under-reaction in the home became shut down when dealing with threat. So, the children who grew up around shut-down parents had less ability to express anything at all, and the children who grew up around over-reacting parents were more out of control.

The children's nervous systems were being born primarily during their first three years of life, but instead of starting life nicely regulated, they were learning to find a set point to match their parents; just like in the secure attachment example, but without something well-regulated to internalise.

Attachment Recovery

Both sets of parents and children were observed to be either just about right, or too reactive, or too disengaged. This is exactly what you would expect from our story of the nervous system.

It seems that the type of dysregulation in the mother translates into a similar problem in the baby. And that's why this first relationship really matters. We actually affect the regulation or dysregulation of babies with our own regulation or lack of it. If we want children to grow up into well-regulated adults, then we have to give them the best possible start for their own nervous system before their independent lives begin. As we saw in Part One of this book, even a well-regulated nervous system can be vulnerable to becoming dysregulated by life's subsequent events. But a good beginning gives us somewhere to anchor back to. The goal of the nervous system is to get back to where it started from; therefore, this set point which it returns to is critical.

The good news for worried parents is that even with our dysregulated nervous systems, we can practice boundaries and containment to simulate a well-regulated nervous system and this is likely to be good enough for a baby to develop healthily. The idea is not to replace yourself with a mythically perfect parent, but to recognise what that would look like and to try to approximate to it.

Even if your children are fifty-years-old, you can still parent and nurture their nervous systems by offering them this dynamic. Although the brain is not growing as it did in childhood, it remains plastic into old age. It is never too late to be a better-regulated parent to your child, or even to someone else's. Just fake it until you make it. The good news is that you now know how to do this: by using boundaries and containment.

Disorganised Attachment

One of our many complexities is that we do not always behave in only one way. Just looking at Gabby's short case-study, you can see that she is a different nervous system in different situations.

So far, we have developed our model of human behaviour out of a very simple, linear way of looking at the nervous system and its dysregulation. It is true that in any given situation, my nervous system will provide me with what is either an over-reaction, an under-reaction or something just right, a Goldilocks reaction, but sometimes it is more complex. Attachment researchers found that some babies did not fit into any of the three types I've mentioned above.

They appeared chaotic, and their style of attachment to their caregiver was labelled disorganised attachment, a name reflecting the observation that their behaviour did not fit into one of the three types of organised attachments seen above. Our neat model of human behaviour starts to break down here because real life can be messier than even my drawings.

When researchers looked more deeply at where these kids came from, they saw that there were high levels of what they considered to be abuse and neglect in the home. It seemed that, as a result, no dominant style of nervous system dysregulation emerged in the babies.

Underlying this disorganisation are the same fundamentals that inform us about the nervous system. Babies, like all mammals, are looking for safety. They are also trying to avoid threat. And when they are young, they need someone to do both for them. We know that babies need a safe caregiver to model a nicely regulated nervous system. Now, if this same person they're relying on to teach them the biological building blocks of dealing with threats becomes a threat themselves, then this is the worst possible scenario. The place the baby needs to go to to learn how to manage threat is a threat itself. This traps the baby's nervous system between safety and danger; the baby doesn't know where to go.

The result is a fragmentation into different behaviours and styles that don't seem to make sense; they are dis-organised because the body is disorganised. If I tell you to quickly stand up slowly, you can see what that feels like. This is disorganised attachment in relationships. It's agony.

9. HOW NERVOUS SYSTEMS FALL IN LOVE

What You Will Learn

We've seen how the story of the nervous system fits into the existing models of attachment for babies with their mothers. These babies grow up. Their attachment styles then affect how they fall in love. This can be messy. However, with some understanding of the nervous system, it can become a little clearer why we do what we do, and we can see that some existing theories of our dysfunctions in love are well-informed by the story of the nervous system.

Adult Attachment

You may have noticed that children grow up and have another go at forming intimate relationships after those with their family, even if their relationships in childhood weren't straightforward or even particularly healthy. However, we tend to end up being the person we learned to be when we were young. Attachment styles seem to predict the kinds of romantic relationships we have in later life and, once again, there is a parallel with our story of the nervous system.

So, how does that work out for everyone involved? If your set point from your early family life is under-reaction or over-reaction, then this is what you're used to. This is your normal and you typically go on to display under-reaction or over-reaction in relationships. Add on top of this dynamic the dysregulation people have accumulated throughout the rest of their lives and we have a recipe for unhealthy adult relationships.

One of the most compelling frameworks for understanding dysfunctional romantic relationships was popularised by Pia Mellody, and it describes the cycles of love addiction and love avoidance. Looking at how its description of the behaviour of people in love fits our story of the nervous system can help us to understand even the most baffling of relationships, including the sad story of Gabby and David.

The Love Addict

There are classic characters in love stories. Think about the archetypal Cinderella. And the perfect Prince Charming who comes along. Through the transformational power of love, all of her problems are removed and she is rescued from a life of neglect, slavery and abuse.

It's a famous and enduring story because we all buy into it. Most of us, at some point have had this fantasy of saving someone or being saved, or both. Gabby quickly came to believe that David was her Prince Charming and bought into the idea that, if only they were together, all her dreams would come true. And he was very charming. But how much of this was in the mind and how much was reality?

According to the theory of love addiction, people enter into this relationship in a state of fantasy. To fuel this fantasy, they have to tell themselves all sorts of stories to keep the idea alive that this person and only this person can make everything okay again. We've probably all been there at some point. We tell ourselves little lies about our crush. We ignore or overlook warning signs. We want desperately to believe in this relationship. Because we think that if we can get the right relationship, then all our pain will go away. And so we fantasise that this relationship is the right one.

Sound familiar? Well, then, you'll know that in the end, something happens to shatter the fantasy. Either we are confronted with a truth we can't deny any longer, or we are unable to maintain our fantasy any longer. Or, perhaps, the other person leaves. However it happens, it hurts like hell. These are the relationship break-ups that have people completely collapsed, crying in their bed for days on end, drowning their sorrows in drink, even killing themselves or others. It is completely shattering because so much of ourselves and our world has been placed in the hands of a mythical other. And then it all suddenly evaporates like a bursting soap bubble, leaving us with neither the fantasy nor a strong connection to ourselves.

Recovering from this wound, the heartbroken love addict will often obsess endlessly, or even go as far as stalking the other person. Eventually, there is the space and energy to start again. At this point, the love addict begins the cycle over again, either with the same person or someone else.

Why? What is the point of having a relationship which is, in fact, an illusion and hurts so much when it ends? And why do it again? Why not learn from the first time? The answer, of course, lies in the story of the nervous system.

Under-Reactions in Love

For the love addict, all their relationships start out as a way to fill some kind of void. And we have seen in our models of relationships and attachments that, nothing creates a void like having a main caregiver who is an under-reactor. The child is likely to behave the same way, with under-reactions as their own default set point in life. This is a bit like Cinderella. Her mother was dead and God knows what her father was doing, which left her in a situation with a stepmother who was not interested in meeting her needs. All three of them gave her nothing.

And so, Cinderella became an under-reactor herself, meekly complying with everything everyone wanted of her. She didn't fight. She didn't run. She gave up. This is the perfect example of a childhood nurtured by someone else's under-reactions. So, it makes sense that her fantasy would be for someone to come and fill the void.

This nervous system has not received enough connection in childhood, and, as a result, it's yearning for, and waiting for, more. That's why it needs everything from outside, from a relationship with a perfect person who can both fill the gap left by an un-nurturing childhood and provide the strength and power to protect her. Only a Prince Charming will do. However, in the real world, how many princes are there, really? The chances are that we will have to do some mental gymnastics to turn an ordinary bloke into that perfect partner. This seems to be what Gabby did with David.

Gabby's mother has been unreliable. Her father phoned in his help from a distance. Gabby's childhood was lacking presence. As an adult, she seemed to replicate the under-reaction she had learned by working in a world where it was normalised to have superficial relationships. Although she could put on a great show and might seem like the life and soul of the party, Gabby's daily life was characterised by a lack of real connection. Truth was, she regularly felt lonely, even though she was never alone. She needed someone to pierce through this veil of disinterest to heal the wounds she was hiding. So, she would go to any lengths to make up a story for herself about David, to believe that he was this person.

But what was going on for David, to make him want to make this same fantasy come true? What is his side of the attachment and nervous system story?

The Love Avoidant

David did everything right. Well, up until he left, that is. This is a dominant characteristic of the love avoidant. Love avoidants enter into a relationship out of a sense of overwhelm from their childhood. This is the person whose nervous system has been set up by their caregiver's over-reactions, which could be anger and violence, or just neediness and smothering. These over-reactions flooded the young person's system, and this became their set point for how to react. As an adult, this person is also out of control; perhaps rebellious, argumentative, maybe even ruthlessly charming.

The twist in this particular tale is that, actually, the charming prince is also desperate for help. It may seem counterintuitive, but that dashing rogue who sweeps you off your feet and seems to give you everything you want is actually just acting out of an over-reaction. This is not especially healthy. It's their way of compensating for a childhood when they were overwhelmed by someone else's reactions. It's as though their nervous system is saying, "If I can make you happy all of the time, then surely I will finally have a relationship with someone who doesn't overwhelm me with their over-reaction?"

So, it begs the question, even if it feels wonderful to have someone sweep you off your feet, is it really a relationship at all? When you are given everything you want, you are being manipulated to be happy all the time. Why? Because that person cannot bear for you to be unhappy. Their own system is already flooded since childhood with other people's over-reactions. They certainly can't handle any more in adult relationships. So, who would be their perfect date? Why, someone meek and in need of rescue; Cinderella, of course!

Over-Reactions In Love

David was like this. From day one, he was making all the right moves, saying all the right things. He was everything Gabby had lacked in a father. He made time for her, even when he was busy. He took her into his world. He was charming and available. He was the one who was pressing to meet her family, because he thought that she would want this. He even got triggered when she resisted letting him meet them at first, because there was clearly something wrong here, and he didn't know how to fix it. The only way he thought that he could make Gabby completely happy with the relationship was to push the issue until it was resolved.

However, part of the love avoidant's pattern is that inevitably they get exhausted by all this caretaking, and so, become overwhelmed again. Remember that they were set up to be out of control, and that's an exhausting way to be. It might look like David was taking care of Gabby, in the cliché of the knight in shining armour, but, in fact, he was taking care of himself by trying to keep her from over-reacting. But, in the end, it was too much. At some point, the mask has to slip. The fantasy crumbles and they can't bear to be overwhelmed by the other's feelings about that, so they take off.

David even dumped her in a very Prince Charming way, taking her to a romantic hotel for the weekend. These habits run deep because they are defences. This was the only way he knew to keep himself safe. Once he had met her family, this fantasy became too real for him. He was starting to deal with the real mess of real life. This triggered his overwhelmed system and he had to leave. Goodbye fantasy life together.

The love avoidant leaves relationships without any obvious pain. It is a relief to them to create that distance. But they tend to get back to being out of control in other ways with other risky behaviours. In the end, and perhaps even quite soon after, the love avoidant is ready to go around again, either with the same person or with a new one. It's a cycle.

Addicted And Avoidant

A lot of us can find something about ourselves that we recognise in both of these people. That can be very confusing. Maybe you're thinking, "Wait, am I a love avoidant or a love addict? Surely, my childhood was set up for me by under-reactions or over-reactions". Sometimes we can't decide which of these two types we are. That's because we can be both.

We don't have just one childhood with just one person. And even if we did, that one person didn't behave in just one way all of the time. As we move from our neat model of the nervous system that was drawn in little diagrams on the page into the messy business of real life, we're going to have to allow a bit more flexibility in how we mix things together. And, when we do, we can start to transform these simplistic stories into something much more powerful and close to home.

I can be a love addict and a love avoidant. I can be one style in one relationship and the other style in a different relationship. And I can be both of them in the same relationship. Remember our model of the nervous system with triggers, baggage and reactions? I have different baggage from different people. And this can get activated at different times in different ways.

These different triggers will cause different reactions in me. You might be a trigger for me to have over-reactions, but your friend might trigger me to have under-reactions. Or you might have two different behaviours which trigger each of them. This is going to change my attachment style, and whether or not I am a love avoidant or a love addict. But, in every case, something from the past is being activated.

For those of us who have had quite complex childhoods, there is a mountain of unfinished business in our baggage. We are not always going to be the same, all of the time.

And that's okay. Once you build this model of relationships, based on the nervous system and its way of managing triggers, baggage and reactions, you don't need someone to be the same all of the time.

In the original story of the invisible lion, there is nothing wrong with the man running down the street. His biology is performing perfectly for someone who is running away from a lion. The only problem is you can't see the lion. But once you add the lion into the picture, nothing is wrong. And more specifically, no one is wrong. No behaviour is wrong.

We can judge people in love all we want, but we only do so because we can't see their invisible lions. With them back in the picture, everything makes perfect sense; the way they have their over-reactions, their under-reactions, how their attachment styles (the set points for their nervous systems) set them up for being either passive fantasists or active charlatans (or both) in relationships, why their relationships suddenly crash and end horribly, how they go about trying to recover and why they do it all over again. It all becomes much more reasonable once you know the story of the nervous system.

Love Conquers All

Like the majority of us, these are just people trying to recover from dysregulation. They were not adequately regulated as children, and then life happened, leaving more unfinished business in their nervous systems. This makes relationships tough. And painful. Yet we persist in trying to have them. And for good reason.

Romantic relationships are an opportunity to heal our attachment wounds from childhood. They shine a light into the deficit of our earliest attachments. Everything that went wrong in early life, everything that contributed to that wonky, too-much or not-enough set point for regulation, everything that set us up for difficult experiences later in life, can all begin to be healed by a healthy relationship with someone who is, at first, like a box of matches for the gunpowder store of our own undischarged baggage. We are attracted to people who will be a trigger for all of our unfinished business. This is why we go for the same person (in one way or another) over and over again. The point is to use that experience constructively.

Deep inside the wisdom of our bodies lies the innate drive to restore ourselves to health. All our problems come from unfinished business in the nervous system. And how do we finish that unfinished business? We need a trigger to get it going again.

People are powerful triggers, and intimate relationships with people are like triggers on steroids. Nothing gets to the source of our dysregulation quite so effectively! But the tragedy is that most of us are unable to use this for healing. Instead, we start with the over-reactions and under-reactions as if they were about what is going on right now, rather than unfinished business from back then. And then the two cycles of addict and avoidant start on their merry way again, like hamsters on two interlocked wheels. While these wheels keep on turning there is no growth, just repetition.

But what if these two people can jump off their wheels and approach the difficult business of relating differently? Then there is so much potential for mutual healing. And we already know how to do that. We have the tools of boundaries and containment at our disposal. Now, amid the mayhem of a romantic relationship, we can take these tools to a weapons-grade level and test them in the battleground of extreme nervous-system activity.

Most people can't do that because they don't know the story of the nervous system, and so, they aren't looking for the invisible lion. They are pointing fingers instead.

This was Gabby's fate. She went through these cycles so many times that she grew to despair of them. Nothing changed for Gabby. Her nervous system remained exactly the same. It's interesting that when life forced her back to the real source of the problem, her original family, she was able to do things differently. Everything she had failed to do with a romantic partner, she was now able to do with her father when he got older.

Her father was now present. He needed her and had nowhere to run away to. The void was filled. And although she had nothing she had thought she wanted in life at that point, she felt happy.

10. OUR PARTS PERSONALITIES AND CHARACTER

What You Will Learn

Remember the idea that we can be a person who has over-reactions and under-reactions? We're going to have to start to understand these three simple notions of over-reacting, or under-reacting, or getting it just right, as all able to happen at the same time. After all, sometimes we appear to be a baffling mixture of all of these possible states. But how could that be possible?

If I said to you that this morning part of me wanted pull the duvet over my head, you would know what I meant. But look at what I've just said; what does that even mean? How many parts of me can there be at any one time? Unsurprisingly, the answer, roughly speaking, seems to be three; an over, an under and a just-right part.

My Child, Teen And Adult

Most people can relate to the idea that there is a part of them that wants to behave like a baby sometimes; to give up and to be looked after. It's that part of us that pulls the duvet over our head when the alarm goes off. Or the vulnerable side of us that affectionately curls up with their loved one and wants to be brought treats and tea. Or the person we become that gives up during work meetings when we can't get our point across or no one is listening to us. It's an aspect of our human experience that's generally characterised by taking no action, submitting and wishing to be rescued or helped. This is the child part.

Then there is the teenager. Most of us can recognise this part by going to visit our parents' house. We might arrive as fine, functional, independent adults, but when we get back to the original family dynamic, we can become difficult, boisterous, grumpy, sabotaging teens. It can happen at any age. This is the part of us that says "whatever" to consequences and does stuff anyway. It might be a prank at work that we know is going to go down badly. Or not turning up for something we'd committed to, because we can't really be bothered. Or being rude to our partner and not caring if that hurts them. This adolescent energy is the place from which we quit our job on a whim and tell everyone at work what we really think of them. It is often great fun and we can have a great time in this part of ourselves, but the high usually wears off as the longer-term consequences become clearer.

These consequences are then taken care of by our adult. Our adult part is cooperative, measured and able to collaborate with the world and the people around us for everyone's mutual gain. This is the place in all of us that makes the world work. It's where we do our best parenting and have the most functional personal relationships. We take care of our health, our environment, our families, our community and our world from this place. The adult sees things clearly, unburdened by too much emotion, and figures out solutions to problems, usually together with others. This is a very useful person to be. Pia Mellody refers to this part as 'the functional adult' which combines both of these important ideas perfectly.

The Hung Parliament

Which of these descriptions do you relate to? Probably all of them, to some degree. Most people intuitively get it. But even people who get it, don't always behave like one or the other of these parts. Adults almost never behave exclusively like the child part or the teenage part, but they can still feel these parts inside of them. Ever been in a work meeting where you wanted to just walk out of a boring presentation, but you didn't do it? Or dragged yourself out of bed that time when you just wanted to give up and get someone to come and look after you? It's almost like a dialogue. There are at least two parts to you, trying to figure out who is going to win. But who, exactly, is managing all of this?

For example, when we were talking about practicing boundaries and containment after being triggered, who did we think would be doing that? Not the out-of-control over-reactor. It was as if we magically suggested that there is someone else there, watching this process, who can gain some control over it. And, actually, there is.

In our models of dysregulation, the adult is the Goldilocks reaction, the child is the under-reaction and the teenager the over-reaction. When we start to look at how each of us experience and manage these parts of ourselves, it's clear that we appear to be able to have more than one of these reactions at once. That seems to contradict our nervous system model that we are only ever one of these at any one time.

To understand that contradiction, we have to go right back to the beginning where we learned that the thing we call our brain is not actually one thing at all. Remember how our brain is made up of many different parts itself, the most obvious different parts being the reptile brain, the mammal brain and the newly-developed human brain?

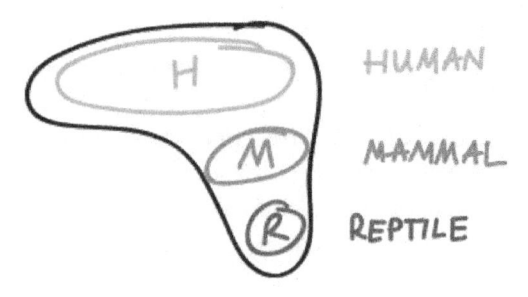

HUMAN

MAMMAL

REPTILE

So, our different brains can have different functions at the same time, and so, we can have a variety of simultaneous reactions. It would be much simpler if these brains would take turns; then we would either just be a child, a teenager or an adult. But that's just not how it works.

It is more like a democracy than a dictatorship, and, most of the time, we have a hung parliament with no clear party in control. As a result, there is a lot of negotiation needed between these members of a coalition government. And even then it's not always clear who is in charge.

We can be dysregulated in one part of our brain and watch that happening from another part of our brain. Even more astonishing is that, with some effort of conscious will, we can actually determine how much priority is given to these different reactions within us.

We know we do this because when we get drunk, we suddenly get very bad at doing it. Most of the time, our idealised, well-regulated, Goldilocks response to any given situation is available to us because there is some part of this brain left that hasn't been hijacked by a trigger. At the same time, another part of our brain can be reacting to the trigger. These two parts of the brain might then violently disagree on what to do next.

So, you might have a smallish over-reaction in your mammal brain. Your self-aware, thinking, human brain probably wants that to stop. This is, in fact, exactly the kind of takeover of the mammal system that we explored in Part One of this book; the one that caused the whole problem of dysregulation in the first place. Back then, we described this as a bad thing, something that had resulted in the lack of restoration of health in the nervous system. But now we can also see the upside. If we were to behave like teenagers, or babies, without any constraints during our actual adult lives, then we might quite quickly find that life becomes unmanageable.

In fact, if you look at people for whom there are no consequences, whether children or adults, they often start to behave more and more wildly. This realisation that if we let our mammal biology run riot, then our lives will be less manageable in the long run, keeps humans doing what they do best. It has been our evolutionary advantage. Out-voting the mammal in our biological hung parliament has allowed humans to plan for higher survival rates. Unfortunately, it has had certain consequences that have caught up with us too.

The Executive

The executive branch of the brain, the president of our hung parliament, seems to have some measure of control over how we apportion our energy to these different parts of the brain.

This place is called our prefrontal cortex, or, to put it another way, our adult. This is who we want to have in charge. The adult manages our boundaries, helps us to practice containment, and then, once properly educated (which is why I wrote this book), it will help us to allow our mammal brain the appropriate time and space to heal our nervous system. You'll see how this works in Part Four of this book.

Now that you're aware of these parts, it can be a useful exercise to start to measure how much of us is in our child, adolescent or adult reaction at any one time. Take that meeting, for example, where you wanted to walk out during the boring presentation. Are you 50% adult in that moment? If so, is the rest all that teenager? Or, underneath that, is there a frozen child, trapped in this room and wishing she could run away? How much of each of them are you struggling to maintain, with your calm, smiling, listening, not running-away adult?

It can help just to acknowledge the conflict and name these parts. Every day when I start writing, if I'm lucky, I'm probably 20% a child who wants to give up, 30% a teenager who just wants to watch YouTube, and maybe 50% an adult, which is why I actually start to write. It's a battle.

This battle can be baffling. Ever wondered why you waste time procrastinating or end up doing things you didn't want to do or have failed to reach your calmly and logically calculated goals? This is why. Not only is our nervous system dysregulated, but each of its dysregulated reactions can take hold of us in different parts of our brains. These parts of the brain can co-exist and fight it out with each other for who is going to get the most control over what we do next.

Believe it or not, our brain's main job is to run our bodies. So, whichever part of our brain has majority control is going to determine what our body is going to do. Doing is how we show our behaviour. And our behaviour affects our relationships, which affects everything we think we need to feel safe, such as a family, a partner or a job.

That's why, if we don't get on top of this warring brain of ours, we can end up making our world less than safe for ourselves.

But we can start to dismantle this vicious cycle of safety and behaviour if we open up a window into the question of where to put our energy while these parts are trying to take control. If we can find our adult, we have a chance of making ourselves feel safer, because adults make things safe. And if we feel safer, we will probably have fewer triggers and fewer reactions. And if we can do that, we might even get more power into our adult. And so on. It's like a government that is working properly, finding compromises in the greater interest of the nation as a whole.

Recovery is possible. We are not necessarily slaves to our brains and biology. Through learning and some directed effort (perhaps starting with this book), we can begin to swing the wild workings of our brains and bodies back in our favour. It starts with self-awareness; in fact, the concepts you've been learning in the preceding chapters are the building blocks for exactly that awareness. And now that you have those, I'll explain how you can put them to work.

Minority Parties

I've kept things pretty simple so far, to give you these building blocks. But before we move on, let's have a quick glimpse at other ways of looking at this that are not so simple. The brain is a fabulously complex organism. This book offers as simple a model of it as possible because that is enough to help our thinking brains to understand ourselves better and take some positive steps to improve our lives as a result.

But other, more complex models are interesting to visit briefly too. Janina Fisher has a very elegant formulation, leaning somewhat on the work of Dick Schwartz and Pat Ogden. In these expanded ideas, you might find some aspects of yourself which you recognise, and it can be a relief to know that all of these life experiences, some of which we even blame or judge ourselves for, are simply the inevitable consequences of being a human mammal with a dysregulated nervous system.

So far, we have looked at only three possible responses to a threat: over-reaction, under-reaction and the just-right Goldilocks reaction. But what if I told you there are also responses we have before we get to this point, and perhaps even after, too?

We know that when we (and other mammals) first

become aware of possible trouble, something in us changes. We think of animals pricking up their ears; imagine a rabbit in a field as it picks up the scent of a fox, for instance. The rabbit narrows its focus and its whole physiology is now orientated towards the possibility of threat. But this is not really a reaction, yet. It's a defensive orientation, preparing you for the possibility of having to react to a threat. You become more vigilant.

The interruption of normal life from a peripheral awareness of a threat can be described as switching off the social engagement system. When we are calm and healthy, we are typically socially engaged with other people. Or to put it another way, we're connecting to them in a collaborative and cooperative way. And that's because we are trying to make allies and to be safe with them. If we get a sniff of not feeling safe, this engagement may stop because we then may need to become competitive and combative to survive, retreating back to our earlier mammal brains.

Some people feel threat in their lives all the time. They might find it hard ever to be in their social engagement system and to connect safely to other people at all. By comparison, other people find great comfort and safety in making these connections, and they reduce threat in their lives by having good relationships and strong networks.

Help Me

Just before we mobilise our fight-or-flight reactions, we have another option. If a threat is detected, we can look for help before we have our own independent reaction to the threat. Non-human mammals do it too.

In fact, it works very well for young mammals to call upon a larger mammal, like a primary caregiver to come and change the dynamic of the threat. Once this larger mammal comes to the rescue, the threat goes away and the young mammal doesn't need to work through a full-blown reaction. The situation is diffused.

We all have this memory from childhood; for some of us, this threat response worked out well. For others of us, it was not so successful. So, each of us now has a different idea of whom to cry for when we need help. From a child running for their mummy or a special forces unit calling in air cover, it is a completely logical response to a threat to try to get the threat taken away by someone else bigger or stronger than you, before any flight-or-fight is necessary. The instinct is very clear.

This also helps to explain why we are all so interested in identifying ourselves with larger groups. People follow sports teams, identify with people who love the same things, join gangs or get very invested in their nationality. All of this helps us to feel safer. We belong to something. We are attached. This activity of forming groups within groups within groups is seen in most higher-functioning mammals. If we have a family or a group or a gang, then we have something bigger and stronger than ourselves to cry to for help when life gets threatening. This keeps us out of fight-or-flight and further away from life-threatening danger. The people who have the most dysregulated nervous systems and experience the most real threat in daily life will cling most strongly to this dynamic, like the inner-city gangs of disadvantaged youths that can be seen in cities the world over.

Dead Faint

At the other end of the spectrum is a variation in our freeze response. We have described freezing as an under-reaction. There are actually two ways that the nervous system does this, and we'll be familiar with both from metaphors from animal life. We say people who are overwhelmed are frozen like a deer in the headlights. When this happens, the deer is still standing up. It is so overwhelmed by the stimulus to take action that it locks up and doesn't move at all. We might relate to this as being so fearful or panicked that we can't do anything. We are frozen.

But there is also the other way to freeze. Sometimes we talk about people playing possum. Possums freeze in a different way. They go completely limp, so would be unable to stand up like the deer in the headlights. What's going on? This is an example of the reptile brain having completely taken over from the mammal brain, sending the animal into a very low state of arousal. This is the freeze we saw the gazelle in during the video clip in Part One of this book.

We might most easily relate to this as a state of submission. Sometimes, we just give up, unable to fight the threat anymore. We give into the inevitable and no longer have any will to change the outcome. Humans don't do this often, but we can feel this flat sense of complete submission, of giving up, in the mix of the various parts of ourselves, courtesy of the hung parliament of our complicated brains. These are all just waypoints along our familiar threat response cycle.

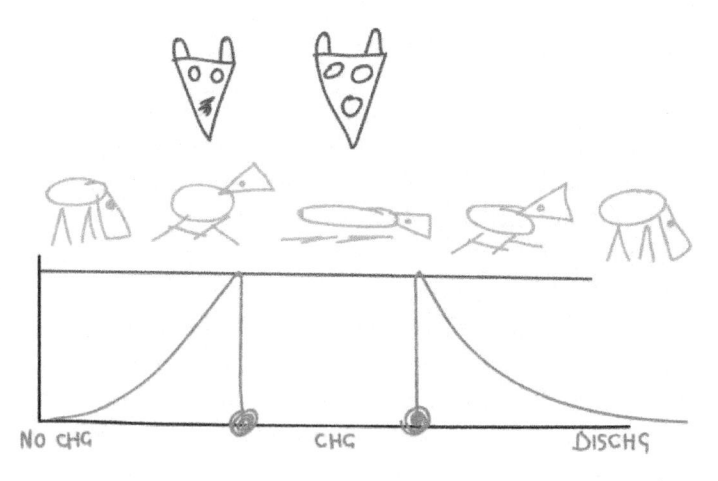

Each of them is being partially felt in a different part of the brain. The war between them for control of my body can lead to a lot more complexity than just pulling the duvet over my head when I need to go to work.

Adding these new ego states or brain parts or threat responses into the mix of our basic model gives us a good approximation to more complex models used in neurobiology and psychology. So, let's look at how these models come together.

OUR PARTS PERSONALITIES AND CHARACTER

Imaginary Lion Alert	Pia Mellody Model	Peter Levine Model	Stephen Porges Model	Janina Fisher Model
Everything is safe	We rest in our functional adult	The nervous system is at its resting point	We are comfortable socially engaging with others	We are relaxed, open and cooperative in our social engagement system
Maybe things are not so safe	We might start to behave like an adapted teenager or a wounded child	The nervous system moves into vigilance and we orientate towards the threat	We disengage from this social engagement lifting the brake on the other responses below	Maybe we also cry for help from the part of us that attaches for security
We feel the threat as real and maybe we can defeat it	We adapt to behave like a teenager	Our body fights	The mammal takes over driving the fight response	We get in touch with the part that wants to fight
We can't defeat the threat but we can escape	We adapt to behave like a teenager	Our body runs	The mammal takes over driving the flight response	We get in touch with the part that wants to run
We can't run or fight any harder	We behave like a wounded child	Our body freezes	The mammal is overwhelmed and the system locks up	We get in touch with the part that is actively frozen
We can't run away or fight it off and now all is lost	We behave like a wounded child	Our body freezes	The reptile takes over with a total shut-down response	We get in touch with the part that submits

They seem to fit our observations of ourselves. What they have in common is that they are all driven by the same underlying premise of the story of the nervous system. They are different ways of explaining what is observed from this foundation stone of all human behaviour.

Fragmentation

You may have heard of dissociation. It describes how we feel when we are not quite all there. You might have experienced it while driving somewhere, then, on reflection, not really remembered anything much of the journey. Where were you then, during that journey?

We can become dissociated when these different states from the different parts of our brain (the different parties in the coalition government) don't line up. For people with a lot of baggage in their systems, this can happen quite often. For example, some people, if the general experience they carry in their baggage is that people are not safe, find it very hard ever to settle into their social engagement system. Their different parts in their brains might, therefore, never be fully able to agree what to do.

The most extreme version of dissociation is when someone is so split by these different parts that they actually have different personalities. This was often referred to as multiple personality disorder, and more recently as dissociative identity disorder, and is usually the result of severe childhood abuse. We might understand it as a defence against the huge pressure of trying to realign all these very stressed parts of the brain back to an awful reality.

Being in a different reality may also show up as

psychosis or paranoia. This could also be a defence against the overwhelming experience of trying to manage a horrifying reality in a dysregulated nervous system with a fragmented brain.

Personality

If someone can have many personalities as a defence against severe dysregulation, then how can you know which one is real? And if you can't, how can you know if any personality is real? For instance, I speak a little Greek and people say I have a different personality in that language. I kind of know what they mean.

Many interesting questions look very different once you understand the story of the nervous system. If you add to that a bit of basic knowledge about the brain and how it connects to the body (neurobiology and anatomy), then we can start to look at many of life's most baffling questions from a totally different perspective. The more complex the problem is, the harder it is to put forward a nice, tidy model of how to understand it from the nervous system perspective, but, with a good grounding of the basics, we can look at most aspects of human behaviour in a totally different light.

Maybe you think that you're quite normal and have a fixed personality that belongs to you. Maybe you identify that personality with the idea of you. This is who you are, isn't it? But what if that personality was actually just a reaction to some unfinished biological processes in your body?

Take the issue of addiction, for example. In the old-school addiction treatment programmes, there was this core idea that if someone was an addict it was because they had a, somehow, deficient personality. They said they would never get better until they understood and accepted this. I see it differently.

To me, the addict is someone who's trying to regulate their nervous system (either up, down or both) by using something from the outside. The more you do this with substances and experiences, the less able you are to regulate your nervous system on your own, and so the more addicted you become. Add to this that most chemical experiences become less potent the more you do them, and you have an escalating problem.

Many addicts talk about hitting rock bottom before they could get any better. This is like reaching a point of surrender. They submit. Oddly, this is also the final response to threat on our chart above. Animals use this state as a last resting place when all is lost. It actually halts the highly activated response in their bodies and puts everything into shutdown, which might be a huge relief for someone who is completely out of control on drugs. In addiction treatment, this is seen as a step forward; from there, recovery becomes possible.

Teenagers are another example. They often get a bad rap for their behaviour, and then this is ascribed to their identity as an example of their woeful personality. In fact, teenagers are a very interesting stage of mammal. If you are smaller than adults, given a choice between fight or flight and freeze, you will be unlikely to go for the fight or flight. This leaves unfinished business in the system.

When the body gets bigger, to about the same size as an adult (like a teenager), this equation changes. Now you can successfully risk mobilising into fight or flight, and look how much energy you have stored up in your baggage to add into the equation. Teenagers are taking their first steps to trying to finish their unfinished business. The chaos that ensues has no boundaries or containment and is therefore unlikely to have a healthy outcome, but it's not because of their personalities. It's their biology.

Character

Almost everyone has a dysregulated nervous system, to some extent. As people grow up, go to schools, universities, become adults, they have to try to find some way to fit into the world so that they can get what they need in life. Sometimes even the basics, like food and shelter, are a struggle if they are very dysregulated and can't collaborate at all with the world. Holding down a normal job and managing normal relationships can become a massively difficult task. Getting on with normal life gets very tricky indeed.

To deal with this twin difficulty of living in a dysregulated nervous system and trying to get our needs met in the real world, adults can adapt into different characters, each of which seems to have its own patterns of behaviour. These are sometimes called character strategies. It seems that we change who we are to fit in or to get what we want. There has been a tradition going back to Freud's first followers that had linked this development of character with perceived changes in the body, most recently formulated by Dr Pat Ogden as part of her Sensorimotor Psychotherapy.

These different character strategies deal with their own needs and the needs of others differently, and are explained by the challenges which they faced in childhood during attachment. This, in turn, is explainable by the workings of the nervous systems of their caregivers which they then inherited. So, even though the result is these quite complex adult behavioural strategies, they link with the simple model we have developed of the origin of distress stored up in the body. It is perhaps therefore not too surprising that the way people carry their bodies has been linked with these different ways of presenting behaviour in different characters.

It is also an example of how a simple biological difference in evolution, such as my self-awareness of my response to threat, becomes a hugely complicated syndrome as it is played out by more and more people in more and more complex ways, settings and societies.

You can trace a single, causal line from the nervous system of self-aware humans becoming not that good at completing threat responses to the most complicated, baffling and peculiar personalities, character and behaviour of individuals today. It's powerful stuff.

Our Dysregulated World

What would happen if everyone was doing this? What would our world look like then? Everything you have read so far in this book gives you the answer.

If you took a perfect world, and then changed one species so that it became self-aware, like the computers did in the classic movies The Matrix and The Terminator, what would happen next? Would the following make sense?

That species starts to function differently. This new self-awareness creates more information, and this information becomes a new way to assess threat.

Where before it could just naturally do what mammals had done for millions of years, now the natural discharge of a threat response did not make sense and became interrupted.

This new species was unable to complete many of its responses to threats, and this caused the first dysregulated nervous systems.

These new dysregulated mammals then reproduced. These children were not raised by regulated nervous systems and so, they struggled to grow their brains and bodies into the regulated nervous systems they should have become.

Life happened to them, too. So, they became more dysregulated.

Many, many generations went by. This new species forgot what it was like to have a regulated nervous system. Only mystics and sages could remember and they told them stories to try to explain this loss.

With all these new mammals unable to correctly identify and process the true level of threat in their environment, the world became a more destructive and dangerous place. Even rich mammals were hunting and fighting to get more. No one ever felt safe, no matter how much threat they avoided.

With more threat being added to the world by their own actions, mammals started to live in a new world where their nervous systems were no match for the difficulties they faced. They started to become ill in a variety of baffling ways and to behave strangely.

Their relationships became disordered. They were addicted to substances or experiences to try to find a few moments of regulation. They altered their personalities to develop strategies for survival.

And they began to destroy their planet, stripping it

of its resources and not replenishing them. Their nervous systems were under such strain that it always felt like they needed more, and they needed it right now. Taking care of things for the future seemed irrelevant.

Ironically, their self-awareness and intelligence allowed them to build a world that had never been safer for a mammal. Fewer and fewer died of hunger, exposure or predation. But it didn't matter.

Life felt like a desperate, urgent problem, causing them to excuse all kinds of terrible actions.

It was as if they were always running away from something they could never escape. And all they did was run faster and faster.

That something is the Invisible Lion.

Our endless accumulation of resources to try to make ourselves feel safe, despite there being less and less need to, has changed and shaped our planet in a very short space of time. More so in a few thousand years than in many millions.

I think it's time to look at how to undo the damage. Let's learn how to repair a dysregulated nervous system, one person at a time, and save the world while we are at it.

Let's start with you.

PART FOUR

HOW TO PUT THE LION BACK TO SLEEP

WHAT HAVE WE LEARNED SO FAR

The dawn of self-awareness created a dysregulated nervous system in humans. All of our problems followed, like a chain of cascading dominoes. We have seen the effects it has on our health, our behaviour, our relationships, our personalities, our society and even our planet.

And the inevitable question we must all ask ourselves is, how would I be if I was not dysregulated? How would we all be? And how might we get back to the way we were supposed to be?

This part of the book will be your very own DIY guide to restoring your nervous system back towards regulation. I want to help you leave your invisible lion in the past, once and for all.

In theory, it's pretty straightforward. It's just a case of moving from the interrupted threat cycle in the diagram below

THE INVISIBLE LION

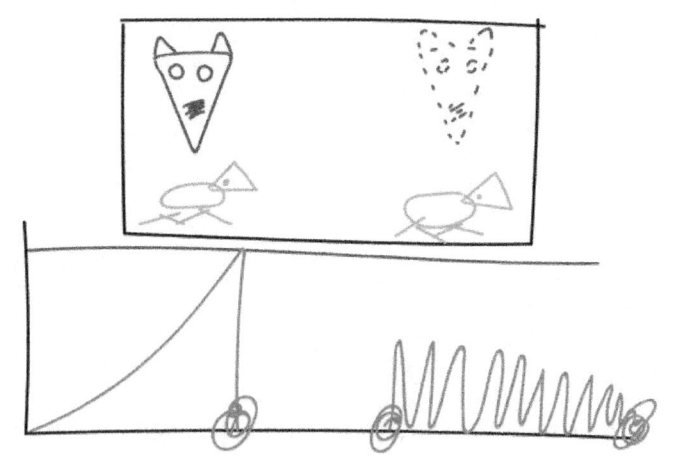

to the far more ideal threat cycle of this one.

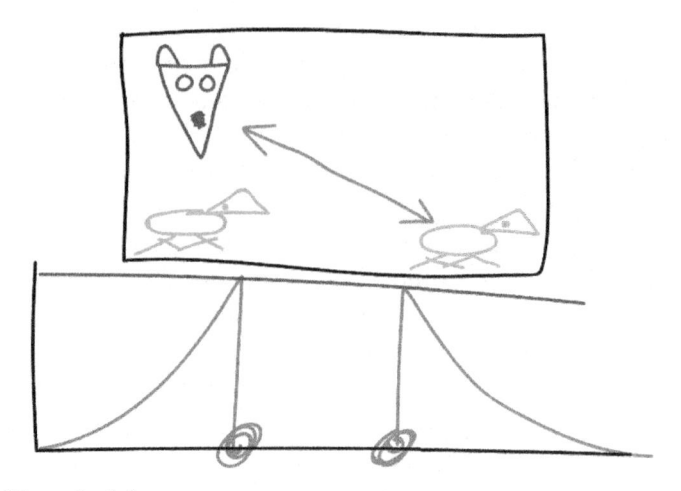

Easy, huh?

11. UNDERSTANDING

What You Will Learn

I'm going to give you the specific tools to make that shift from being dysregulated to having a more regulated nervous system, and I'm going to structure it as an easy-to-follow 28-Day Plan with exercises at each step to guide you through the process of applying your new understanding of the nervous system to yourself.

Read the steps below and then customise the guide for however you intuitively feel is right for you. If you like structure and feel that it is useful to be held through this step by step, follow the 28-Day Plan and, by the end of it, you should have the tools to apply this method in real time to any situation in your life. If after reading Part Four of this book you understand the overall plan and feel like you want to freestyle, then that's fine too.

You might not be able to do this on your own. We all learn differently. Many people who read this book and embark on the 28-Day Plan will find that it guides them perfectly. Others will get the theory and want to follow the plan but may find it too hard to do alone. That's completely fine and to be expected. Each one of us has different challenges to contend with in terms of our nervous system, and some people may need more help to get through the more difficult experiences they are trying to resolve. Whether it's support from a trusted friend or from a professional, don't be afraid to gather all the help you need for this journey.

Four Steps To Freedom

There are just four steps to the process of freeing yourself of dysregulation. They are:

1. Understanding the dysregulation in your body
2. Reframing how you experience your life in this body
3. Connecting with the baggage that this reframing leaves in your body
4. Discharging this baggage and completing the original response to threat

Another way to look at this is with our favourite diagrams. Remember these?

UNDERSTANDING

1. Understanding the dysregulation in your body	
2. Reframing how you experience your life in this body	
3. Connecting with the baggage that this reframing leaves in your body	
4. Discharging this baggage and completing the original response to threat	

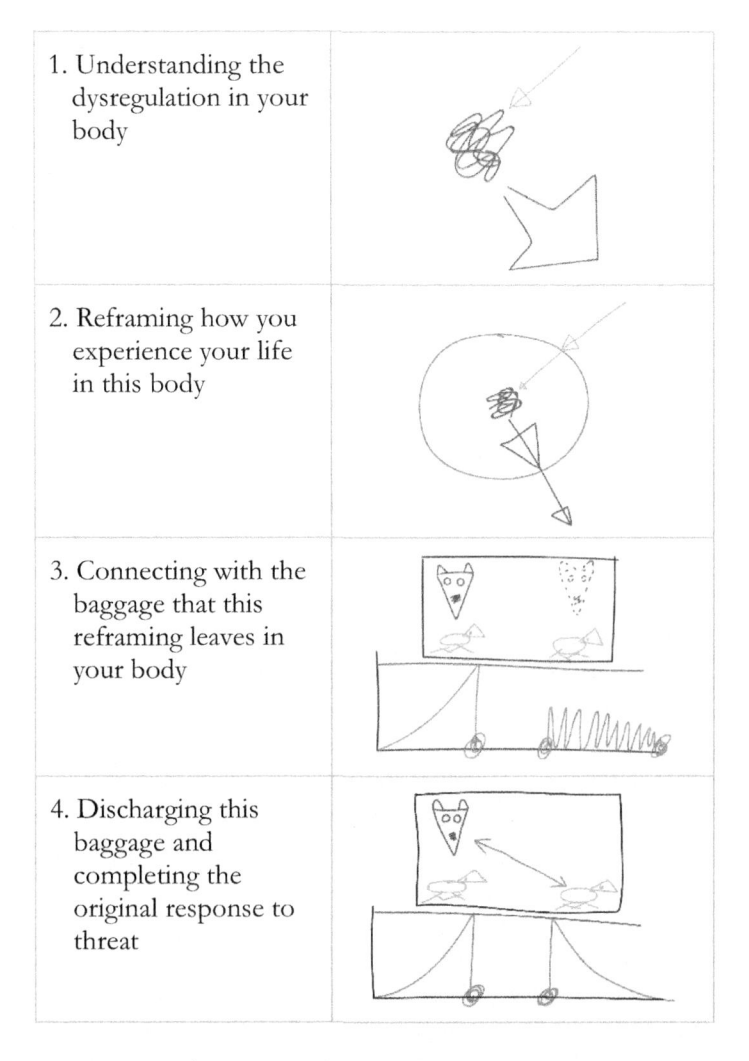

The good news is, by reading this book, you are already well on your way to completing the first step. The rest, we'll cover in the 28-Day Plan.

You might find this overall process easy. You might find it hard. However you experience it, I can guarantee you that your body can do this. At its core, it knows what to do.

It is easier to say than to do, though. Doing it requires some practice. This DIY toolkit is designed to get you started with that practice. Hopefully it will become a lifelong awareness of how to do you differently, and will allow you to make the changes in your life which you most desire.

Understanding

The first step towards a regulated nervous system is to train your thinking brain to allow the mammal and reptile part of your brain to take over. Essentially, you need to agree to get out of your own way.

I'm afraid there's no way to skip this step; it's the foundation of everything that comes after. Until we return control for some things back to the mammal brain, we will remain forever stuck in these loops set up by our self-awareness. The only way to do this is to fully understand what's happening, and why. That's actually why I wrote this book.

Psycho-education was always one of the primary aims in my consultations with clients. It's why I then delivered a lecture series on the subject. I want people to understand the nervous system and, more specifically, their own nervous system, because that is the first step to freedom.

I hope I have developed a simple way to explain the basics, not in an academic or medical way, but enough to persuade your thinking brain that it makes sense and fits with your experience. If we are lucky, your brain will then agree with us that it would be a good idea for it to get out of its own way for long enough to let your body heal its nervous system.

To help appeal to this logical brain of yours, this book is built on a logical progression of ideas, one after the other, which when taken in order give a clear, compelling view of the workings of your nervous system. So, the very best thing to do first is to learn this book and to study it as you might study a text-book for an exam.

Yes, I am serious.

Maybe you feel like, from what you've read already, you get it and it makes sense. If that's the case, brilliant. Or maybe you're still feeling uncertain about exactly how all this stuff works. After all, there is a lot to take on board. That's okay, too. Or maybe you're completely confused, even though you want to understand it. Also okay.

Wherever you sit on this particular spectrum, if you are really serious about returning your nervous system to a state of blissful regulation, my advice to you is to take a moment and be honest with yourself about how much you have understood so far. You don't need to get it all perfectly. You just need to be able to connect the dots.

The good news is that I've done most of the hard work for you. I've created a simple, multiple-choice test to help you gauge your understanding of this book so far. It's easy to take the test and score it for yourself. You can even do it online. And you can do it as many times as you like throughout this journey of working on your nervous system.

You'll find the test in the first week of the 28-Day Plan. Take it seriously, and if you find a question you don't know the answer to, don't guess; go back into the book and read the suggested pages.

I know this sounds like a lot. But believe me when I say that your greatest enemy in this process is your own thinking human mind. Sadly, it's not like some distracting app you can delete or shut down when you're trying to get something else done. You have to make an ally of your mind and persuade it to allow you to do the rest of the work of recovery. And to do that, you only have to show it that this all makes sense. This is what makes us feel more in control. And that's how your human brain feels safe.

12. REFRAMING

What You Will Learn

Once your brain is in agreement with the plan to let your body restore itself to regulation, you're ready to use that newly educated brain to begin to look at the world slightly differently.

Remember how this book started? There was a man running from a lion, but we couldn't see the lion. We formed all kinds of opinions about him in that moment. But the second we see the lion, he went from seeming crazy to seeming pretty sane. Now we need to work on transitioning you (and the world around you) from feeling crazy to feeling sane. To do that, you'll need to understand the nervous system (reading this book, check), and then use that understanding to change the way you look at the world.

This is still something that requires the thinking, human brain. It takes a bit of practice and some discipline to do. I will explain the basic technique here, and then you will practice these exercises in the 28-Day

Plan. The more you practice, the better you will get at it. I promise.

Reframing

The point of this step is to construct a gateway into the body that sets us up for the final two steps. As with all the steps, this one is non-negotiable. You can't progress to the next steps without it. These steps are giving you skills for life and may, as a bonus side-effect, even make you easier to live with. There is much to gain by sticking with it.

To recap, the goal is to go from the diagram on the left to the one on the right.

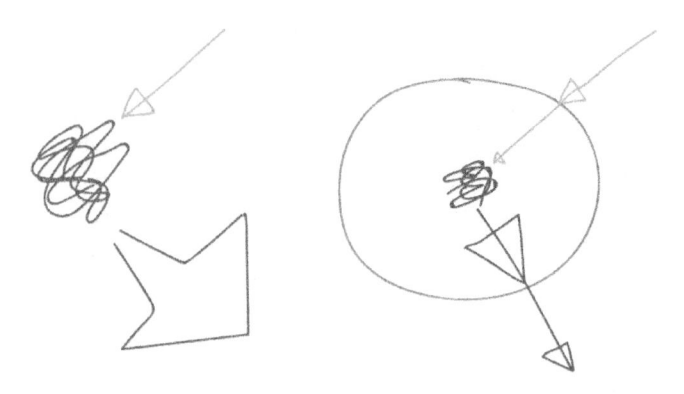

You already know and understand that boundaries and containment are a good idea, in theory. The problem is, they can be a pain to apply consistently in practice in the real world. It means looking after yourself. It means trying your best not to do any damage to other people in the process. Both can be surprisingly hard to do, particularly if your nervous system is dysregulated.

To help with that, in the following pages you will learn a simple formula for managing your communication when you need to give a voice to what is happening in the diagrams above. The idea is to create an easy format which limits the amount of damage you can do to yourself and to others, without you feeling the need to shut down entirely.

At its heart, this is about making you feel safe. Others' behaviour can alarm us, and our own behaviour can frighten us, too. If we make a dent in filtering out some of that alarm and fear, then our nervous systems get to experience the same events in relationship with others in a safer way. This, in turn, helps to shine a light on our baggage in a more subtle, useful way. This is the prep work for the third and fourth steps.

This step comes in three parts, and you already know the main characters: the trigger, the baggage and the reaction. I'm going to teach you how to put a voice to them in a way that's simple enough to apply to any situation you find yourself in. You can sometimes take these in a different order (and they do loop round on each other) but the format is the same.

I've worked with these constraints in groups and individual sessions for many years. Some people love it. Some people hate it. Some people get it instantly. Others find it hard work. All I can tell you is that when you get it, and if you are lucky enough to be around others who get it at the same time, it can be transformational for your relationships and your nervous system.

The Trigger

Life happens. And it can happen very suddenly. When events carry with them even a tiny echo of something we haven't yet finished reacting to, they become triggers. As triggers, they arrive at our nervous system and hit our baggage. This typically sets off a reaction in us, which can paradoxically sometimes be to have no obvious reaction at all. These reactions then seem out of proportion to the original trigger, at least to someone who is unaware of our baggage.

So, to straighten all of this out for ourselves and for others, we must first identify the trigger. With a bit of practice we can get good at knowing that we have been triggered, becoming aware of how reactive we are being or how shut down we're being. The question is when did it start? What was the beginning of the trigger?

Often, we see this most clearly in how we want to react to another person. Being triggered often makes us want to verbally abuse someone else or to never talk to them again because, of course, we're triggered. That's the reaction taking over. Instead of doing this, our goal now is to look at this reaction as if from outside of yourself and to talk through an objective description of your own process.

It's difficult, which is why it takes practice. The following formula is designed to guide you in this practice. Remember, the goal is to open up a window into your nervous system so that the other person can see all of you, not just what's presented on the outside.

When you identify a trigger, you want to keep it as simple as you possibly can. One way to think about it is:

What did I see?
What did I hear?

Try to answer these questions as if you were writing a film script to show the director what action to film and which noise to record. This is important because, most of the time, when we are triggered, we want to focus on these other questions instead:

Why is the other person an arsehole?
Why are they wrong?

See the difference? All I want you to do is describe the trigger in the diagram below with specific reference to an actual incident.

So, we start with the green arrow. It is not a judgement about another person. It is not a character assassination. It is not forgiveness, either. It's just a green arrow. Something happened; an action or a sound or both. That's it.

Your job, as you recalibrate your nervous system, is to describe this diagram to yourself or others with words that are about you, not about someone else.

When you do this, you're finding a healthy way to talk about triggers. That also makes it safer for others too.

Let's see what happens when we apply this technique in practice:

John has agreed to pick up Mary from a work drinks event and take her to a dinner with his friends. He's supposed to collect her at 7pm. At 6.55pm, she tells everyone she has to go, gets ready and is expecting him. He doesn't show up. There's no call, no message, nothing. As she's waiting by the lobby of the bar, some of her colleagues leave together and comment that they thought she'd left. They ask her if she's okay. Mary smiles bravely and tells them that everything's fine. But inside she's dying. She has no idea what's going on and having played it all cool, like she had to leave because she had another event to go to, now she's the one standing on her own, looking foolish. It doesn't help that one of the people passing her in the lobby is her work nemesis! John finally turns up at 7.50pm. Mary is still waiting, but not exactly pleased to see him. As he walks into the bar, all flustered, and greets her, she must make a choice in what to say.

Now you are an expert in the nervous system, which of the following would you recommend?

A. Hi.
B. Don't you dare come near me!
C. Where the *@!% have you been?
D. (sobs) I've been so alone (sobs uncontrollably).
E. If you ever so much as think of trying to make another plan with me again, I will kill you.
F. When we agree to meet at 7pm and you show up at 7.50pm, that's a trigger for me.
G. Let's go. I don't want to talk about it.
H. Don't worry about being late. It's no big deal.
I. You are such a huge arsehole.

You can probably think of a few choice lines of your own, too. It's kind of satisfying, isn't it? Thinking about how to swing the verbal bat or how to squeeze every last ounce out of a guilt trip, not to mention the pure twisted pleasure of a passive-aggressive attack of seething, smiling rage is great fun. But none of it is going to benefit your nervous system.

Give yourself a big pat on the back if you went for answer F, because that's the right answer. See how simple it is?

Let's practice with some more examples.

You work in an open plan office and you are on a tight deadline for an important project. Eric sits opposite you and often tries to engage you in conversation. You are quite shy, but don't want to just say outright that you don't want to talk. You feel trapped, and the stress of your deadline just keeps growing. What can you say, to open up a window for Eric into your experience, using the diagram above?

- A. Hey Eric, when you keep interrupting me, it triggers me.
- B. Eric, being distracted by you really triggers me, and I find it difficult.
- C. Eric, please be quiet. You are triggering me with your constant chatter.
- D. Hey, Eric, I'm on a deadline and the conflict of also wanting to talk to you is a trigger for me.
- E. Dude, this is a nightmare. You are making me go crazy.
- F. Eric, can you shut up? You are triggering the $*&! out of me.
- G. Uh, huh. Yup. Right. Got it. Yes.
- H. You're so funny. I love chatting with you. But I'm

busy.

Tricky isn't it? The ideal response is actually D because it is the most simple description of what is really going on inside you, with no embellishments or judgement. There's no added insults or exaggerations or untruths, just an explanation of what is going on for you, which, in turn, will open up the window in to the rest of the diagram above.

You might have felt inclined to go for B, or even A or C. But look at it from the other end of this conversation. Be Eric for a moment and imagine hearing A to D being said to you. Which one are you more likely to listen to? Which one is more likely to make you care about the person saying it? It's probably the one where I only talk about myself and don't point fingers at you.

Try another one.

Sue and Anne are flatmates. They met through friends and although they get on well enough, they have quite separate lives. One day, Sue comes home, looking forward to the leftovers from a dinner she cooked for a friend the night before. But the food has already been eaten; the Tupperware is empty and not even washed up in the sink. She's upset because she'd made no other arrangements for dinner. She's exhausted and could have picked something up on the way home. However, now she's nervous because she doesn't know what to say to Anne. She doesn't want there to be an atmosphere in the house, but equally, it doesn't feel right just to ignore it. After all, things like this have happened before. Anne comes in later, while Sue is watching TV. What should Sue say?

A.   Hi, did you have a nice evening?

- B. You ate my quinoa salad, and I was looking forward to that all day.
- C. We really need to talk about who is allowed to touch what in the kitchen.
- D. Did you think I was finished with that food in the Tupperware in the fridge?
- E. When I think people have taken my stuff at home, that's a trigger for me.
- F. Can't you make your own food and leave mine alone?
- G. I don't think we can live together anymore.
- H. Would you like some dinner?

This is a difficult one for people who don't like conflict, especially because they are living together. They can't go home for safety and sanctuary after the conversation, like you would do in an office. They are at home, which is supposed to be their refuge from all the other triggers in life. In that sense, there is more at risk. It's tricky.

The answer, of course, is E. Again, all you have to do is to look at the diagram, think of the events and see how simply and truthfully you can describe it. The less you make it about the other person, and the more you make it about yourself, the better.

Sue's thought process might have been something like: Did I get triggered? Yes. What was the trigger? I found an empty Tupperware when I was expecting to find a full one of food. I thought Anne did it.

That's it. That's the whole story. That's all we need, to start to straighten this out. Everything else is just part of your reaction to being triggered.

Is that unsatisfying to you? Did you want to add in a bit more? To get a little nasty? If so, think about what you are trying to achieve. What would have been

Anne's reaction to that? Again, try to hear it through Anne's ears. Because the reason you are speaking is to be heard.

Here's one last one.

Peter went home to his parent's house for Christmas. His brother and his sister are there, and his sister has brought along her new boyfriend, Frank. Peter's family is quite tight-knit and his parents are also fairly strict. There's a certain way they like things to be done around meal times. Everyone helps to set the table and get the food served. Then they eat. Growing up, this was not optional, and his parents could be harsh if they felt he was not pulling his weight. On their first evening together, he noticed that Frank was not contributing to this at all. He just stood there, chatting to Peter's mother while everyone else worked around him. This happened again the next day. Twice, in fact, at lunch and dinner. By the evening, Peter was fuming. What should he say? Whom should he even say it to? Does he have a problem with Frank, with his mother, or with everyone? How can he process this experience?

Here are some options.

A. Hey Frank, pick up a plate and make an effort. Don't you see us all helping, here?
B. Mum, is it okay if I don't help either, like Frank?
C. Hey, Sis, when are you going to civilise your boyfriend for mealtimes with the tribe?
D. Frank, I'm uncomfortable with you getting away with doing no chores here with us.
E. Hey, Mum, I see you not saying anything to Frank when he doesn't help, and it feels like a trigger to me.
F. I'm really pleased that Frank is here. It's a more relaxed vibe.

G. Good evening, everybody, and please go @&%*! yourselves.
H. Happy Christmas, Frank. I'm learning so much from you.

Are you beginning to get the picture? You have to start to think about everything, first and foremost, from the point of view of the nervous system. This diagram should be your visual starting point whenever you feel uncomfortable. Is should be in your mind's eye all of the time.

That is why it is on the cover of this book. Use it. Memorise it. Commit this diagram to memory and bring it up whenever something feels difficult.

Then go find the green arrow. In this case, Peter wasn't really triggered by Frank not doing anything. He was triggered by his mother not reacting to it. Peter could sense that this did not feel okay for him. He went looking for the trigger, and that's how we can see that E is the right answer. He described what he saw and what he heard, that had become his trigger.

It's not always easy. This process can become highly subjective and often a bit confusing. But if you hold onto the idea that you are painting a picture of the diagram above, and that your first job is to describe the green arrow, then it gets much clearer. If, instead, you find yourself judging or abusing someone, then you are not in the right place and it's time to take a moment, reset and come back to the diagram above.

This diagram is so useful because it shows that the important person in the story is you. It is not being caused by someone else. It is being caused by your experience; the sights, sounds, smells, sensations that are arriving at your nervous system. Just describe these. Leave out the temptation to judge everything that led up to it, and to attach motivations to the people involved. Then we can move on to the next part of the puzzle.

The Reaction

You might think that the next part of this exercise would be to go into the baggage, opening up this experience in chronological order of trigger, baggage, reaction. But, actually, that's not yet possible. The baggage is the most hidden part of this scenario, so, before we go there, we need some further clues to help us to see it clearly.

So, the next part of the experience to articulate is the reaction. This can actually be very simple. One way is to take a menu of basic emotions and to check the ones which you are aware of as you talk about the trigger.

There is also a great resource called a feeling wheel, which breaks down the simpler emotions into more complex ones as you get towards the rim of the wheel. Search online for examples. Or you can come up with your own list to help you. Here is an example of a list

I was taught in treatment. These are common emotions you might experience in your reaction.

Joy	Passion
Love	Fear
Sadness	Anger
Shame	Guilt

Another way to approach exploring this reaction is to start to notice what sensations you have in your body when you are talking about the trigger. Pay close attention to this experience. You might start to notice that you feel shaky or shut down or hot or numb. Or that you want to run away or not be talking right now. It's just as important to be aware of these sensations as we are of what we traditionally think of as our feelings, or emotions.

So, to go back to the example scenarios we've just looked at, we might be able to add to the communication about the trigger by also including a good description of the reaction. For example:

John is late to pick up Mary at the bar, and when he arrives, she says, "When we agree to meet at 7.00pm, and you show up a 7.50pm, that's a trigger for me." And then she adds, "And now I notice that I feel very angry, upset, hurt, confused and scared. My stomach is tight, and everything feels hot in my abdomen. I don't feel safe."

As you can see, Mary has been practicing! This is the result of some very committed work in couples counselling using these methods. She's ready for being triggered, and has done some really good work on developing awareness of herself. Before she had learned how to do that work, she might have just said,

"I feel terrible and I want to go".

And that's okay, too. As long as you are just trying to describe what you notice in your reaction, it doesn't really matter yet how well you do it. It just matters that you say something about your reaction after identifying your trigger. This then sets you up to use the experience productively for your nervous system.

Mary's description of her reaction was a very intimate explanation, the kind of thing you'd probably only share in a loving relationship. In a work setting, it is likely to be more appropriate to err on their side of neutrality, while still being very clear. So, when dealing with Interrupting Eric at work, you might say something like:

"Hey, Eric, I'm on a deadline and the conflict of also wanting to talk to you is a trigger for me. I notice that it makes me stressed, and I'd like to avoid that."

Or even, if you want to keep it as work related as possible,

"It makes me less productive because I feel like I'm in two places at once."

These are all layers of being a witness to yourself. The goal, in working with reactions, just like working with triggers, is just to notice them in the simplest way possible. Again, keep blame and judgement out of it; don't use this as a platform to get all the abuse you left out of the trigger back into the conversation.

Explanations like this are not part of the plan:

"And now I feel like you are a giant arsehole, and you should go jump in a lake."

That's not actually a feeling; it's an insult. You could say, *"Now I feel like I want to insult you"*, but, if you do it instead, then you are not on track. Again, this takes practice. It's also important to start when you are not overwhelmed. In the 28-Day Plan, the second week exercises are all about training yourself in the art of self-observation and appropriate expression, so you're about to get really good at this if you follow the instructions.

Let's look at two more examples with friends and family.

Sue is explaining to Anne how she got triggered; *"When I think people have taken my stuff at home that's a trigger for me."* And she wants to continue to open the window into her experience, so she says, *"And I'm feeling really scared to talk about it, like it's not okay or something bad will happen to me"*.

This is entirely accurate, isn't it? Sue was worried to bring it up at all, but, by noticing that and being able to add the trigger to the story, she's actually making a lot of sense. Even if you were the quinoa salad thief, it would be hard to hear these words and not to have some empathy. Sue has not been abusive, or even accusatory. She has simply stated her experience. She has put the diagram into words. She had an experience, and then she noticed some difficult feelings. Most people would react to this with warmth and compassion; even Anne, as she guiltily picked bits of quinoa out of her teeth.

And, of course, the place where we are most used to getting nowhere (being most stuck and feeling like there's no point in speaking up) is in the family. Decades of behaviour feel like they will never change. Often in the family dynamic, our unspoken deal is to react the same way as we always did forever. To do anything else can be daunting, and even feel very dangerous both for you and the other family members, too.

So, Peter decided to take a chance with his mother. He just felt so uncomfortable. He didn't see his parents all that often anymore, and this was a chance to do something differently, maybe even to feel differently, so he decided to start with what he had learned in this book and said, *"Hey Mum, I see you're not saying anything to Frank when he doesn't help and it feels like a trigger to me."* And then he carried on, opening up a window into his nervous system, *"I notice how distressed I feel, but I can't even really explain it. I just feel uncomfortable, and it makes me want to run away. But I don't want to run away. I miss you guys."*

Again, this is a dialogue that could have gone a very different way. It could have had an ugly, petulant tone with blame and judgement. But with this way of expressing himself, Peter brings his mother closer, rather than pushing her away. He's having a hard time, but he'd rather be having a nice time instead because he doesn't see her that often. Hearing that, she's likely to want to help him, not to push him away.

The Baggage

To set up this process of drawing the other person in, rather than putting them on the defensive, you start with the careful explanation of the trigger. If you don't attack, blame or judge with the trigger, you will usually find that the person you are talking to (even if it is yourself) can also find some degree of empathy and compassion with whatever difficult experience, sensations or feelings you are having in reaction to this trigger.

All of this then sets the stage for the final part of opening up the window into your nervous system, which is when we go from the diagram on the left to the one on the right.

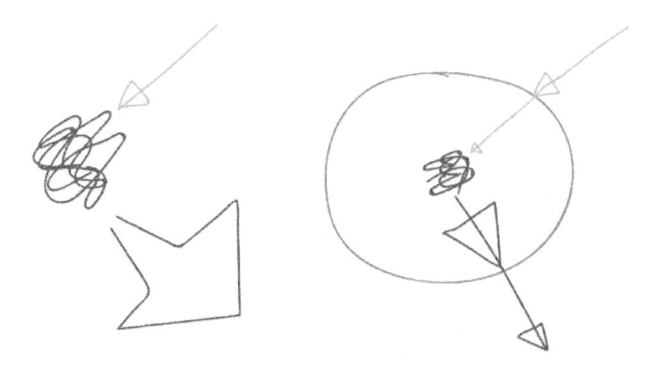

By not alienating or abusing the other person, and by even generating some empathy for our experience, we are creating the right conditions safely to explore and expose our baggage. We now get to tell them why we had the reaction we did. Or, at least, have a really good guess.

Our baggage, of course, is at the heart of all of our problems. It is the unfinished business from our responses to threat in the past. In nervous system recovery terms, it's our greatest opportunity but also our greatest threat. Revisiting unfinished threat responses is always going to be difficult because we are returning to the experiences which most overwhelmed us in the past, but completing them is our surest pathway back to regulation. All the same, it's something to approach very carefully.

Baggage is dealt with in each of the four steps during the 28-Day Plan, but at each stage it's approached in a different way, from different angles. And it's this careful combination of these approaches safely nurtured together which will create some lasting change in you.

So far, you have carefully identified your trigger. Then, you have diligently noticed and safely articulated your reaction. Now it's time to open up the bit in the middle, the bit that links the trigger to that reaction.

This is where we start to guess at the origin of our baggage.

It is a fairly simple formula. Once you've described the trigger, and the reaction that went with it, you try to make sense of the distance between the two by telling yourself, or the other person, what this combination of your trigger and your reaction reminds you of. It might not work; it might not remind you of anything. But, usually, especially if you have got the first two parts right, you will find that the baggage comes into view.

So, in our examples above, it might be something like this from Mary:

"When we agree to meet at 7.00pm and you show up a 7.50pm, that's a trigger for me. And now I notice that I feel very angry, upset, hurt, confused and scared. My stomach is tight, and everything feels hot in my abdomen. I don't feel safe."

After a moment's reflection on that, even hearing her own words, Mary says, *"This reminds me of when I was always waiting for my mum. She was always late for me when I was younger."*

Or, in a less vulnerable, more practical way, in a work context:

"Hey Eric, I'm on a deadline, and so the conflict of wanting to talk to you is a trigger for me. It makes me less productive because I feel like I'm in two places at once."

And then you might add, *"I felt like that in my last job and it didn't work out so well. So, I'm trying to do something differently here."*

Or with your housemates:

"When I think people have taken my stuff at home, that's a trigger for me, and I'm feeling really scared to talk about it, like it's not okay or that something bad will happen to me".

Then, after a moment, *"It reminds me so much of being at home with my siblings. I never felt like I had any privacy, but we couldn't complain because my parents were already overwhelmed by my sick brother."*

Or in the family:

"Hey, Mum, I see you not saying anything to Frank when he doesn't help, and it feels like a trigger to me. I notice how distressed I feel, but I can't even really explain it. I just feel so uncomfortable, and it makes me want to run away. But I don't want to run away. I miss you guys."

Reflecting on that, it gets very close to home: *"That's how I always felt growing up when things seemed unfair. I think that's why I moved away."*

What each of these very brief snippets of conversation does is to open up a window into the link between your nervous system, your behaviour and, therefore, your relationships. It puts this picture into language that's specific to that situation.

And it keeps you in relationships while you do it. Staying connected is the very best thing you can do for your nervous system. It regulates you and gives you a chance to repair attachments. To be able to process unfinished business, whilst staying connected is priceless.

I could give you a thousand examples, but this only works if you practice it for yourself, in situations that are meaningful to you. That's why the second week of the 28-Day Plan is dedicated to working through examples from your own life. You'll be guided to take some of your own remembered experiences and re-do the conversations you had with yourself and others about it. This will begin a safe approach to dealing with the baggage in your body, which will be the work of Steps Three and Four.

Boundaries

The whole process of regulating the nervous system would be far easier if we experienced fewer triggers less often. So, keeping things manageable is a priority, and, to do this, we can use these boundaries to begin to build a bubble of containment around our dysregulated nervous system.

But how do we know in practice exactly what those boundaries should be?

Well, it becomes obvious when we follow the process above. In each of the examples we've been working with, there is an opportunity to extend the dialogue with a follow-up observation or a request based on what you to have now noticed about your nervous system.

"When we agree to meet at 7pm and you show up at 7.50pm, that's a trigger for me. And now I notice that I feel very angry, upset, hurt, confused and scared. My stomach is tight, and everything feels hot in my abdomen. I don't feel safe. This reminds me of when I was always waiting for my mum. She was always late for me when I was younger."

What does this help Mary to learn about herself now, as an adult? She has an over-reaction to people she cares about being late for her. She obviously has some work to do on this, but, in the meantime, how can she keep the triggers to a minimum, so that this work is easier to do? She can ask John to help:

"So, in the future, it would really help me if you could be on time, or let me know if there's a problem as early as possible. And what I will do to help myself is if you are late and I'm

getting uncomfortable, I will just go home."

This does two really important things. First, Mary is letting John know how he could be her buddy in this whole process. This is not a demand she's making; it's a request. It is not John's job to manage Mary's nervous system, but he can help out if he wants to. Like anyone, he can only be helpful if he knows what to do. This level of awareness and communication from Mary sets him up to succeed in helping her if that's what he wants to do. He now has a roadmap to follow.

Second, Mary states what she is going to do for herself if John can't help. This is her backstop. The very worst thing you can do with a so-called boundary is make it someone else's responsibility, and then act like a victim if they don't do it. You can see from this whole book that that is the opposite of what we are trying to do here. The goal is for you to get your own nervous system more regulated. Only you can do that. Others can collaborate. They can even cooperate. But they are not responsible for the outcome. That's all down to you.

The bottom line is that Mary needs to find a way to rescue herself from her trigger, baggage and reaction when someone is late for her. She needs to show up for herself and take herself home to somewhere safe. This, it turns out, is more important than going out to dinner with John.

In fact, if you've been paying attention to this book, you'll recognise that rescuing the nervous system is the most important thing of all. It is the foundation of a better life for you, your colleagues, your family, your village, your society, your world and your planet. Definitely more important than dinner.

So, once you find the boundary, which protects you from a trigger, take responsibility for making sure that you take care of you. And when you do this, then you can start to solve all your other problems from a different, more regulated place.

Here are some more possibilities, based on what we've just explored:

"Hey, Eric, I'm on a deadline and the conflict of also wanting to talk to you is a trigger for me. It makes me less productive because I feel like I'm in two places at once. I felt like that in my last job and it didn't work out so well. So, I'm trying to do something different here."

Could be followed by, *"I think it would help me to be able to signal to others when I need to be left alone. So, I'm going to start wearing headphones, even if I'm not listening to anything!"*

Notice how this is the opposite of telling Eric what to do or making it his job to take care of your trigger. I cannot emphasise this point too much. It is often misunderstood when people talk about boundaries; no one can let you down here but yourself. You have to know what is okay for you, ask for it, and then take action to make sure you get it. It's never anyone's job but your own.

"When I think people have taken my stuff at home that's a trigger for me, and I'm feeling really scared to talk about it, like it's not okay or that something bad will happen to me. That reminds me so much of being at home with my siblings. I never felt like I had any privacy, but we couldn't complain because my parents were so overwhelmed by my sick brother."

One way to go from here is, *"I'm going to make it really clear what's mine and what I need to have left alone, rather than to share with you. I hope that's okay. I'll find a way to do that in the kitchen and the bathroom to make it easier for you."*

Again, this avoids shifting the blame onto the other person. Sue is setting up Anne to be able to help her to get what she needs. She is also making her needs crystal clear. If this doesn't work, then she is most likely going to have to move out, but she is giving both of them the best chance to avoid that by being really clear with herself where the original problem came from, and, then, from this place of clarity, making a plan to reduce this trigger in her home as much as she can. Also, it is kind to Anne. Sue is allowing Anne to see into the window of her nervous system to understand where all of this is coming from. That makes it less weird for Anne and makes her more likely to want to help.

It can even work in families, too.

"Hey, Mum, I see you not saying anything to Frank when he doesn't help, and it feels like a trigger to me. I notice how distressed I feel, but I can't even really explain it. I just feel so uncomfortable, and it makes me want to run away. But I don't want to run away. I miss you guys. That's how I always felt growing up when things seemed unfair. I think that's why I moved away."

Where does Peter go from here? Logically, you might say that what he needs is to see his Mum taking up the issue with Frank. This is one of the reasons why families are so difficult; our triggers are right there. They don't need much explanation or recreation. We don't have to really think hard about what this reminds us of. It is happening now, again, right under our noses. What Peter really wants in this situation is to be heard and understood. This doesn't often happen in families, so he needs to go gently. He might say, *"Can we talk about this more and see if maybe in the future we can do things a bit differently? Otherwise, I'm worried that I will continue to keep my distance to protect myself."*

There are other ways to go with this until you find the one that works for you. Again, practice is the key. In the 28-Day Plan, you're going to practice coming up with the right words that work for you, away from the stress of doing it in a real-life trigger situation. Then, you'll be ready when the time comes to respond skilfully in the heat of the moment.

Listening

Just before we move on, think for a moment how you would respond to any of these conversations if you were the one listening. It can seem like a bit of an odd dialogue. It's not really how we normally talk. So, what would it be like to be spoken to like this?

Usually, our reaction to something new and different is some form of resistance. We might be a bit alarmed. Add to this that we might easily hear these kinds of comments as if they are an attack, a judgement or blame, even when they are not. This might then become a trigger for the listener. And you know what can happen next if we then have our own reaction while listening to the first person's reaction. We can get into a vicious cycle of mutual triggers, instead of a healthy, regulating conversation.

The very best thing to try to do if someone is opening up to you like this is to listen. That might sound easy, but it's actually one of the hardest things we ever do. Listening means hearing all the words and imagining what it is like to be saying them, rather than hearing just some of the words, and then wanting to react or interrupt. Let's be honest, most of us just react and interrupt most of the time. Even if we don't actually interrupt the speaker with words, we interrupt our listening with our thoughts. Listening takes real effort. And guess what else? Practice, of course.

Clinically, we use a handy device for getting people to listen more deeply. We simply ask people to repeat back what they heard. When someone is listening to another's vulnerable account of their nervous system, they know that at the end of it, they will be asked to try to repeat back what they heard, like a tape recorder. This focuses the mind on the task of listening, but it also shows up where it has been hard to listen. When the dialogue is reflected back to the first person, even if it is only partially accurate, it can be very reassuring for the person who spoke up to know that they have really been heard.

This is especially helpful for couples, for dispute resolution and for family work. If you find it hard to hear this stuff, or to be heard when doing it, this kind of exercise of repeating back what you have heard can be very effective.

13. CONNECTING

What You Will Learn

Once you reach this step, you have successfully prepared yourself for some direct work on the nervous system itself. Even if it doesn't feel like it yet, that's a pretty major advance.

To recap, in the first step, you educated your thinking brain and invited it to get out of its own way. In the second step, you used that brilliant thinking brain to reframe how you see some of your problems in life. Specifically, you have mapped your experiences of distress onto a diagram about your nervous system and given a voice to the three elements of that diagram in a way that is safe for you and for others.

This is all wonderful preparation, but it is still all about the thinking, human brain. The third and fourth steps dive down into the lower parts of the brain, the mammal and reptile brains. This is where the mechanism for dysregulation lives, so, it is there, ultimately, that we have to do our work if we want to bring about deep lasting change in our lives.

Connecting

Here's where we encounter something of an obvious problem. If we are going to disengage the human thinking brain and activate the mammal brain, it's not very easy to do that while reading words. We need to go instead into the part of the brain that's aware of sensations, which show up in our five senses; touch, sight, smell, sound and taste. They are experienced, not thought about or read about.

So, this third step sees us using the sensations from our own body as a bridge through time. That's right; we're going time-travelling, back towards the original trigger that created your baggage. You are going to visit the real lion that had you running in the first place. That reaction was so strong that you had to pause it. And you never completely un-paused it. So, the reaction is unfinished and remains dormant in your nervous system. Using sensation to time-travel back to that experience is the first step to resolving it.

So, you are going to use your awareness of sensation to turn the diagram on the left below, into the diagram on the right.

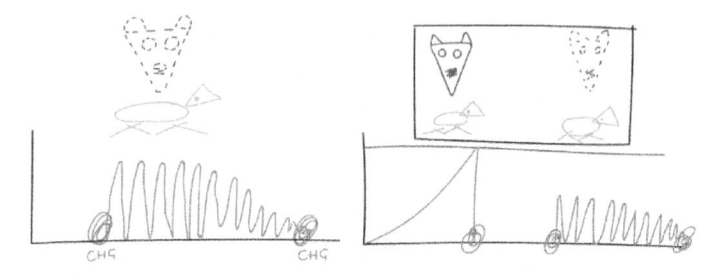

Don't worry, I'll show you how. All you are doing here is expanding the time axis of your total experience. You are including in your awareness today an awareness of this same experience before today. It's just a bigger window of awareness we're opening up, going from the now to the now-and-then. This time-travel is done by your body. No thinking required.

The nervous system is linked to the event in the past, as if it is happening right now. So, you just have to train your body to listen to your nervous system, and your mind to listen to your body. With the right preparatory work, you can tap into this magical somatic dialogue at any time. Fortunately, everything you've done in the first and second steps has prepared you for it.

Time Traveling

In the 28-Day Plan, I'm going to lead you through a series of exercises that will help you to create written examples of your experience of your nervous system, both then and now. Each of these will include some really important information about how you were experiencing yourself in a particular situation and what the experience reminds you of. Then, we are going to take it to the next level, into the body.

Take a statement, like Mary's:

"When we agree to meet at 7pm, and you show up a 7.50pm that's a trigger for me. And now I notice that I feel very angry, upset, hurt, confused and scared. My stomach is tight, and everything feels hot in my abdomen. I don't feel safe. This reminds me of waiting for my mum. She was always late for me when I was younger."

Imagine, in this example, that she's not saying this to John, but actually working through this on her own, or with a friend or even a therapist. She now wants to use this statement describing the sensations she felt to do some work on her nervous system, to get better at handling these kinds of triggering events in the future.

So, while remembering what it felt like when she was waiting for John, Mary goes into her body and looks for sensations. She has already noticed that her stomach is tight and that everything feels hot in her abdomen. Now is her chance to go towards those feelings, not away from them. The goal here is to stop analysing and to allow the experience to start to take over.

Once we find these sensations and focus clearly on them, we have a very important question to ask. This question is not asked of the mind; it is asked to the body. You might feel like this makes no sense at all, but just go with me here. It works. I've seen it work hundreds of times. What it really comes down to is just a trick of language, but it means something to us all in a way that's hard to describe with words. You will know it when you feel it.

Once you have a clear awareness of your sensations as you recall the trigger, reaction and your baggage. Now is when you ask your body this question:

"Can you float that back in time and see where it goes?"

And then you let that hang there for a while. You might want to repeat it. Your body might resist answering. Your thinking brain might be desperately trying to get in on the act. Come back to your sensations, back to your body. Its initial response might be to draw a blank. That's okay. Hang out with blank for a while. If you stay with it, eventually, something will happen. Something will pop up on the radar.

Sometimes, we think it doesn't make sense and so we resist it. Go with whatever comes up, however crazy it may seem. The memory might be an unwelcome one and your mind might tell you not to go there, but the reality is that your body is already there. It's not a memory anymore; it's something happening right here right now. So, there's no point in listening to your mind telling you not to go there. You are there. And now you have a way out.

Hello Lion

The next thing to do is simply to talk it through, in your head or out loud with someone else. Connect with that memory by using language, sensation and feelings. The exercises in the 28-Day Plan will help you do this. Try to allow yourself to go into whatever your mind or body wants to do next. In most cases, no matter how unpleasant the memory and however negative the feelings or thoughts that come with it might be, there is also a sense of relief. This relief is in the nervous system. You might notice that on some level, deep down, you feel calmer, because you are doing what is happening in the diagram below.

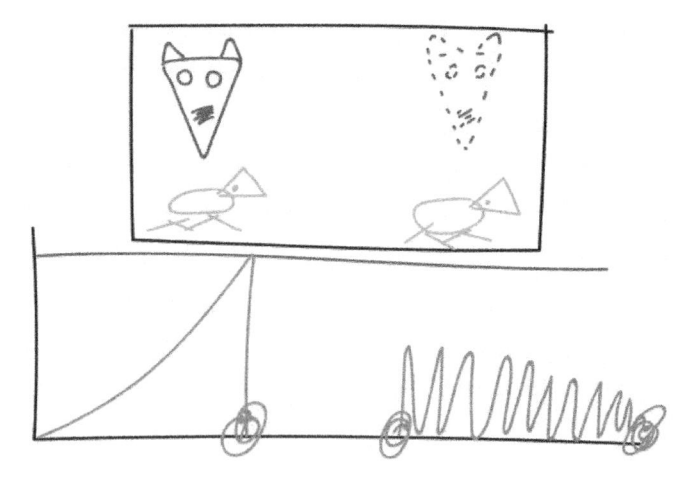

Your body connects the original problem with the reaction you are having now, in the present. This expands your frame of awareness and now it makes sense. To the thinking, human brain, that feels sane, grounded and calmer.

The end result of completing the third step is that you will have added more depth and colour to your description of what this experience reminded you of. For example, Mary already said, *"This reminds me of waiting for my mum. She was always late for me when I was younger."*

Now, she might be able to add:

"I remember this time, when I was at primary school. I must have been very young, maybe four or five, and I was looking out of the window with all the other kids, hoping to see my mother's face. One by one, all the kids left, and, as they left, I started getting more and more panicked because I couldn't see her. I can remember how I got knots in my stomach. I felt ashamed and embarrassed and hot and scared. I couldn't bear to be the one left behind. I refused to turn around and look at the teacher when

she said my name; eventually, she led me away to an office. I just stared at the floor. My face felt flushed, and my stomach clenched. That's how I feel now as I remember it. I just want to disappear and for no one to see me. It's horrible."

When we hear this story, it's now obvious how tough it would have been for Mary to stand in the lobby of that bar, waiting for John and wondering where he was. Look at what was being stirred up in her nervous system. For many of us, that particular trigger might have been no big deal. Stuff happens. People get delayed. But for Mary, it was a lightning bolt that shot right into the unfinished business of her baggage. Suddenly, she's four years old again; abandoned, afraid, ashamed, lost and scared. That's a lot to manage in the body of a cool, self-possessed thirty-eight-year-old executive at a work-social function.

And you can see now why her boundary request to John makes perfect sense: *"So in the future, it would really help if you could be on time, or let me know if there's a problem as early as possible. And what I will do to help myself is if you are late, and I'm getting uncomfortable, I will just go home."*

Of course. She can just take herself home now. She's thirty-eight-years-old! But her baggage takes her back to feeling four-years-old and totally dependent on someone else rescuing her. When John didn't show up, Mary had an under-reaction; she froze and forgot that she had the option to just leave. Then she had an over-reaction when he did turn up because, finally, she now felt a bit safer. You can imagine what that thawing out felt like as it was downloaded into John's face upon his arrival. And we haven't even got into why he was late yet. There's no room for that because of all this baggage Mary's dealing with.

Putting It Into Practice

So, in this phase of the 28-Day Plan, you'll be taking the information you uncovered about your nervous system in the second step and putting it to work.

I'll teach you an introductory exercise where you'll learn to do a body scan to prepare you each day to be more aware of sensation. Having opened up this window into your nervous system, you'll have the opportunity to use the body as a time-machine to expand your awareness of the whole of that experience.

Once you can do this, you'll be teetering on the edge of the final step. You might be ready immediately, or you might need to take your time. The most important thing here is to respect the pace at which your body wants to work. There is nothing to be gained by rushing anything. The body can't do more than it can do when healing anything, whether it's a broken toe or a dysregulated nervous system. It takes the time it takes. So, if you need to, give yourself permission to do this slowly, carefully, in stages.

We now know a better way to do things. It takes discipline. And awareness. And practice. But once you've made a start on reframing all of your experiences this way, and time-travelling with sensation back to your original lion, you'll be ready for the fourth step. That's when we try to bring some lasting change to your life.

14. DISCHARGING

What You Will Learn

As you reach this step, you're now ready for the final transformation, taking your nervous system from the diagram below on the left, to the one on the right.

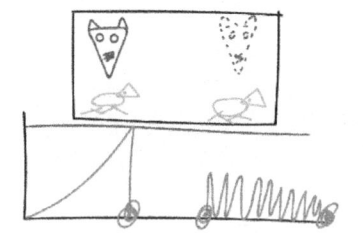

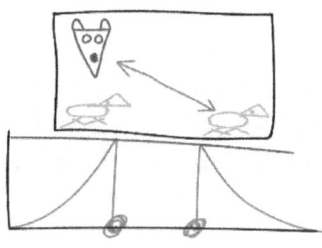

You've come a long way. You have learned to understand your nervous system so that your thinking, self-aware brain can let go of the problem it created in the first place. You've used this knowledge to start to look at difficult experiences in your life as a window into your nervous system, full as it is of triggers, baggage and reactions. And you've understood how to use your body's sensations to time-travel back to the triggering event you are experiencing, realising that this event from the past is still being experienced today.

So, in this final fourth step, I'm going to teach you how to use this connection between the body and these earlier events to allow the body to fully finish its reaction and, as a result, to restore itself closer to its natural, regulated resting point.

Discharging

The goal now is to get even closer to the sensations in your body, which belong to your reaction to the original lion. It's important to recognise that you've worked hard to get to this point; you've practiced boundaries and containment to find your baggage, and used sensation to time-travel back to the original lion. Now you need to invest in the felt experience of this original lion to try to finish your response to it.

There is a simple technique for doing this. Your body, which includes your nervous system, is throwing out clues to you all the time. If you invest time and commitment in listening to these clues, the part of your body that already knows how to finish this experience can take over. And this will allow the activation of your unfinished reaction to begin to discharge. This will return your nervous system to balance.

The problem with doing this is that these clues take your body back to a place when it was most overwhelmed. You're likely to have at least two kinds of negative reactions to that. First, you may not like the way it feels; it might be unpleasant, or odd, or peculiar. Second, if you are time-travelling back to the original event, you will inevitably feel some of your original overwhelm as well. You might even feel like you're just too small, too fragile or too vulnerable to cope with it. Maybe you were, back then. But now, as an adult revisiting these experiences, everything is different. You are bigger. You are stronger. You can cope.

But you have this conflict. The body is trying to go into the sensations of this experience, to get into, through, and out the other side of it. Meanwhile, the brain is resisting, with thoughts about how unpleasant or even un-survivable this is. You have to choose a path and pick a winner. In fact, the whole point of this book is to prepare you for this moment. That's why I wrote it, to help you to pick the right path and to have the courage to stick with it. You have to let the body take over. And when you do, it can be transformational.

I use a visualisation to help with this process:

Think about the sensations in your body as representing a child crying in the street. You're walking along and you see this child, sitting on the front step of a house, sobbing.

You can see other people walk by, not wanting to engage with the child's suffering. Some people approach the child, trying to fix the problem. That doesn't work, either.

Instead, I want you to visualise sitting down next to that child and just paying gentle attention to her. Wait. And watch. I want you to be interested, attentive, alert, concerned. But I don't want you to try to change anything, to comfort her or to shut her up. Instead, I want you to be her compassionate witness.

Then just see what happens next. And witness again. And see what happens next. And witness again. And so on.

Perhaps it sounds crazy, but this is all your body needs from your thinking brain, to allow it to do something healing, which it has been doing on its own for hundreds of millions of years.

This might get a bit weird. Remember the video of the gazelle we looked at in Part One of this book? People can feel shaky, or hot, or trembly, or any combination of these or their opposites. Certain emotions may or may not surface. Specific images or memories may or may not come. There is no way to know what is going to happen, but there is one mantra you can use to help you as you try not to get in the way. There are only five words you need from your thinking, human brain, and they are:

Can you let that happen?

Usually, the answer is yes. We can let pretty much anything happen if we believe that it is a good idea.

Tracking

In the 28-Day Plan, I'll also be introducing you to a helpful technique you can develop as a way of using your thinking brain to help you to reach these places in the body. Pioneered by Peter Levine, the founder of Somatic Experiencing, it is known by the acronym SIBAM, which refers to all the things you might look out for while you "let that happen".

Sensation: for example, tension, heat, relaxation
Images: memory, dreams, and metaphors, or even just an object in the room
Behaviour: posture, facial expressions, speech,

movement

Affect: feelings and emotions

Meaning: beliefs, judgments, thoughts, analysis, even when expressed through words

When using this technique, you (or a friend or practitioner) can ask you questions to expand your awareness of these elements, such as "What colour is that sensation?", or "Is it hot or cold?", or "What shape is it now?".

Then you can watch these qualities change. As you hang out on that visualised doorstep with the crying child, you can develop further awareness of the other elements in this list and use that as a guide to report on your experience. They all help you to be closer to your body and worry less about what's going on in your thinking brain. If you can stay with the body as it processes, then you can make progress on completing the original reaction to the original lion. This will leave you feeling more regulated and much less reactive to that trigger, which you started with at the beginning of this work.

You may even end up like the diagram below, connecting your present reaction with the original lion, and finally discharging the nervous system to the point that it can come back to rest.

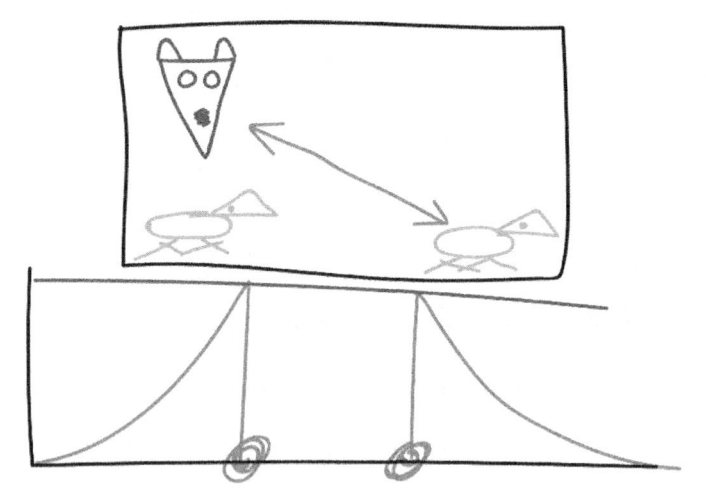

The 28-Day Plan will help you to resolve your body's experiences of the baggage getting triggered, without your thinking brain getting in your own way.

It might turn out to be too much for you to do alone. To feel safe enough to do this work, you might decide that you need a little extra support. If you have someone you trust, who can read this book with you to help you through the work, go ahead and ask. Or if that feels like it's too much, a professional trained in these methods can help too. There is a list of resources, types of treatment and organisations in the Further Reading section at the back of this book.

However you do it, your nervous system can recover. Your life can change. All you have to do is ask:

Can you let that happen?

EPILOGUE

The Path

One of the main ideas of this book is that our species has become so sophisticated that our biology no longer functions properly. The breakdown was caused by the dawn of human self-awareness, and the result was widespread dysregulation in our nervous systems. This has caused significant damage in almost all aspects of our lives, from our health to our behaviour, our relationships, our families, our society and even to our planet.

I have compared this to the story of the Garden of Eden. The original humans ate from the fruit of the tree of knowledge, and thus became self-aware. The first thing they did was to cover themselves up with fig leaves, a perfect metaphor for self-awareness.

While I think this is a compelling comparison, I'm not especially interested in religion in this book. Yet, at the same time, I am advocating some of the things that appear to have parallels with religions. After all, I talk incessantly about practice, which is part of many spiritual programmes. I also talk about being aware of your own behaviour, also included in many religious teachings. And I advocate that, in some specific ways, you change your behaviour.

In parallel with that, I am also asking you to go inside yourself to investigate your internal world and experience. I am suggesting a practice of deeper connection to yourself, inside of yourself, which will bring you great benefits. Sound familiar? This bears more than little relation to the ideas of prayer, meditation, chanting, devotion and so on.

Consider the more secular example of mindfulness. Its popularity has grown hugely recently, now scientifically validated in healthcare and neurobiology. The practice of yoga is on a similarly explosive path, entering into the mainstream of our modern world. They both appeal as a gateway to the wellbeing and awareness we strive for.

Almost every major religious or spiritual practice contains these same elements. At its very simplest, they are: do this, don't do that, pray and join the community (like a church). You can see this in all of the main religions, and also in the prescribed paths of many parallel ideas of spirituality, healthcare and human growth. I'm saying the same thing: have boundaries and containment, track your body's sensations, and improve your relationships.

But this book is a story about the nervous system. I wasn't talking about religion!

From Fear

I have written about neurobiology and biomechanics. I

started with the idea that sometimes we don't finish reacting to a threat, and so, we try to finish that later on, and combined this idea with the dawn of self-awareness. This led to all the healthcare, behavioural and social problems we already see on this planet.

The world after dysregulation looks like this.

We are all now that little red squiggle. The world is full of triggers. And, as a result, we generate escalating reactions, which are themselves threatening. Then we start to adapt, to cope with simply existing in a threatening world, which creates our attachment disorders, relationship dysfunction and societal conflicts.

Look at the diagram above, and ask yourself, what is the one main quality of a world experienced like that? Which single word describes how that little red squiggle feels in that world, a world where everything seems like a bigger threat than it really is, where there are invisible lions on every street corner?

The answer is FEAR.

Fear is the normal, biological, mammalian response to threat. It is the very currency of our survival. In fact, the foundation stone of evolution is that where there is a threat, we react with fear. Without it, we would be extinct. Your very ability to be here, now, reading this, is the legacy of your mammal ancestors who got very good at using fear to survive.

So, we now live in a world driven by fear. And this creates the desire to eradicate all of the triggers that caused it. We want to build walls, hoard money, be secure for life (even at others' expense) because our nervous systems are run by fear.

To Love

But if this book has shown you anything, I hope it's that there is another way. Instead of the exhausting work of managing all of your triggers outside of you, you are now able to organise yourself to manage your nervous system inside you.

Imagine that you could reduce all of your baggage to nothing. Imagine you could go even further from there. You become super regulated so that even real lions in the room with you wouldn't bother you too much. What if you could get your reactions down to almost nothing, even under the most intense, real and present danger; not because you are frozen, but because you are such a master of self-regulation that you can almost choose not to be afraid anymore? Perhaps you'd be a good candidate for the next Dalai Lama. What would that look like in the nervous system? I think it would look like this.

EPILOGUE

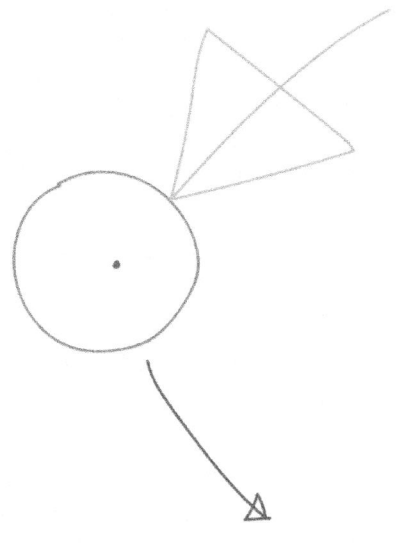

This nervous system is super-regulated. It has both no baggage and great boundaries, so, whatever you throw at it, you get less out than you put in. It is the opposite of the fearful one we saw before; the negative image of dysregulation. This is what we might all dream of achieving, once we start working with our nervous system.

When you look at this diagram, what quality does it suggest? What do you think it would be like to live like this? How would this person experience the world? What would you feel living with this nervous system where the world bounces off you and you are able to have such small reactions? Every time you encounter something or someone that is really upsetting for most people, you would not be overwhelmed. Instead, you might be able to see their difficult behaviour as an expression of their own dysregulation. What feeling would result from that?

The answer is LOVE.

I believe that working on the nervous system transforms fear into love. And I say this not as a mystic, but as a scientist. It might sound like the kind of thing you'd hear in a religion, but, for me, this is simple nervous system biomechanics.

In Practice

This transformation of fear into love is fundamental to every spiritual teaching and great religion that has ever been. All the ancient and modern programmes and religions also have the idea of practice in common. You can't transform fear into love just by reading about it. You have to follow the practice and do it regularly.

So, in theory, you can get all the benefits of all of the greatest paths in human history, just by learning to regulate your nervous system. If you believe in nothing else, start to believe in that. And if you do, then it follows that you will be changing the world. Profoundly. One wannabe Dalai Lama at a time.

I wish you all the best on your journey. Thank you for sharing it with me this far.

YOUR 28-DAY RECOVERY PLAN

The good news about the 28-Day Plan is that you don't have to do much work. Fifteen to twenty minutes a day should be enough, and you get weekends off!

The goal is to build up some basic skills. You are not trying to become a nervous system superhero overnight. I want you to change a little over time, and then to keep going because, oddly enough, change is also a threat to us. If you take it slowly, you won't freak your nervous system out. Do it a little, but often, so that you don't get overwhelmed.

We are very attached to our existing reactions, realities, personalities and characters. So digging into them and moving them about is not without some peril. But don't worry. If you take it slow, don't expect too much of yourself and are consistent in your practice, you'll start to be okay with the improvements in many areas of your life.

For much of this 28-day plan you will need to have a notebook. There are written exercises, which you could write here if you are reading this in a paperback, but I suggest that you do that in a separate, private journal where you have more space too. I will leave a line or two to make it clear when you should be writing. Or you can buy The Invisible Lion Workbook and do it there; or download a printable version with space for the exercises from www.theinvisiblelion.com.

My advice is to start on a Monday. If you miss a day, try to make it up. And if you miss many days, don't worry too much. Just try to pick up where you left off. Your body has its own intelligence and it will all take the time it takes. There is no way to do this wrong.

Your way is the right way.

Week One

Learning

This first week, you are going to revise the basic theory of this book, so that you can apply it to the next three weeks. Each day, you'll have a section to re-visit and then you'll test your knowledge with ten multiple choice questions. I really recommend doing the reading before you do the questions. But if you get a question wrong, just go back to the suggested pages and review the information you missed.

I know it's a bit reminiscent of school tests, but this is important and once you get it, hopefully you'll know it for life. We just need to get your thinking, human brain to agree to help the nervous system. Then we can do what comes next.

You can take the test online if you want. Just go to www.theinvisiblelion.com. Otherwise you'll find the tests for each section here in this book. I'm not going to tell you where the answers are, but if you are determined you will find them!

Week One, Day One

Revision

Today you're going to recap from the beginning. Of time! Remember what you learned about evolution? I want you to revise that Chapters One and Two, recalling how we got from a gazelle's ideal nervous system to a human's interrupted response to threat.

YOUR 28-DAY RECOVERY PLAN

Week One, Day One

Test your knowledge

Take the test!

Question 1: What is natural selection?

A. When you chose a bigger kid to be on your team
B. The process by which some animals survive in the wild and some don't
C. How animals decide which children to keep
D. The reason we vote for our politicians
E. Gene selection by natural disaster

Question 2: Why would a jawless fish want to freeze?

A. Because they are cold
B. To hibernate for the winter
C. So that they avoid other fish
D. To be invisible to predators who are looking for movement
E. They don't like warm water

Question 3: How many brains do I have?

A. It depends on my level of education
B. One but it is not always being used
C. Three, one from the each of the mammal, reptile and human
D. One collective universal brain for the whole planet
E. Just the one above my neck

Question 4: What is a social engagement system?

A. It is the source code of social media
B. It is how PTA committees are organised
C. It tells mammals whom to mate with

D. We use it for paperless invitations to parties
E. It is the branch of the nervous system, which makes us engage with each other

Question 5: In which order would I respond to a threat?

A. Social Engagement System, Vigilance, Fight-or-Flight, Freeze, Death
B. Vigilance, Social Engagement System, Freeze, Fight-or-Flight, Death
C. Freeze, Fight-or-Flight, Vigilance, Social Engagement System, Death
D. Fight-or-Flight, Freeze, Social Engagement System, Vigilance, Death
E. Death, Freeze, Fight-or-Flight, Vigilance, Social Engagement System

Question 6: What does activation mean?

A. Getting the software to work in your brain
B. Making friends with someone at the gym
C. Getting excited about things that might go wrong
D. Stimulation in the nervous system's accelerator
E. Swiping right on Tinder

Question 7: What is the relationship between activation and a charge in the nervous system?

A. Activation builds up a charge in the nervous system, like acceleration builds up speed
B. You can activate the nervous system without creating any charge
C. Charge and activation are not related
D. Charge and activation are the same thing
E. There is no charge for activation

Question 8:   When an activated system freezes, what happens to its charge?

A.   It disappears into the body and leeks away
B.   It is not known, and it is never seen again
C.   It makes the nervous system vibrate at a high speed
D.   It is stored in the nervous system in a dormant state
E.   It is refunded to the same credit card which paid for it

Question 9: When does a nervous system discharge its frozen activation?

A.   Never
B.   Whenever it wants to
C.   When it is safe enough to resume its organic response to threat
D.   When it is told to by the human brain
E.   On the first anniversary of freezing

Question 10: What does the human quality of self-awareness do to the process of discharging activation from the nervous system?

A.   It makes it much quicker
B.   It makes it much slower
C.   It doesn't make any difference at all
D.   It introduces a parallel dimension to the nervous system activation
E.   It observes a threat response with no threat, and, therefore, stops it

Week One, Day Two

Revision

Today is all about the consequences of interrupting the natural threat cycle. This is in Chapters Three, Four and Five. Remind yourself of how a nervous system becomes dysregulated, and how this messes with so much of what we think of as our health.

Week One, Day Two

Test your knowledge

Take the test!

Question 1: What happens if you meet a second lion before you have discharged the threat of the first one?

- A. There is no time to return to the set point before being activated again
- B. You should run for your life from both of them
- C. It depends on if they are related or not
- D. Nothing because it makes no difference
- E. You won't notice because you are still running away from the first one

Question 2: When we are dysregulated, how does our sense of reality change?

- A. We start to think that reading self-help books is more important
- B. We see lions where they are not really there in the present moment
- C. We become less aware of what is going on around us
- D. People are easier to get along with and annoy us less
- E. We become more gazelle-like and want to go on safari

Question 3: The difference between an internal and an external threat is?

- A. There is no difference because danger is always a threat
- B. One you get by email, and the other by messenger
- C. An internal threat comes from our thoughts, unlike real external dangers

D. People don't know the difference because they feel the same
E. Only street magicians know the difference

Question 4: We know that someone has experienced a trauma because…?

A. They have told us a shocking story
B. A psychiatrist has diagnosed them with PTSD
C. Why else would they behave so crazily
D. All of their friends agree that their life has been traumatic
E. Their nervous system has not yet recovered to its set point

Question 5: Yoga and meditation are related to the nervous system because…?

A. Everyone does it these days, so it must be important
B. You get really nervous if you don't do these things at least once a day
C. They were the first forms of medicine, so they must be important to mammals
D. They quieten the human brain and let the reptile and mammal brains take over, allowing the body to heal itself
E. Nobody knows, except for the ancient mystics

Question 6: Historically, healthcare has been thought of in these different categories?

A. Insured, uninsured and charity cases
B. Mental health and physical health
C. Mind, body and spirit
D. Treatable, untreatable and inexplicable
E. For profit and not for profit

Question 7: Medically unexplained symptoms are…?

A. Something your doctor has confused you about
B. A way to stay off work sick, without having to tell your boss why
C. When everyone knows what's wrong with you, except you
D. Nothing to worry about
E. Diagnoses which do not explain how the problem is caused

Question 8: When I say 'mental health' what is a 'mind'?

A. Only a philosopher can answer this question
B. The opposite of a body
C. Everything inside your brain
D. Nobody knows and you can't see it or touch it
E. A helpful classification of scientific phenomena

Question 9: A diagnosis in capital letters, like from the DSM 5, is an explanation because…?

A. It tells you what your doctor knows
B   It isn't an explanation
C. It brings together all the available evidence base into a diagnosis
D. Academics and doctors have validated these classifications
E. It is not just made up from what you've already said

Question 10: Mental and behavioural health problems, like addiction, are…?

A   Just medically unexplained symptoms
B. Healthcare problems equivalent to infection or cancer
C. Ways in which our bodies explore how to heal
D. Usually, examples of deficiencies in our personalities
E. Not interesting to scientist and academics

Week One, Day Three

Revision

Today's re-cap is about behaviour. Understanding this is a vital part of our day-to-day recovery. Re-visit Chapters Six and Seven to remind yourself of how dysregulation starts to show up in everyday life, through the ways that we behave and how that affects our relationships.

Week One, Day Three

Test your knowledge

Take the test!

Question 1: Triggers and Baggage work with each other in which of the following ways?

A. You can carry your triggers more easily in your baggage
B. They are independent of each other
C. Baggage can cause triggers to turn up in the real world
D. They are just different names for the same thing
E. Triggers set off the stored energy in your baggage

Question 2: The three types of reactions to triggers have what relationship with evolution?

A. Each of them evolves over time
B. They were started in the Garden of Eden
C. They are not related to evolution
D. Each fits a different layer of evolved response to threat
E. There is only one type of reaction to a trigger

Question 3: Boundaries are used in which of these ways?

A. To measure the distance between me and another nervous system
B. To explain to me what is okay for me so I can manage it
C. To get other people to do what I need, so that I can feel safe
D. For exerting influence and pressure over people who

are rude
E. To make me easier to live with at work and home

Question 4: Containment is done in which of these ways?

A. By not using the word "you", and by also speaking up
B. Making sure that you don't say what you are thinking
C. Doing and saying nothing until much later
D. Putting everything you are thinking and feeling in a box
E. Spraying your thoughts and feelings around for others to hold

Question 5: Boundaries and containment combined are useful because…?

A. They help you to control other people's behaviour
B. They are the same thing
C. It creates a bubble of safety around the nervous system in which it can heal
D. They are not useful to combine because they contradict each other
E. This is all you need to be happy

Question 6: Stabilising our behaviour stabilises the nervous system because…?

A. We annoy people less
B. Our mammal is nicer to other mammals, and this helps the mammal brain
C. Stable nervous systems create stable behaviour
D. It doesn't work like that and they are unrelated
E. When we protect our nervous system, it can act as if it is more regulated

Question 7: When an over-reaction has a relationship with an over-reaction, what happens?

A. Both of them increasingly trigger each other and they move apart
B. They hold each other comfortably in a balanced way
C. One dominates the other who becomes frozen and stuck
D. Sometimes it works, and sometimes it doesn't
E. True love is possible, but not guaranteed

Question 8: When an over-reaction has a relationship with an under-reaction what happens?

A. Both of them increasingly trigger each other and they move apart
B. They hold each other comfortably in a balanced way
C. One dominates the other who becomes frozen and stuck
D. Sometimes it works, and sometimes it doesn't
E. True love is possible, but not guaranteed

Question 9: How do we know the difference between a Goldilocks nervous system in a relationship, and one with just good boundaries and containment?

A. There are just different ways of saying the same thing
B. There is no difference, other than the internal experience of the latter
C. The Goldilocks nervous system looks like it works much better
D. You can't compare them, like apples and oranges
E. The Goldilocks nervous system is just a fairy tale

Question 10: Why do we choose the people we do to have relationships with?

A. Because of our chemistry
B. We don't choose, them they choose us
C. Our nervous systems fall in love with their nervous systems
D. Their triggers match our frozen baggage, which gives it a chance to activate
E. Mammals will be mammals

Week One, Day Four

Revision

Today, we look at love, particularly our first attempts at loving the people who raised us, what we learned from them about love and our own attempts to find loving relationships in life. This is in Chapters Eight and Nine.

Week One, Day Four

Test your knowledge

Take the test!

Question 1: Babies are born with which kind of a nervous system?

- A. They don't yet have a nervous system
- B. All kinds of different nervous systems, depending on their parents
- C. Their nervous systems look like they are dysregulated
- D. They only get nervous when their mothers are not present
- E. Parents can choose their babies' nervous systems when they are born

Question 2: Attachment styles are formed by early relationships because…?

- A. There is no other time to form them
- B. Babies and young children tend to copy their primary caregivers' regulation
- C. Most people screw up their children, and start doing that from birth
- D. They are just as likely to be formed in later relationships
- E. Attachment styles change all the time, however old you are

Question 3: An over-reacting early caregiver will lead to which problem?

- A. It leads to a resistant attachment style in the child
- B The child will not be affected by this kind of behaviour

C. It's impossible to tell because every family is different
D. It leads to an avoidant attachment style in the child
E. The child will not form any relationships

Question 4: An under-reacting early care giver will lead to which problem?

A. It leads to a resistant attachment style in the child
B. The child will not be affected by this kind of behaviour
C. It's impossible to tell because every family is different
D. It leads to an avoidant attachment style in the child
E. The child will not form any relationships

Question 5: You can help people to recover from an attachment problem at any age by…?

A. Explaining to them everything in this book
B. Telling them to change their behaviour and find new relationships
C. You can't recover from an attachment problem
D. It can only be done in childhood, by changing their parent's behaviours
E. Having a relationship with them with boundaries and containment

Question 6: A love addict comes from which kind of a nervous system?

A. Love isn't related to the nervous system
B. An over-reacting nervous system
C. Anyone can be addicted to love
D. An under-reacting nervous system
E. It can come from any kind of a nervous system

Question 7: A love avoidant comes from which kind of a nervous system?

A. Love isn't related to the nervous system
B. An over-reacting nervous system
C. Anyone can avoid love
D. An under-reacting nervous system
E. It can come from any kind of a nervous system

Question 8: I can be a love addict and a love avoidant at the same time if…?

A. Anyone can be if they have experienced both kinds of attachment in childhood
B. You are either always one or always the other, and you can't swap
C. Everyone is always one or the other but never both
D. You can't be one without the other if you are in love
E. Most people are very unlikely to be either, ever, so both is almost impossible

Question 9: Romantic relationships are a chance to heal because…?

A. Love makes us feel less triggered and, therefore, we seem better
B. Falling in love is the only way to heal a broken heart
C. If we can use them to activate frozen baggage while staying safe, then we can heal
D. Romantic relationships usually damage us and cannot heal us at all
E. St. Valentine was the patron saint of nervous systems

Question 10: Healthy romantic relationships require…?

A. Two willing participants and a bit of luck
B. Love conquers all and solves all problems
C. All romantic relationships are unhealthy, even if they

are fun
D. Weapons-grade boundaries and containment
E. An ability to keep secrets, and the willingness to lie frequently

Week One, Day Five

Revision

On the last day of Week One, we bring it all together. Today, I'm asking you to look at the more complicated effects of dysregulation on personality and character, and how this has affected our whole world. This is all in Chapter Ten.

Week One, Day Five

Test your knowledge

Take the test!

Question 1: Which combination of child, teen and adult can I be?

A. Child, teen, adult, or any two, or any three, all at the same time
B. I can be a child or a teen or an adult
C. I can be either an adult, or a teen or a child
D. It is only possible to be one person at a time
E. It depends how old I am

Question 2: Why do I have a hung parliament in my brain, and who is in charge?

A. Your politics are often very confused, and it's not clear who is president
B. My brain is not a hung parliament, and is very clear about its choices
C. Sometimes I'm a bit confused about life, but I sort myself out in the end
D. It's not possible to generalise because every brain is different
E. The brain has many decision-making centres, and one of them eventually wins

Question 3: What other responses can I have to threat after social engagement other than fight, flight or freeze?

A. There are no other choices because these are the only evolved responses
B. You can become vigilant before a reaction, and have

active and passive freeze states
C. You can simply deal with it without having to get so worked up
D. You can simultaneously deploy a mixture of all three
E. You don't have to respond to threat at all if you are at peace with yourself

Question 4: What possible nervous system explanation could I give for dissociation?

A. If I can't decide which attachment style I like best, I dissociate
B. Dissociation is not related to the nervous system
C. It is when the brain can't resolve the fragmented coalition government
D. Dissociation is just another mammalian response to threat
E. Nobody knows what dissociation is

Question 5: How many personalities do I have, and which is me?

A. You are always the same person, just with different moods
B. You might be different people in different relationships to suit your partner
C. Everyone has multiple personalities they are unaware of
D. Depending on your regulation and reactions, you can have different personalities
E. It's not a relevant question for the nervous system

Question 6: Which character strategies am I born with, and are any of them actually me?

A. A strategy is an adaptation to your dysregulation style and therefore not really you
B. You are always born with a dominant character

strategy that defines you
C. You can have any that you like and each is an aspect of your true self
D. They don't really exist and are just ideas psychologists use
E. You are born with all of them and use them when you need to

Question 7: Our world is affected by our individual nervous systems in which ways?

A. It makes very little difference, other than to our sense of self
B. Each person is greatly affected, but the effects cancel out over larger populations
C. The environment suffers from our lack of safety but our health is not affected
D. All people, relationships, families, communities, countries and the planet are affected
E. Nothing really matters because it is all going to be okay in the end

Question 8: What are the theoretical steps required to get back to an ideal state of regulation?

A. There is nothing you can do to get to an ideal state of regulation
B. Only by meditating up a mountain for many years can regulation be recovered
C. In theory, discharging all the responses to all threats will restore regulation
D. As long as you are having fun in your life, personal regulation is unnecessary
E. Scientists are working on equipment to do this for you

Question 9: What are the practical steps I could take on my own to get better-regulated?

A. Getting a friend to treat you better will start to make you feel more regulated
B. I need to not be in a relationship and to start to love myself instead
C. There is nothing I can do but others can do it for me
D. Just deciding to start to be regulated is enough; the body will follow
E. Recovery starts with stabilisation from changing your own behaviour and boundaries

Question 10: When I am going to do the rest of this 28-day plan?

A. Sometime
B. Maybe
C. Now
D. Never
E. There's a plan?

Week One, Day Six

Review

It's the weekend. Relax. You don't need to do anything today, but if you want to, you can look back over the questions and your answers in this section, picking out the things you found difficult or confusing. You could even talk to a friend about it and see if another perspective helps.

If not, let it go. It will all make sense in the end when it is supposed to. Don't worry if you can't get it all straight, right away.

Week One, Day Seven

Rest

Seriously. Rest. It's the seventh day.

Week Two

Reframing

So, you've read the instructions in Book Four. We spent a lot of time there, looking at how to reframe our experience of life through the lens of our model of trigger, baggage and reaction.

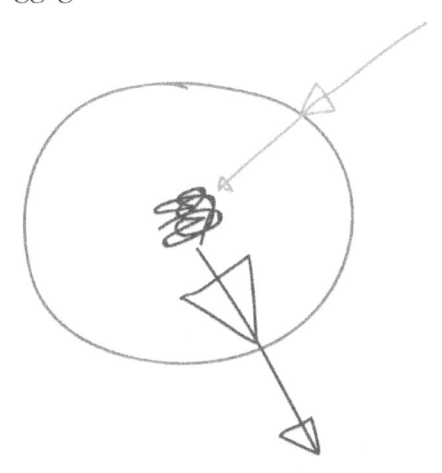

Sometimes, it can be tricky. The key to success here is to keep it simple and to keep it about yourself. To do that, we are going to use a formula to break down our communication, and the first person you are going to be talking to is yourself.

Each day this week, I invite you to start with thinking of three times that you were triggered in life. This could be from a time ten minutes ago or fifty years ago. You just need to find some material to practice with. You will take the first three examples that come into your head and write them down as brief headlines of the events. Then you will rank them from one, to three, in order of importance to you. We are going to work on the top one to reframe this experience.

You just have to think about the headline, and then follow the instructions. It should be quite easy.

Again, there is no right answer you're aiming for, but if you find yourself trying to point fingers at someone else, that's a red flag, showing you that you need to come back to what's going on for you in the diagram above.

Once you have your reframe, we are going to prepare for finding a boundary for this trigger that works for you.

And that's a good day's work. If you follow the script, you can't go too far wrong.

Week Two, Day One

Three Times I was Triggered

Take a moment. Give yourself some space and peace. Put the phone on airplane mode or turn off the Wi-Fi if you have to.

Try to settle a bit on what is going on inside your mind and body. Now go and look for trouble. Where inside of you is there a ripple of discomfort, discontent or distress?

Left to its own devices, that ripple will turn into a thought, often a memory and usually about someone else. Write down a short headline about this thought, memory or person.

Headline 1 _____

_____

Do it again, looking for another trigger to work on. Take your time. Try to settle a bit on what is going on inside your mind and body.

Somewhere inside you there is a ripple of discomfort. Let it become a thought or a memory. Write down a short headline about it.

Headline 2 _____

_____

One more time. Find the ripple. Let it become a thought or a memory. Write it down.

Headline 3 _____

_____

Well done! You now have three headlines for historical events that live on in your nervous system. Let's pick one to work on.

Week Two, Day One

Reframing

Imagine you are the editor of a newspaper, and, at your morning editorial meeting, three of your best writers come to you with these three stories. You can only have one headline on your front page. Which one do you want to work on?

Pick the story you think has the most widespread appeal. You want people to read your paper. You want stories that translate to the largest possible audience. You want to cover things that feel important. Ask yourself, which of these three headlines feels most important to you?

Now you are going to do the reframe exercise on this story. Don't try to do this if you haven't read Part Four. And don't read Part Four if you haven't read parts One to Three! You need to know why you are doing this more than you need to know how to do it.

Write down the headline again _____

_____

Now find the trigger that began this story. You are like a film director writing your script to recreate the event. Just recall what you saw and what you heard. Actions and sounds. That's all.

I noticed this trigger.

What I saw was _____

_____

_____

_____

What I heard was _____

_____

_____

_____

It doesn't need to be longer than this. Sometimes, it's tempting to use this as a way to attack someone else's behaviour but try to resist that temptation. Keep it really simple and about you.

Next, I want you to write down your reaction. This can be more complicated, but again, let's aim to make it really simple. Record what you remember or noticed about your sensations, emotions and thoughts. Crucially, you only want to focus on thoughts about yourself, not others.

I noticed this reaction.

I became aware of these sensations in my body_____

_____

_____

_____

I became aware of these emotions happening _____

_____

_____

_____

I became aware of these thoughts about myself _____

_____

_____

_____

Now you're ready to have a quick guess at the baggage. Go with what comes to mind immediately after writing out the trigger and the reaction. Don't dwell on it. There is no right answer. Just fill in the gap below.

When I look at this trigger and reaction something

about it feels familiar _____

_____

_____

_____

_____

If nothing about it feels familiar, that's fine. Just let it go. It might come to you later.

This might feel a bit difficult the first time you do it. And you might feel like you are not getting anywhere, or that it doesn't work. Don't worry; that's very normal. This is a skill that you will build with practice. And practice is what this week is for.

So, have another go tomorrow.

YOUR 28-DAY RECOVERY PLAN

Week Two, Day One

Boundary Prep

You can now use this story to prepare for setting your own boundaries around this issue. Go back to your main headline.

Write down the headline again _____

_____

Write down even more simply what triggered it.

What I saw was _____

_____

_____

What I heard was _____

_____

_____

How would you need that to be different, if you were not going to be triggered by it? You can usually find out by asking yourself, "What was okay for me" and "What wasn't okay for me".

It doesn't feel okay for me when _____

_____

Now you have some helpful knowledge. You know what the problem was.

In the future, you can try to make what's not okay for you happen less. That's your job. No one else's. We will do that in more detail in Week Four. But that's enough work for today. You now know what happened, where the trigger might have come from, and what you would like to be different in the future to make it less difficult.

Think about how this story now reads in your newspaper. How very different is that to the story you might have written if you had not done this exercise? It is this difference which gives you the opportunity to begin to make a real, lasting transformational change in your life.

Week Two, Day Two

Three Times I was Triggered

Today, we'll do the same exercises again, delving into any new stories that you sense you'd like to work on. Take a moment.

Try to settle a bit on what is going on inside your mind and body. Now go and look for trouble. Where inside of you is there a ripple of discomfort, discontent or distress?

Left to its own devices, that ripple will turn into a thought, often a memory and usually about someone else. Write down a short headline about this thought, memory or person.

Headline 1 _____

_____

Do it again, looking for another trigger to work on. Take your time. Try to settle a bit on what is going on inside your mind and body.

Somewhere inside you there is a ripple of discomfort. Let it become a thought or a memory. Write down a short headline about it.

Headline 2 _____

_____

One more time. Find the ripple. Let it become a thought or a memory. Write it down.

Headline 3 _____

_____

Well done! You now have three headlines for historical events that live on in your nervous system. Let's pick one to work on.

Week Two, Day Two

Reframing

Imagine you are the editor of a newspaper and pick the story which you want to be the headline of your paper. Ask yourself, "Which of these three stories feels most important to my life".

Write down the headline again _____

_____

Now find the trigger that began this story. Remember that you are like a film director, writing your script to recreate the event. Just recall what you saw and what you heard.

I noticed this trigger.

What I saw was _____

_____

_____

_____

What I heard was _____

_____

_____

_____

Remember to keep it simple and short. Next, you're going to write down your reaction. Again, make it really simple and about you, not others. All you need is what you remember or noticed about your sensations, emotions and thoughts.

I noticed this reaction.

I became aware of these sensations in my body ____

_____

_____

_____

I became aware of these emotions happening _____

_____

_____

_____

I became aware of these thoughts about myself ____

_____

_____

_____

Now have a quick guess at the baggage. What comes to mind immediately after writing out the trigger and the reaction? Fill in the gap below without overthinking it.

When I look at this trigger and reaction something about it feels familiar _____

_____

_____

_____

_____

Well done! Just like yesterday, you have one more task to complete.

Week Two, Day Two

Boundary Prep

Go back to your main headline.

Write down the headline again _____

_____

    Write down again, even more simply, what triggered it.

What I saw was _____

_____

_____

What I heard was _____

_____

_____

    How would you need that to be different if you were not going to be triggered by it? You can usually find out by thinking about what is okay for you and what is not okay for you.

It doesn't feel okay for me when _____

_____

_____

_____

You've now done your work for today.

Week Two, Day Three

Three Times I was Triggered

Today, we're looking for three more headlines. Find a ripple and write down short headline about the thoughts, memories or people that come to mind.

Headline 1 _____

_____

And again. Find the ripple. Let it become a thought or a memory. Write it down.

Headline 2 _____

_____

One more time. Find the ripple. Let it become a thought or a memory. Write it down.

Headline 3 _____

_____

Week Two, Day Three

Reframing

Ready, editor? Pick the headlines that feels most important to you right now.

Write down the headline again _____

_____

To find the trigger that began this story, write down what you saw and what you heard.
I noticed this trigger.

What I saw was _____

_____

_____

_____

What I heard was _____

_____

_____

_____

Keep it brief and simple.
Now let's recall what happened next. I noticed this reaction.

I became aware of these sensations in my body _____

_____

_____

_____

I became aware of these emotions happening _____

_____

_____

_____

I became aware of these thoughts about myself _____

_____

_____

_____

Try a quick guess at the baggage; this might be feeling like a more intuitive process by now. What comes to mind?

When I look at this trigger and reaction something

about it feels familiar _____

_____

_____

YOUR 28-DAY RECOVERY PLAN

Nearly there.

Week Two, Day Three

Boundary Prep

Choose your main headline.

Write down the headline again _____

_____

Write down again even more simply, what triggered it.

What I saw was _____

_____

_____

What I heard was _____

_____

_____

How would you need that to be different, if you were not going to be triggered by it? Think about what is okay for you and what is not okay for you.

It doesn't feel okay for me when _____

_____

_____

_____

_____

That's enough for today.

Week Two, Day Four

Three Times I was Triggered

I hope this is feeling less strange by now. Today is just the same as the other days this week, building on the work you've already done. Let's find three new stories that your body is asking you to look at.

Find a ripple, and write down short headline about the thoughts, memories or people that come to mind.

Headline 1 _____

_____

And again. Find the ripple. Let it become a thought or a memory. Write it down.

Headline 2 _____

_____

One more time. Find the ripple. Let it become a thought or a memory. Write it down.

Headline 3 _____

_____

YOUR 28-DAY RECOVERY PLAN

Week Two, Day Four

Reframing

Which of these three headlines feels most important to your life?

Write down the headline again _____

_____

To find the trigger, write down what you saw and what you heard.
I noticed this trigger.

What I saw was _____

_____

_____

What I heard was _____

_____

_____

_____

Don't be tempted to use this as a way to attack someone else's behaviour. Keep it really simple and about you.

What was your reaction? What do you remember or

notice about your sensations, emotions and thoughts?
I noticed this reaction.

I became aware of these sensations in my body ____

_____

_____

_____

I became aware of these emotions happening _____

_____

_____

_____

I became aware of these thoughts about myself ____

_____

_____

_____

Now have a quick guess at the baggage.

When I look at this trigger and reaction something

about it feels familiar _____

_____

_____

YOUR 28-DAY RECOVERY PLAN

_____

_____

And, as you'll know by now, you have one more task to complete.

Week Two, Day Four

Boundary Prep

Go to your main headline and write it down again __

_____

_____

    Write down again even more simply, what triggered it.

What I saw was _____

_____

_____

What I heard was _____

_____

_____

    What would need to be different, if you were not going to be triggered by it? Let's explore what's okay and not okay in that context.

It doesn't feel okay for me when _____

_____

And that's Day Four wrapped up.

Week Two, Day Five

Three Times I was Triggered

This is the last day you'll need to dig into those experiences that are causing any kind of discomfort, discontent or stress. You're probably quite good at this by now.

Find a ripple and write down short headline about the thoughts, memories or people that come to mind.

Headline 1 _____

_____

And again. Find the ripple. Let it become a thought or a memory. Write it down.

Headline 2 _____

_____

One more time. Find the ripple. Let it become a thought or a memory. Write it down.

Headline 3 _____

_____

Week Two, Day Five

Reframing

Which of these three headlines feels most important to your life?

Write down the headline again _____

_____

To find the trigger, write down what you saw and what you heard.
I noticed this trigger.

What I saw was _____

_____

_____

_____

What I heard was _____

_____

_____

_____

Don't be tempted to use this as a way to attack someone else's behaviour. Keep it really simple and about you.

What was your reaction? What do you remember or

notice about your sensations, emotions and thoughts? I noticed this reaction.

I became aware of these sensations in my body _____

_____

_____

_____

I became aware of these emotions happening _____

_____

_____

_____

I became aware of these thoughts about myself _____

_____

_____

_____

Now have a quick guess at the baggage. Just fill in the gap below with whatever comes to mind.

When I look at this trigger and reaction something

about it feels familiar _____

_____

_____

_____

Well done! The last step now is prepare for boundary work.

Week Two, Day Five

Boundary Prep

Go to your main headline, and write it down again __

_____

_____

    Write down again even more simply, what triggered it.

What I saw was _____

_____

_____

What I heard was _____

_____

_____

    What needs to be different so that you are not going to be triggered by it in future? Think about what is okay for you, and what is not okay for you.

It doesn't feel okay for me when _____

_____

_____

YOUR 28-DAY RECOVERY PLAN

That's it! You've got through the week.

Week Two, Day Six

Review

You've done a lot of work this week, which, I hope, got a little easier each day. The more you practice this, the better you get at it. If you did this every day for the rest of your life, it would do you no harm at all.

Eventually, you might be able to do it all the time, live, in every situation as it happens. That would completely change how you view your life and how you experience it.

So, today, you only need to have a look back at what you have written this week, reviewing it more as a witness than a participant. See what you notice. Things might look a bit different from the outside, looking in. You might notice where your language was a bit spikey or where you were really talking about someone else, rather than your own experience. These are your opportunities to clean things up a bit.

Just noticing how things can seem different when you are not caught up in the energy of them is a big step. Re-write anything you read if you think you want to make it better. The goal is to get to the point where you are watching your nervous system and describing it, rather than just bring trapped in it and reacting to it.

Week Two, Day Seven

Rest

Rest. That's all.

Week Three

Connecting

Each day last week you worked in some detail to reframe your experience of an event that had triggered you. We are going to take that same important event from each day last week and use it to practice doing some time-traveling.

In each of these examples last week, you found your baggage by reflecting on what felt familiar about your reaction. You may have thought of something very specific, like an actual event, or something more general, like a pattern of events, behaviours or experiences.

This week we are going to move you down your brainstem a bit, away from thoughts, from ideas and even from language, into the body and its experiences.

The reframe was an observation of your nervous system today; a trigger, your reaction and an idea about the baggage behind it. The aim of this section is to link that baggage to something unfinished in your body from the past. This opens up your awareness from the limitations of just today, to the whole timeframe from when the baggage was created, right up until now, represented by the black box in the diagram below.

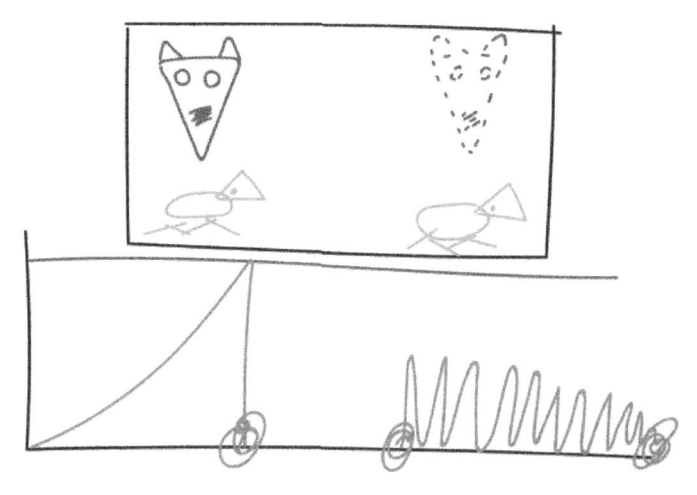

We do this by becoming a gazelle again, connecting to our inner mammal and leaving behind the problems created by the self-awareness of our thinking, human brain. This allows new connections to be made, and is the gateway into the transformational work of the final week of this plan.

One irony of all of this is that you are, right now, reading a book. Gazelles tend not to read. By reading, you are activating your thinking brain. And I am trying to get you to do the opposite.

So, to get you ready, you are going to learn how to do something called a 'body scan'. I'm going to recommend you do this with a video rather than reading it on the page here. You can search on the internet for body scan videos or find one you like at www.theinvisiblelion.com.

Each day this week, you are going to review the piece of work you did on the corresponding day in Week Two that will be your material for this exercise. You are going to read that story again, put down the book, and then do the body scan exercise while this story is still present for you.

Your goal is to use the body scan to find a place in your body where the sensations match the activation from the baggage of that story. You will, somewhere, somehow, feel it in your body, and that's why the body scan helps you to find it.

Once you find it, you will be able to use that sensation and float it back in time. Sounds weird? It is, a bit. But you can do it by asking your body one simple question:

Can you float that back in time and see where it goes?

Remember, don't ask your brain! Ask your body.

Whatever comes back to you from this question, try to allow it to be whatever it is. It might not make any sense at first. So, don't judge the answer. People often discount the thoughts or memories that come up because they can't understand the connection. Be prepared for that. This is not about logic; this is about allowing the body to make connections through its senses. Don't judge.

Once you settle on an experience or a memory, I want you to shift gear, get out your journal and write down as much about it as possible. You will write about both what you remember and what you notice about your sensations, now, as you remember it. This will then be your material for Week Four.

A word of warning; if you get really good at this, you might go deep enough into the experience that you don't want to wait until Week Four to process it. That's why it might be a good idea, right now, to also read on to Week Four and have those resources ready. If it feels right to you to continue straight from one to the other, then go for it. The body knows best.

On the other hand, it is also more than enough just to do some time-traveling on its own and to write down what that was like for you. That's okay too.

Week Three, Day One

The Body Scan

Review your stories from Day One of Week Two. Find your headline and write it out again. Writing it again is part of the process of getting back into your body.

Write down the headline _____

_____

Then, read though everything you wrote about it in Week Two until it is something you can hold in mind without looking at the page any more.

Now do the body scan to completion. While it is happening, notice where your body is grabbing your attention. These are the places you want to come back to.

You can search the internet for body scan videos or find one you like at www.theinvisiblelion.com.

Week Three, Day One

Time-travelling

Once the body scan is finished, ask your body:

Can you float that back in time and see where it goes?

and just allow whatever comes up to linger there. Go towards that memory or experience with curiosity. Hang out there for as long as you need to, as you rediscover it. Then, come back to this book.

Now write down in as much detail as you can (in your journal) what you notice about remembering that experience.

This takes me back to _____

_____

_____

As I rediscover this, I notice the following in my body

_____

_____

_____

See, it's quite simple. We will do another one tomorrow.

Week Three, Day Two

The Body Scan

Review your story from Day Two of Week Two.

Write down the headline _____

_____

Find your headline story, and write it out again. Read through everything you wrote about it in Week Two until it is something you can hold in mind without looking at the page any more.

Then, do the body scan to completion, noticing where your body is grabbing your attention. These are the places you want to come back to.

YOUR 28-DAY RECOVERY PLAN

Week Three, Day Two

Time-travelling

Once the body scan is finished, ask your body:

Can you float that back in time and see where it goes?

and just allow whatever comes up to linger there. Go towards that memory or experience with curiosity. Hang out there for as long as you need to, as you rediscover it. Then, come back to this book.

Now write down in as much detail as you can (in your journal) what you notice about remembering that experience.

This takes me back to _____

_____

_____

As I rediscover this, I notice the following in my body

_____

_____

Well done. Keep going tomorrow.

Week Three, Day Three

The Body Scan

Review your stories from Day Three of Week Two.

Write down the headline _____

_____

    Find your headline story, and write it out again. Read through everything you wrote about it in Week Two until it is something you can hold in mind without looking at the page any more.
    Then, do the body scan to completion, noticing where your body is grabbing your attention. These are the places you want to come back to.

Week Three, Day Three

Time-travelling

Once the body scan is finished, ask your body:

Can you float that back in time and see where it goes?

and just allow whatever comes up to linger there. Go towards that memory or experience with curiosity. Hang out there for as long as you need to, as you rediscover it. Then, come back to this book.

Now write down in as much detail as you can (in your journal) what you notice about remembering that experience.

This takes me back to _____

_____

_____

_____

As I rediscover this, I notice the following in my body

_____

_____

_____

Nice work. Two more to go.

Week Three, Day Four

The Body Scan

Review your stories from Day Four of Week Two.

Write down the headline _____

_____

    Find your headline story, and write it out again. Read through everything you wrote about it in Week Two until it is something you can hold in mind without looking at the page any more.
    Then, do the body scan to completion, noticing where your body is grabbing your attention. These are the places you want to come back to.

Week Three, Day Four

Time-travelling

Once the body scan is finished, ask your body:

Can you float that back in time and see where it goes?

and just allow whatever comes up to linger there. Go towards that memory or experience with curiosity. Hang out there for as long as you need to, as you rediscover it. Then, come back to this book.

Now write down in as much detail as you can (in your journal) what you notice about remembering that experience.

This takes me back to _____

_____

_____

_____

As I rediscover this, I notice the following in my body

_____

_____

_____

Nearly there.

Week Three, Day Five

The Body Scan

Review your stories from Day Five of Week Two.

Write down the headline _____

_____

Find your headline story, and write it out again. Read though everything you wrote about it in Week Two until it is something you can hold in mind without looking at the page any more.

Then, do the body scan to completion, noticing where your body is grabbing your attention. These are the places you want to come back to.

Week Three, Day Five

Time-travelling

Once the body scan is finished, ask your body:

Can you float that back in time and see where it goes?

and just allow whatever comes up to linger there. Go towards that memory or experience with curiosity. Hang out there for as long as you need to, as you rediscover it. Then, come back to this book.

Now write down in as much detail as you can (in your journal) what you notice about remembering that experience.

This takes me back to _____

_____

_____

_____

As I rediscover this, I notice the following in my body

_____

_____

_____

You made it. That's a good week's work.

Week Three, Day Six

Review

This week, you might have had some great experiences and felt like this is beginning to make sense. Or it may have been very hard, maybe even unproductive. It is important to remember that this is just practice. You are building a skill set day by day, week by week, to allow you to look at your life differently and to experience it with less difficulty.

If you were able to do some time-travelling, have a look at what came up. These are unfinished moments for you, showing you where your unfinished business is. Somewhere around these kinds of experiences, your activation got stuck, so a part of you is still there, always there, waiting to discharge and finish your response to this threat. Next week, I'll show you how to start to do that.

For now, if you were able to get this far on your own, then well done. That shows that your nervous system has resilience and that you are ready to do this work. If you drew a blank, don't worry. Just by understanding what you are trying to do, and by preparing the ground to do it, you are already moving in the right direction.

If you need some help to keep moving from here, a friend or even a relevant professional might be useful to walk through this process with you. We all find safety in different ways and the company of someone we trust is always great for regulating the nervous system, to help to prepare it for completing its unfinished business.

Week Three, Day Seven

Rest

Now let your system rest.

Week Four

Discharging

So far, you have worked hard to create the building blocks for this final piece of work. You have learned the theory and have reframed some of your difficult experiences. You have sensed into the baggage you discovered there and time-travelled back to some earlier experiences which felt the same.

This week, let's see if you can complete some of that unfinished business and discharge some of your baggage. If you can, then you will be less triggered in future and will, therefore, find your boundaries easier to maintain. As a result, containment gets easier, and so, you'll find this work more accessible in general. It gets better and better, once things get moving.

But it's not always easy. It may be that doing this exercise on your own, from a book, is a step too far. And while some people take to it intuitively, others need more preparation, support and time. That's okay. Just do what you can and remember that this book is about creating the discipline of a practice.

Whatever you get out of this week, you will be building the skills to live with your nervous system in a different way. Then, you can see what extra help you might want to make it work for you as well as it possibly can. No one would suggest that everyone's problems can be resolved just by reading the exercises in a book, but some of some people's problems probably can be. And it will be a lot easier to find the right help for everything else, once you know what you are trying to achieve.

So, this week, we are doing this:

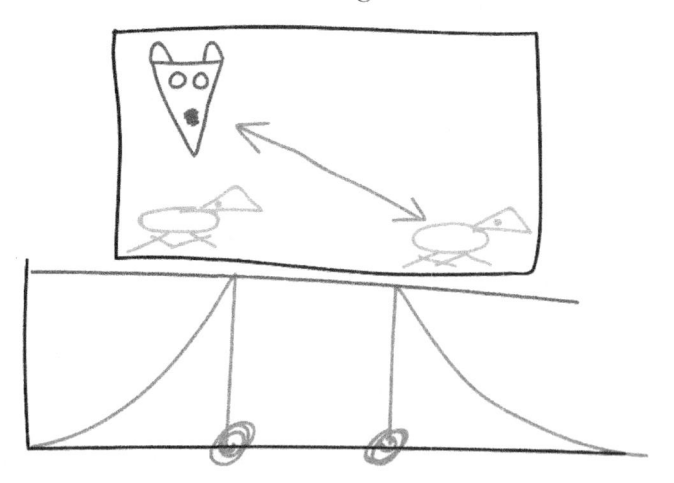

We use the innate wisdom of the body to reconnect with the threat response started by the original lion. Then we let that happen. And, then, we let that happen some more. And we keep going until we feel a sense of something completing.

If we don't get that far, that's okay. This is a beginning and a practice. The first time you meditate or hold a yoga pose or hit a tennis ball, it doesn't usually work very well. That's why you are supposed to practice a little bit every day.

Each day, at the end of this exercise, you'll have a chance to review the whole thing. After reconnecting your body with the original lion, you will be able to see the whole time-line of your problem a bit more clearly. This will help you to set the boundary you need for the future and, even more importantly, to know how you are going to manage that boundary to make sure you keep your nervous system feeling safe.

The safer you feel, the better you will be at this work.

If you get good at this process, the benefits will continue to build in your life. You can then begin to do all four weeks' exercises at once, all in a row, live, in the real world. Eventually, you will be able to habitually catch yourself being triggered in the moment, reframe the experience, time-travel and discharge the baggage on the spot.

That's the ultimate goal. To become a gazelle again. And if you can do that, while remaining human, not only will you change your life, but you will transform the lives of those around you, your families, communities, societies and the planet.

You really can change the world, one nervous system at a time. And Ghandi was right; you really do only have to start with you. Good luck!

YOUR 28-DAY RECOVERY PLAN

Week Four, Day One

Tracking Sensation

Each day this week, we are going to start again with the body scan. This is a really important tool in understanding and regulating your nervous system, so I'm hoping that, over time, it will start to feel very natural to you. Make sure you create a quiet space for yourself to do this work, turning electronics off and settling into the possibility of getting back into your body. You will, by now, have identified your favourite body scan video or audio recording, so try to get into a routine so that it is something familiar to your nervous system. And then begin.

After the body scan, you are going to re-read your time-travel from the corresponding day on Week Three. Try to read it mindfully, slowly, with great care and attention. I want you to get back into the experiences that your body was communicating to you while rediscovering that moment. And this time, we are going to stay with it, to see if anything will move.

So, once you have done the body scan and read the time-travel, it's time to pay attention to your sensations. There are a number of ways to do this. One very simple way do that is to ask yourself a number of questions about the sensations you're aware of, starting with the one which seems most important.

You can ask:

Where is the sensation?
What colour is it?
How big is it?

What shape is it? Round? Jagged? Square?
What textile is it? Smooth? Shiny? Rough?
What temperature is it? Hot? Cold? Warm?

Then, answer these questions in your head. This helps you to pay attention to the sensation, which might be, say, a hot, small, blue, smooth, square egg in the middle of my stomach. And, as you concentrate on this description of it, connecting it to my sensation, ask yourself:

And what happens next?

What you are looking for is whether any of these qualities change. An easy example would be that it gets cooler. Make sure you notice this, by saying to yourself, "It's getting cooler". It's just about noticing the details of the sensation.

Then, ask yourself a very important question:

Can you let that happen?

The correct answer is yes! In some respects, the whole point of reading this book is to bring you to this right answer at this vital point in your recovery. You might remember that the problem started in Box 4, with self-awareness; this moment is the antidote.

Can you let that happen?

Yes!

When you let this happen, you are restarting your interrupted response to the threat of the original lion. Then you keep going, letting it happen until you come to a natural pause in the process.

Then, go back to the questions about the sensation:

Where is it?
What colour is it?
How big is it?
What shape is it? Round? Jagged? Square?
What texture is it? Smooth? Shiny? Rough?
What temperature is it? Hot? Cold? Warm?

Then, ask yourself:

And what happens next?

Then, ask yourself:

Can you let that happen?

And then let it happen.

Keep going until you feel that things have come to a natural conclusion. You might feel calmer, or notice your posture relax, or let out a deep exhalation. These are your clues that something has been finished. This is how mammals feel once they have completed their escape from, and response to, a threat.

Then, from this new place, you can review the whole piece of work to find out what you need to do, when similar triggering situations come up.

Week Four, Day One

Boundary And Review

Now go back to the story you chose to work on from Day One of Week Two.

You're now going to finish this piece of work, creating a boundary from the work you began at that end of that process. Find the boundary prep from Day One of Week Two and write it out again.

It doesn't feel okay for me when _____

_____

_____

_____

As you write this out again, and read it back to yourself, you might find that you have a different relationship with those words. When you first wrote them, they were an idea. Now they might be closer to a really clear instruction from your body. There is an expression "the body knows". When you feel it, you know what it means. Hopefully, you are getting a glimpse of that now.

From this new embodied place of deeper understanding of your needs, you are now going to make two new, vitally important statements. You are going to tell yourself:

What I need in the future
What I am going to do for myself to make sure I get it

YOUR 28-DAY RECOVERY PLAN

You can figure out what you need in the future because it is related to what doesn't feel okay for you, as you stated in your boundary prep. If it doesn't feel okay for you to be shouted at, in the future you need to make sure that you don't get shouted at. This bit is usually that simple. The hard part is not making that someone else's problem.

If what I need is not to be shouted at, then I might think that this is something I need to persuade others to do for me. But then I've lost all of my power, when what I really need is exactly the opposite. That's why we need to take control of reducing the triggers in our lives ourselves.

Then ask, "What can I actually do for myself if the problem is being created by other people or situations" The answer is usually that we can do only two things. We can ask people to do things differently, explaining why, if we feel safe enough. Or if they can't, won't or don't, then we can choose not be around those people in these situations. That's it.

Ultimately, this might create some very difficult choices, like leaving a job or a relationship in extreme cases. But if that's what is necessary to rescue your nervous system, then it might well be worth it. Only you can decide. Going through this exercise of allowing the body to inform you about how it feels about the problem will help you know, deeply, what you really need. Usually, once someone knows this, nothing feels more important. The body knows.

If you can get this far, and have made clear to yourself and others what you need in the future, and are making sure that you get it, one way or another, you have reset the conditions for your world and made yourself more safe.

And once you are safer, your nervous system has more room to work with sensations, and, therefore, more chance of completing unfinished responses to earlier threats. If you keep going, it should get easier and easier.

So, what I need in future is _____

_____

_____

_____

And this is how I am going to take care of myself if I don't get it _____

_____

_____

_____

See how that feels. Let it settle into your new nervous system. And breathe.

You have just completed one piece of work around one earlier threat in your life. If you want to, read back what you wrote on Day One of Weeks Two and Three. Then, read your boundaries above again.

Imagine what it would be like if you could do all of this automatically, the moment the trigger first happens. It's possible. That's your goal. It's what all this practice is for. Keep going. It will get easier.

Week Four, Day Two

Tracking Sensation

Today, we'll do the same again. Create a quiet space for yourself to do this work, and start with your favourite body scan video or audio recording.

After the body scan, read your time-travel from Day Two of Week Three. Read mindfully and slowly. Pay attention to your sensations and find one sensation that seems urgent. Then ask yourself:

Where is it?
What colour is it?
How big is it?
What shape is it?
What textile is it?
What temperature is it?

List the answers in your head. As you concentrate on your description of it, connect it to this sensation, and ask yourself:

And what happens next?

See if any of these qualities you've described change. Then, ask yourself this very important question:

Can you let that happen?

Let it happen until you feel a pause in the process. Then, go back to the questions about the sensation:

Where is it?
What colour is it?
How big is it?
What shape is it?
What texture is it?
What temperature is it?

Then,

And what happens next?

See if any of these qualities change. Then, ask yourself:

Can you let that happen?

And then let it happen.
Keep going until you feel that things have come to a natural conclusion.

YOUR 28-DAY RECOVERY PLAN

Week Four, Day Two

Boundary And Review

Go back to the story you chose as your main piece of work on Day Two, Week Two. Find the boundary at the end, and write it out again.

It doesn't feel okay for me when _____

_____

_____

_____

Now that the body knows this, make two new, vitally important statements.

So, what I need in future is _____

_____

_____

_____

And this is how I am going to take care of myself if I don't get it _____

_____

_____

See how that feels. Let it settle into your new nervous system. And breathe.

You have just completed one piece of work around an earlier threat in your life. If you feel like it, read back what you wrote on Day Two of Weeks Two and Three. Then, read your boundaries above again.

Keep going.

Week Four, Day Three

Tracking Sensation

It's the same process again today. Have you settled into a rhythm for your quiet body scan yet?

After the body scan, read your time-travel from the same day last week, mindfully and slowly. Pay attention to your sensations, identifying one sensation that seems most urgent. Then, ask yourself:

Where is it?
What colour is it?
How big is it?
What shape is it?
What texture is it?
What temperature is it?

List the answers in your head, and as you concentrate on your description and connect it to this sensation, ask yourself:

And what happens next?

See if any of these qualities change. Then, ask yourself:

Can you let that happen?

Let it happen until you feel a pause in the process. Then, go back to the questions about the sensation:

Where is it?

What colour is it?
How big is it?
What shape is it?
What texture is it?
What temperature is it?

Then ask yourself again:

And what happens next?

See if any of these qualities change. Then, ask yourself this very important question:

Can you let that happen?

And then let it happen.
Keep going until you feel that things have come to a natural conclusion.

Week Four, Day Three

Boundary And Review

Go back to the story you chose as your main piece to work on from Day Three of Week Two. Find the boundary at the end, and write it out again.

It doesn't feel okay for me when _____

_____

_____

_____

Make two new, vitally important statements, helped by your body's wisdom.

So, what I need in future is _____

_____

_____

_____

And this is how I am going to take care of myself if I don't get it _____

_____

_____

See how that feels. Let it settle into your new nervous system. Breathe.

You have just completed a further piece of work around an earlier threat in your life. If you like, you can read back what you wrote on Day Three of Weeks Two and Three. Then, read your boundaries above again.

Keep going.

Week Four, Day Four

Tracking Sensation

Let's do it all over again. Is it starting to feel more natural yet? Don't worry if it isn't; it'll happen.

After doing the body scan, read your time-travel from Day Four of Week Three mindfully and slowly. Pay attention to your sensations, pinpointing one sensation that seems urgent. Then ask yourself:

Where is it?
What colour is it?
How big is it?
What shape is it?
What texture is it?
What temperature is it?

List the answers in your head, and, as you concentrate on your description of it, connect it to this sensation, and ask yourself:

And what happens next?

See if any of these qualities change. Then ask:

Can you let that happen?

Let it happen until you feel a pause in the process. Then, go back to the questions about the sensation:

Where is it?
What colour is it?

How big is it?
What shape is it?
What texture is it?
What temperature is it?

Ask yourself:

And what happens next?

Do any of these qualities change? Now ask:

Can you let that happen?

And then let it happen.

Keep going until you feel that things have come to a natural conclusion.

YOUR 28-DAY RECOVERY PLAN

Week Four, Day Four

Boundary And Review

Go back to the story you chose as your main piece to work on from Day Four of Week Two. Find the boundary at the end and write it out again.

It doesn't feel okay for me when _____

_____

_____

_____

Now make two vitally important statements.

So, what I need in future is _____

_____

_____

_____

And this is how I am going to take care of myself if I don't get it _____

_____

_____

_____

How does it feel? Let it settle into your new nervous system. Breathe and feel.

You have now completed another piece of work around an earlier threat in your life. If you want to, read back what you wrote on Day Four of Weeks Two and Three, then read your boundaries above once more.

Keep going. You're making great strides.

Week Four, Day Five

Tracking Sensation

Last one! Work through the body scan, and then read your time-travel from Day Five of Week Three. By now, you'll be more used to getting back into the experiences your body was communicating to you and paying attention to your sensations. Find one sensation you'd like to focus on today. Then, ask yourself:

Where is it?
What colour is it?
How big is it?
What shape is it?
What texture is it?
What temperature is it?

List the answers in your head, and, as you concentrate on your description of it, connecting it to this sensation, ask yourself:

And what happens next?

Do these qualities change? Ask yourself this very important question:

Can you let that happen?

Let it happen until you feel a pause in the process. Then, go back to the questions about the sensation:

Where is it?

What colour is it?
How big is it?
What shape is it?
What texture is it?
What temperature is it?

Then ask yourself:

And what happens next?

See if any of these qualities change. Then, ask yourself this very important question:

Can you let that happen?

And then let it happen.
Keep going until you feel that things have come to a natural conclusion.

Week Four, Day Five

Boundary And Review

Go back to the story you chose as your main piece to work on from Day Five of Week Two. Find the boundary at the end and write it out again.

It doesn't feel okay for me when _____

_____

_____

_____

Now make these two important statements.

So, what I need in future is _____

_____

_____

_____

And this is how I am going to take care of myself if I don't get it _____

_____

_____

_____

How does it feel? As before, let it settle into your new nervous system.

You have now completed your fifth piece of work around earlier threats in your life. Feel free to read back what you wrote on Day Five of Weeks Two and Three and your boundaries above again.

You are done!

Week Four, Day Six

Review

Wow. You've made it. Congratulations on completing your 28-Day Plan. You've been through the whole process of retraining your thinking, human brain, reframing your life experiences, using what's left over to time-travel, and resolving where that took you back to.

One end result from this process in a boundary. Look back over the five boundaries you discovered this week, and reflect on what you have told yourself you need and what you have promised yourself you will do if you can't get it. You can't typically regulate your whole nervous system forever in one go, but you can start your own practice of boundaries in your life, which will keep you safer and make the work easier to continue.

I hope you have found some places in you that feel safer now and have good clues about how to adjust your life to make it safer, too. If you continue to combine these two elements of nervous system recovery, you should find that your life changes significantly for the better in the long run.

There will be many ups and downs because that's how the nervous system works, but you will find that, in time, the ups are better and more sustained and, the downs less far down and last less long, and that the swings between the one and the other happen less often.

Welcome to a life an increasing regulation. Give yourself a pat on the back. You deserve it!

Week Four, Day Seven

Rest

Now let your system rest. Celebrate the beginning of the rest of your life.

CLINICAL CASE STUDIES

From Harley Street To High Street

This book is written for everyone. It is about all of our lives, ourselves, our relationships, our families, our workplaces, our communities and our world. But the knowledge behind it comes from more specialist sources. Much of it stems from work done by a small band of pioneers in the field of mental, behavioural and physical health, typically in areas where treatment has often not been very successful.

I have been a patient of that system, which is how I discovered what I now think of as the future of healthcare. I set up a residential clinic to put these theories into practice, and have been lucky enough to have spent years working at the coal-face of these innovations. All of us who have been involved in this work have learned a lot about the messy business of being human as a result. But this knowledge shouldn't just remain cloistered in clinical work. Everybody needs to know it because being human is a shared problem.

The clinic has gone from strength to strength, due to the heroic efforts of the staff who have worked there and the trust, courage and commitment of our clients. It typically treats people who have been failed in treatment elsewhere, either in hospitals, rehabs, private therapy or in medicine. We are often told that we have become an option of last resort for our clients who feel that their problems are both not understood and not successfully treated by existing ideas and methods.

We have had some remarkable results. But we are not always successful. I have lost count of the number of people who have thanked us for setting up the clinic and have credited the work they did there with saving their lives. Equally, there are people I remember who did not feel this way and whose outcomes have been much less successful. It has been an enduring mission of mine to understand the difference and, therefore, to improve our treatment outcomes.

People tend to come to us when they've reached some kind of crisis, when their symptoms are beginning to affect their life in a seriously adverse way. They might tell us about severe depressive episodes, or about panic attacks or describe symptoms of stress and anxiety. They may be experiencing problems in their relationships and feel they don't know what to do. Sometimes, they talk about feeling stuck; they explain how they know that they should be doing certain things, but that, instead, they are behaving differently to how they wish to.

Or they have addictions that they cannot break, that are starting to render them unable to function properly. These addictions could be anything, from substance addictions, like drugs and alcohol, to behavioural addictions, such as eating disorders, hoarding, spending or sex. They can have baffling physical health problems too.

Whatever the specific problem a person brings to the consulting room, everyone we see has one thing in common: they are experiencing something which they seem to feel unable to change. The start of the recovery process, therefore, can look a bit like a diagnostic puzzle. Rarely does someone come in and explain exactly what is wrong with them or give us the whole story about the relevant underlying history that created it.

I have chosen case studies that I believe will give examples of situations that most people can relate to, if not from their own lives, then from the life of someone they've known. I've introduced each case by posing the presenting question, the question that's on the client's mind when they come to us. Eventually, we will try to answer the question, but not until we have reframed the whole story through the lens of the nervous system.

SHOULD I LEAVE MY HUSBAND?

Presenting Problem

Maddy is fifty-two. She is a high-functioning chartered accountant and mother to a son, aged sixteen, and a daughter, aged eighteen. Maddy's husband is a property developer, and they live together in south-east London, where they are active members of their local Anglican church, the centrepiece of their social and spiritual community.

On the surface, this is a perfect family. Most people who know them would never suspect anything was wrong. However, Maddy has been suffering from overwhelming bouts of anxiety, on and off, for almost twenty years. The anxiety attacks started in her mid-thirties, around the time the children were born. At its most severe, anxiety has included symptoms which were labelled Obsessive Compulsive Disorder, when she would become obsessed with cleaning the home or she would repeatedly check the front door was locked over a short space of time, or become convinced she had left the oven on after leaving the house and insist on going back to check (it was never on).

Maddy experienced occasional bouts of paranoia. She would be suspicious that people in church were talking about her and become deeply concerned that they had guessed her condition. In response, she would isolate herself.

She also has a history of self-harm. She has cut and hit herself on a number of occasions. Like many women with some social standing, Maddy has got herself into a situation where she feels it is vital to maintain her outward appearance. She feels a need to be perceived as successful, at all costs, even when she feels as though she is dying inside.

Six years ago, things came to a head when Maddy realised that she simply could not manage her symptoms any more. She had previously tried CBT and antidepressants, but this time both she and her GP knew she needed residential care and broader scale intervention. She was admitted to a private psychiatric hospital for twelve weeks.

In the past, it had been hard to monitor the effectiveness of Maddy's treatments because she had worked so hard on controlling her symptoms. She carried on functioning as if everything was normal, even though she was struggling internally. So, it was hard to tell if it was the treatment or Maddy's enforced coping strategies that had made things seem better at the time.

Maddy stayed in hospital for around three months. This was a major watershed moment for the family. The children (then aged ten and twelve) were told that their mother was unwell, and Maddy's husband had to take some time off work to help with them. The bubble had burst on that picture of the perfect family. It was impossible for them to fake it anymore, to pretend everything was fine.

But the problem with this hospitalisation, as Maddy found, was that it didn't do anything to cure the root cause of her problem. The aim was to manage the symptoms and keep her safe.

When Maddy was stable enough to be discharged, she started to look for other psychological treatments, and, eventually, found us. We listened to her story and started to look for the other layers of Maddy's problems to get a deeper picture of the whole timeline of her life, trying to find some links and clues to the inner workings of her nervous system.

One thing that started to emerge strongly was the extreme sense of duty that Maddy felt towards her husband and her community. She got on with things to the point that she was running herself into the ground and neglecting her own needs. It was also very clear was that Maddy found her husband to be overbearing and, at times, verbally and psychologically abusive. This could be seen as a threat to her nervous system.

Maddy began to worry that perhaps she was ill because of her husband's behaviour. This thought was unbearable to her because, in her community, separation or divorce were unacceptable. Maddy knew that this would mean being shunned by the community she lived in and relied upon. Her husband, his family and their friends would utterly condemn it. So, she felt trapped. Her choices, as she saw it, were bleak; stay married and continue to be ill, or to be effectively exiled.

At this point, we needed to look at how she arrived at this situation, to ask ourselves whether it was a real situation (was it really down to her husband's behaviour, or was he just the imaginary lion) and to explore what options she had.

Client's History

Maddy grew up in an American military family, one of four daughters. Her father was in the U.S. Air Force, and he would be posted away on missions for long periods of time. This was the pattern of Maddy's childhood; Daddy disappearing for long periods, and then returning home and being around all the time.

The family also moved around a lot, as is typical of military life. So, although they had a very strong sense of belonging to the wider Air Force community, the family had a far weaker sense of immediate community because they were always on the move. For this reason, they maintained a very strong family unit.

Maddy's father was the only male in the family and was often absent. Whenever he returned, there was a lot of competition for his attention from the five women in his family, all of whom needed that attention in their own ways. Like many of his counterparts, he found it difficult to adjust from military postings to domestic life. And, as was common, he relied a little too much on alcohol, which, although socially acceptable, made him volatile.

So, the family dynamic became about two things. First, it was about competing to see who could please Daddy the most. Second, it was forbidden to upset Daddy because he wasn't around that much. Therefore, it was imperative to make sure that the time he was there was perfect for him. Of course, when Daddy did get upset, it was very frightening for his young daughters because they were unaccustomed to having a powerful male presence around the place.

Add to this a fairly austere mother who constantly reinforced the message about pleasing their father and compound it with the military culture of macho respect, and you have a situation in which a child with normal needs, like being playful or exploring the occasional outburst, is a threat. Being herself simply didn't feel safe to Maddy. When a child gets upset, they instinctively need to complain and ask for more love. But Maddy and her sisters knew that doing this would not be allowed. In fact, Maddy had been conditioned by her mother that this normal need, to express pain and seek comfort, would make her unacceptable to both parents.

A child craves love from their parents, but, in Maddy's case, to ask for it would have been instantly to lose it. And this unbearable dichotomy is enough to overwhelm a young, fragile nervous system. You can see how there is no major traumatic event here, just how this family grew up and what they thought was right. This way of thinking and behaving would have been conditioned in Maddy's mother long before her children were even born. She simply believed that her husband needed to be protected and that this was how they should operate as a family. To go against this or to challenge this family's behavioural structure would have been unbearable.

No one is to blame. No one meant any harm. This is just how everyone was raised to behave. It was incredibly hard to step out of line and go against the grain, an act too overwhelming to contemplate.

Formulation

Let's look at Maddy's story from the point of view of her nervous system, using what we know so far to reframe her problems from a different perspective.

We can see how Maddy's nervous system got dysregulated from a young age. It's also clear that she did not have a secure attachment to her primary caregiver because her mother's attention would wax and wane, depending on whether Daddy was home or not. Early on, Maddy's nervous system would have started to store up this undischarged material, so she started to under-react.

Like any child, Maddy encountered situations during her childhood that she perceived as threatening. A young mammal's first reaction to threat is to seek help. They know they are not strong enough or fast enough yet to compete with adults, so they look to the primary caregiver to help them. In Maddy's case, this normal, biological, hardwired, instinctive need became, itself, a source of threat.

When her father was away, Maddy was in the middle of five females where the primary objective was to keep her mother happy at all costs. Her mother showed signs of stress, so she and her sisters knew they had to rally round. Maddy's instinctive knowledge that if she needed help from her mother, first she had to look after her mother to get it, activated her own sense of threat, overwhelmed her and created her first unfinished business in her nervous system.

The story was no better when Daddy came home. Then, Maddy was competing with four other women for his attention. While she was doing her very best to keep Daddy entertained and pleased, she couldn't seek the help from a primary caregiver she needed to feel safe, to regulate her nervous system and to finish the unfinished threat cycles in her system.

As a child, Maddy did not have the amount of support she needed from primary caregivers to build her own healthy threat response, so she couldn't regulate the normal stresses of family life. Instead, they overwhelmed her. This doesn't mean her parents neglected her. They loved her and thought they were doing the right thing. But they were completely unaware of what their actions were doing to Maddy's fragile, semi-formed nervous system.

So, as Maddy grows up, her regulation decreases, with more and more overwhelming threats. She hits her red line sooner and sooner. Eventually, by adulthood, she has so much unfinished business in her nervous system that she is almost constantly triggered, producing a size 9/10 reaction to a size 3/10 trigger.

This is the Maddy we met in treatment. A woman unable to function in the world because anything can plunge her into a state of utter panic while her body desperately tries to cope with years of accumulated baggage. Maddy has carried countless pieces of unfinished business into her adult life, piled on top of the original overwhelm she experienced as a child when she couldn't get her primary needs met.

So, what does she do as an adult? She does what so many of us do. She replicates the whole scenario in her family life, to re-activate the baggage in the hope of discharging all those incomplete threat cycles. The military system she grew up with is replaced by the church system, where she can feel like she belongs to a trusted organisation with rules and conventions. She accumulates wealth from a professional career in order to have the material possessions that she finds comforting. She even marries a man whose needs are more important than her own. And she raises a family where she puts everyone else's needs before hers, too.

Because of this, and because she has been unable to create healthy coping strategies, Maddy's already-overwhelmed nervous system gets more and more problems stored up in it. So, when stressful things happen, like when her husband loses an important deal, or the kids have problems at school, she simply doesn't have the capacity to cope. Instead, she experiences episodes of extreme anxiety throughout her life.

We can see mild paranoia or OCD as our thinking, human brain desperately searching for ways to make sense of the non-verbal fire-alarm signals coming from the nervous system. Obsessive behaviour, like constantly checking the oven is switched off, looks a lot like our thinking brain inventing a threat. But that threat never got discharged and is repeated, over and over, in all kinds of perfectly normal, unthreatening everyday scenarios. It is the Invisible Lion, almost literally.

Was this understanding a complete relief to Maddy? Yes and no. After all, the more she understood how she had become dysregulated in the first place, the more she understood that she had literally married a trigger! She could also see quite clearly that, in her current state, her husband was making her ill. She had to ask herself whether she needed to leave him in order to prevent herself from becoming a long-term mental patient.

The digging into her past and the diagnosing of her issues was all fascinating to Maddy, but, at the same time, it made her realise how much work needed to be done. She knew it could take years to repair her nervous system. She also needed to work on boundaries and containment so that her newly regulated nervous system, when she got there, would be safe and secure.

In treatment, she was able to start the process of connecting to and discharging energy from her nervous system, small step by small step. We also gave her tools to help with boundaries and containment. Ultimately, for Maddy, divorce was a worse fate than being mentally unwell for the rest of her life, so she wanted to do everything she could to stay in the relationship and to change things so that she wouldn't get so triggered.

Maddy was an intelligent, considered and highly rational person. But there's a difference between understanding a theory and actually applying it to your life. Most clients like Maddy totally get the theory. Then they can reach the diagnosis with their therapists and formulate a recovery plan. But it's still a stretch to put that plan into practice, because old habits die hard when we are dysregulated. Recovery requires a lot of faith and courage; and can demand that we make significant changes in our lives.

So, even when the problem is identified, when the theory makes sense, and the treatment plan is laid out, there's still work to be done.

Treatment

Maddy understands why and how she has a dysregulated nervous system. She can see how the family and social dynamics that she has created around her are all consequences of the countless incomplete stress cycles she has stored up since childhood. Her mental health problems now make perfect sense to her. But what to do about it?

We are all on a continuum when we begin the slow process of creating a structure to support a healing nervous system. But this process is not black-and-white, and it certainly doesn't happen overnight. It can take some time to see the world exactly as it is, without events triggering our baggage and causing us to over-react or to under-react.

We learn how to protect ourselves by setting boundaries and how to function better in the world by practicing containment, but we can still be left in a lot of pain. Before Maddy finished treatment with us, we wanted to help her find a coping strategy for the work ahead. Her husband came to some of her therapy sessions, and it was obvious that he was also highly dysregulated. This came as no surprise. Dysregulated people are often attracted to each other because they trigger familiar baggage in one other. The problem was that his demanding behaviour was Maddy's biggest trigger. It would be impossible to complete her unfinished stress cycles and reduce her own baggage if her husband's behaviour kept triggering this baggage that she was trying to clear.

And so, to come back to Maddy's original question of whether or not to leave her husband, you can see that it was a tricky one. Those of us without a strong commitment to an establishment (like Maddy's church) might say, "Divorce, of course!". But for Maddy, the idea of giving up on her marriage felt like giving up on everything she believed in and subscribed to, so she was committed to finding a way to make it work. It would also have been a threat to get divorced.

Setting boundaries was tough and following through on the rules she'd set up was even tougher. She had to learn to do something when her boundaries were crossed. She was used to doing nothing, freezing when she was triggered, her baggage causing anxiety attacks and OCD episodes. She needed to make the somewhat uncomfortable progression towards a more active, defensive response that would protect her when triggered.

That's why some of Maddy's new boundaries needed to involve her leaving sometimes. You can imagine how completely unfamiliar this was for her; it took an incredible amount of work for Maddy to adhere to her own boundaries. She had no idea what was right for her and what wasn't. This is typical of someone whose focus has been on everyone else's needs, while their own have been neglected for so long.

Her nervous system offered lots of information and clues here. If something was not okay for Maddy, it was going to notice. So, she had to learn to observe her responses carefully. Mindful practices like yoga and meditation helped her a lot because they started to build a connection between her mind and her body, starting a dialogue between the two.

When Maddy had worked out her boundaries, she communicated them to her husband, she was shocked that his first reaction was one of extreme relief. For years, he had been clueless about what to do. Finally, here was an actual plan. Maddy's husband was very solution-driven, responding positively to a set of instructions that will work towards fixing a problem. He'd been unable to figure out what would make Maddy happy, so to be given a list was ideal for him. To him, it was as though he had been given a map of how to make his wife happy, and it filled him with hope.

Maddy was not expecting this reaction. But, in setting boundaries, Maddy was simulating the behaviour of a regulated person, which was ultimately what he wanted from her. However, as you can imagine, practice was very different from theory. Maddy's husband was also sitting on his own accumulated baggage. Very soon, his neediness kicked in and he wanted to be in charge again. His ability to do what Maddy was asking of him was questionable. She had to make it very clear how she would take care of herself to maintain her own boundaries.

One of Maddy's boundaries was that she was not okay with her husband shouting at her. She decided that if he did, she would take care of herself by packing an overnight bag, leaving the house and going to stay with a friend or at a hotel. With no drama and no fuss, she would simply carry out this plan that she had let him know about.

So, the answer to the original question of whether Maddy should leave her husband became very simple to answer. No, so long as she can manage her boundaries and the relationship at the same time. If her husband can successfully collaborate with her on that project, then she can stay in the marriage and recover her nervous system.

Unfortunately, it turned out that he could not. After many attempts to make things work together, Maddy's nervous system let her know that she needed more safety in order to recover than he could allow her to have at home. After a trial separation, Maddy's continuing work on reducing her own dysregulation helped her to have far fewer symptoms than before of anxiety or OCD. Ultimately, she decided that the best thing for her and for her children, and even her husband, was to put her nervous system health first, and so, despite the concerns of her community, and she formalised the end of her marriage.

Whilst sad and difficult, this was a reflection of the quality of the relationship itself. Had they been able to work together on this project, everyone would have been much safer in the end. But, given where she was, this was the only way she could make sure that her nervous system had the boundaries it needed to start her own long-term recovery.

HE'S BROKEN MY HEART: WILL I EVER BE ABLE TO LOVE AGAIN?

Presenting Problem

Brenda is thirty-six. A secondary school teacher, she is married, with a three-year-old child. A year ago, she had a very passionate extramarital affair. When her lover ended it, she was devastated. Now she has told her husband she wants a divorce.

The breakdown of her love affair has completely crippled Brenda. She has become clinically depressed and suicidal. She has even asked her husband's family to take care of her child because she feels incapable of being a fit mother. She has collapsed, unable to function at home or at work. Everyone says she is having a nervous breakdown.

This is how Brenda was when she contacted us for treatment. She was heartbroken, not sleeping or eating properly. She had stopped taking care of herself. Instead, she was consumed with thoughts about the man she'd had the affair with.

They had met at work. Brenda was beautiful. Brenda's husband Mike, on the other hand, was quite normal by comparison. In fact, Brenda had married an unassuming, average man, who was quite possibly completely baffled by her interest in him as she seemed to be out of his league. She described how she had chosen her husband because he was reliable and had come along at the right time, rather than having had any real attraction to him.

Client's History

Brenda grew up in post-colonial Africa, and her father had left early on in Brenda's childhood. An only child, she was raised by her mother, who was very beautiful. Brenda recalls her mother having had a series of boyfriends. All of them seemed to her to be powerful men. So, as a child, Brenda had a string of very charismatic men in her life, who offered her differing versions of fatherly love. But, they all left eventually, and the early promise of a consistent father figure never came to anything.

Brenda became sexually active at thirteen. She discovered early on that she had huge power over men because of the way she looked. She recognises in adulthood that she abused this power, getting a high from the effect of attention and physical contact, even though she never really enjoyed the sex. She did well at school, however, and managed to establish more stable relationship patterns later in her teens.

She came to England to go to university and things began to settle down as she threw herself into student life and pursued her early career path. She describes her mid-twenties as probably the healthiest and happiest years of her life. She qualified as a teacher, and then she met Mike. After a few years, they got married. Brenda was twenty-nine. As soon as the wedding and honeymoon were over, Brenda started to have doubts about her marriage. She was concerned that she had married someone that she was too easily able to control, someone stable, but not very challenging. After a few years, they had a baby, but rather than bringing them closer together, it made things worse. She felt no real passion for her husband and couldn't deal with how mundane life seemed to be after the baby was born. She missed her work, so, she eventually went back, part-time. Her mother-in-law offered to look after the baby.

Brenda met a charismatic manager in the local education system, and he lavished her with flattering attention. Their secret affair was exciting to Brenda. She felt euphoric after years of feeling dull and sterile. She craved her lover's attention and contact all the time. The affair brought her back to life and she started to take more care of herself. As everyone watched Brenda flourish, her friends and family assumed she was getting back to her old self after a difficult few years with the baby and that her return to work was suiting her. Her husband was relieved to see her more upbeat and optimistic about life.

However, Brenda soon started to unravel. She became utterly obsessed with her lover. Because the affair was secret, their contact was very sporadic and this drove Brenda mad. She couldn't stop thinking about where he was, what he was doing, and when she was going to see him next. She was frustrated by the fact that the affair seemed to be completely on his terms; he dictated where and when they met. And, in between their trysts, he was very elusive. Brenda struggled to cope.

One day, Brenda had an outburst at her lover. Angry and emotional, she told him she was going to leave her husband to be with him. The very next day, her lover sent a message, breaking it off. He didn't answer any of her subsequent messages and she never heard from him or saw him again. He even passed on responsibility for Brenda's school to a co-worker, to make sure their paths never crossed.

At first, she was in denial that it was over. She tried everything to get in touch with him. When she couldn't, she began to fall apart, and, within three weeks, she was a complete wreck. The story Brenda told herself was that if she hadn't been married, it would have worked out with her lover. And so, she abruptly told her husband she wanted a divorce and immediately instructed lawyers. But, as proceedings began, she crumbled and, having talked of suicide, came to our clinic.

Formulation

Brenda was the only child of a woman who was bereaved and serially heartbroken. Brenda's earliest experience was her mother's huge need for companionship. Her mother relied on her only child as a companion whenever she was abandoned. An infant cannot manage its own nervous system. It needs its mother to regulate its nervous system to keep it feeling safe. But, in this instance, the situation got reversed. Brenda's mother used her child for comfort, and so, Brenda met her mother's needs instead.

A pattern emerged. The beautiful mother would get

a new boyfriend and become incredibly happy, so the child becomes happy. But when the boyfriend leaves, the mother is depressed and looks to the child to comfort her. This frightens and overwhelms the child. As a result, she is swinging between safety and overwhelm all the time. No surprise then that Brenda has grown up associating a boyfriend with safety and the absence of a boyfriend with threat.

From the point of view of the nervous system, regulation was provided by a charming man walking into the picture. This would fix her mother and fix her. But when her relationship with the man broke down, Brenda's mother would unravel completely, and young Brenda would be unable to regulate herself.

There is no blame here. Brenda's mother was not making these decisions and taking these actions consciously. Everything she did was a result of her own dysregulated nervous system, which had probably formed as a result of her own mother's dysregulated nervous system, and so on.

By the time Brenda hit puberty, her nervous system was regulated by male attention, and this became a kind of drug she craved to help her to feel safe. As a young beautiful girl, she finds that this drug is easily obtainable. She got into relationships effortlessly and then finished them, always on her terms. Brenda was used to men not hanging around for long from her childhood, so she didn't feel too bad about finishing things when she did. She was simply mimicking what she was used to growing up. Her mother had used the intensity of attention and short-lived, exciting relationships, and so, Brenda had learnt to do the same.

By the time Brenda hit her twenties, romantic relationships kept her regulated. Her dysregulated nervous system was able to simulate regulation when there was a man on the scene. But when she married Mike in her thirties, she chose someone she knew she could control, who would not leave her. Life then got boring. Marriage meant no more exciting serial relationships. No more avalanches of sudden, adoring attention. So, when a new man came along and hit Brenda with the full force of his seduction, Brenda was toast. Having been off her drug for years, she got a massive high. But when Brenda became more and more desperate and needy, he finished the relationship.

This relationship had successfully triggered her baggage. But she could neither discharge it, nor get the one thing she seeks to soothe herself, which was the attention of this charming man, because he had cut off all contact. No wonder Brenda was a mess when she came to us. Her baggage had been fully activated and she couldn't begin even to understand it, let alone to clear it. All this unfinished business loose in her system had led her to a total nervous breakdown.

Treatment

Brenda learned to accept that the relationship had been symptom of a deeper problems. But it was hard for her to stop fantasising and romanticising about it. Brenda had to set boundaries for herself. No more contact. No more obsessive thoughts and fantasies. That was very hard. Then Brenda started to work. With guidance, she accessed what it felt like in her body to be two-years-old again and to have to deal with her mother being in and out of regulation and overwhelm.

It took Brenda a while to adjust her focus and to realise that her fundamental problem was nothing to do with having a boyfriend who left her. Her problem was the constant overwhelm she experienced as a toddler, because her mother could not regulate her, leading to a lifetime of unfinished business which her dysregulated nervous system was unable to process. And because she was dysregulated, she couldn't form healthy attachments with either romantic or platonic partners. Instead Brenda learned from her mother to allow her sexuality to play a leading role in her relationships.

Brenda's containment work, in this case, involved forming healthy, platonic relationships and practicing her ability to relate to people without allowing her sexuality to dominate. And she had to fake it until she made it. Instead of manipulating situations, saying whatever she needed to say to get her fix, or exploding or shutting down when triggered, Brenda had to be honest and authentic, and risk feeling vulnerable. This is where group meetings, group therapy and the community of residential treatment really helped her.

The more she continued to work on her internal boundaries, and the more she processed her baggage, the easier Brenda found it to contain her behaviour and work towards having a more regulated nervous system.

Brenda was in residential care for about four months. When she left she was alone, but she was able to look after her child again and she got another job. Through treatment, Brenda has learned for the first time in her life not just that love and sex are not the same thing, but, most importantly, why. She is now able to pursue genuine loving relationships with friends and family. She is also able to form appropriate, healthy relationships with colleagues and associates in a way she could not have previously imagined.

Her childhood wounds began to be repaired by giving the child in her what she really needed; connection, not sex or obsession. Before, Brenda threw every bit of herself into each highly intense relationship with one man after another, just as she'd watched her mother do. Now she can bear to connect to dozens of people at the same time in a non-sexual way, and feel a loving bond with each of them. This is a much safer and more nurturing way to have relationships, rather than immersing herself in that one, all-consuming, intense affair.

Brenda had never really understood the difference between physical and emotional intimacy. Now she recognises that while physical intimacy is much easier, emotional intimacy comes from connection, regulation and attachment. For her, with no experience of that in childhood, this was very scary. It meant taking risks. And she now understands that this is about her nervous system and how it was trained to react to relationships in the past. Brenda is effectively redoing her childhood, providing her own attachment figure for herself, and in doing so, is successfully creating a new template for what love means to her in an intimate relationship.

MY LIFE IS GREAT, SO WHY AM I FALLING APART?

Presenting Problem

Patrick is forty-two, and is married to Helen. When we first met Patrick, Helen was three months into her first pregnancy after years of trying. Just before Helen announced she was pregnant, Patrick got a promotion at a logistics firm where he is a manager. He is popular at work, and the couple have a nice circle of friends. Most of them have young children. Patrick and Helen are delighted that they are soon to be parents themselves.

On the surface, Patrick's life seems great. But behind closed doors, it's a different story. For several years, Patrick has been suffering from bouts of severe depression. He has a serious sugar addiction, which Helen knows about. But he is also addicted to watching pornography on the internet, which Helen does not know about. Now it's affecting his work. He once stayed up nearly all night, watching porn and was too exhausted to go to work the next day. He called in sick, claiming he had a stomach bug.

Patrick feels intense shame over his pornography addiction. In the fifteen or so years that he has been with Helen, he has been unfaithful twice. Both times were during depressive episodes and were really extensions of his pornography addiction and the direct result of bingeing on alcohol. They were one-night stands, seven years apart, and he never contacted or saw either of the women again. He has never told Helen about this, and he feels terrible guilt and shame about it. Patrick has worked hard to drink less and give up the pornography addiction, but now he binges on sugary foods instead, and has become a workaholic.

Patrick has been using food, pornography, alcohol and work to regulate himself when he suffers from depression. Helen has been aware of Patrick's depression for some time, but has been at a loss as to know what to do. After she got pregnant and Patrick's stress levels immediately increased, she insisted he get some help before the baby was born. And that's when Patrick came for treatment.

The first thing we noticed about Patrick was a lot of nervous energy. He was wound up and had not been sleeping. At that point, he was in a period of extreme anxiety, working around the clock and binge-eating. Helen's pregnancy had also triggered a paranoia about losing his job. Patrick was feeling the pressure because Helen had told him she wanted to give up her job and be a stay-at-home mother for at least two years. If he lost his job, Helen wouldn't be able to be the mum she wanted to be. He'd also been imagining Helen's reaction if she found out about the porn addiction and even the one-night stands.

Patient's History

Patrick is the youngest of three brothers. His father was a self-made man from a working-class background. Patrick's two older brothers were carbon copies of Patrick's father and the apples of his eye. His father also set up a lot of rivalry between the two older brothers, always encouraging them to compete with each other, and instilling in them the huge importance of winning. As a result, Patrick's dad and his two older brothers had an ongoing love-hate relationship.

Patrick was closer to his mother. She was a submissive character, who was routinely belittled and put down by her husband, often in front of the children. The abuse stopped just short of physical, but the family culture was very misogynistic. A household with four men, three of which were competing to be macho, was as unpleasant atmosphere for her. Patrick was similar to his mother in many ways and, as a result, Patrick's father all but ignored his youngest son. Although Patrick was more academic than his brothers, and more successful in other ways, he never got any acknowledgement or praise from his father. Nothing he ever did was good enough.

To Patrick's extended family and their circle of friends, his father was a hero. He joined the police force after serving in the British Army from the age of sixteen to twenty-four. He retired from police service and went on to establish a private security firm, which he built into a successful business and had sold for a lot of money. When Patrick was four-years-old, there was a credible threat made against his father and the family. They were forced to move, and even needed police protection for a period of time. Even now,

Patrick doesn't know all the details, but he's always suspected that the threat was linked to organised crime, and that perhaps this was gang retaliation for his father infiltrating a particular crime ring.

The story, however, has always been very murky and is never discussed in the family. But Patrick clearly remembers his mother being terrified for a long time. He has always found it hard to maintain family relationships, not just with his brothers and father, but also in the wider, extended family, with uncles, aunts and cousins. He feels like an outsider and gets paranoid about what people are thinking and saying about him.

Formulation

Patrick was born into an environment where the prevailing activity was men either competing or fighting with each other. The nurturing presence of his mother was diminished in this macho family set-up. As a young child, Patrick couldn't cope with the aggression between his father and two brothers, and so, he went to his mother to regulate himself. This automatically put him in a different camp from his father and brothers.

The young Patrick saw his mother as a point of safety, where he felt comfortable. But he then had to watch his father attack his mother. The natural instinct when someone attacks one of your key resources is to defend it. But Patrick was a toddler and couldn't possibly win a fight to protect his mother. His nervous system would go into overwhelm with his emerging fight response trapped inside it.

So, by the age of four, Patrick's system is already overloaded with unfinished business. And then something new happens, a real external threat. The family is under attack.

In some ways, this new threat would have come as a relief for little Patrick's overwhelmed nervous system. At least the external threat was real, so there was something to validate all of his unfinished reactions to threat. In the context of the family being threatened, all the sensations he was already having now made sense. Patrick recalls this time as being a relatively positive period, because it united his very tempestuous family for a short time, at least.

Then Patrick grows up. Capable and hard-working, he gets on well at school and university and has a couple of nice girlfriends before finally settling down with Helen. He's done well on all fronts. But one thing that defined Patrick's early adult years was that he is a conformer by nature, always trying to fit in. All his life, Patrick hasn't really paid attention to what he wants because he just wants to be doing what is expected of him. He learned from his family to go along with the big kids. And so, if everyone is drinking, Patrick will drink. If everyone is going to a club, Patrick will go too.

While he's just getting on with it, Patrick is oblivious to all the unfinished business dormant in his nervous system. But what happens when Patrick gets older? He gets bigger and safer. He's more secure. He has a home, a good job and a wonderful wife. He's built an incredibly safe world. Once the nervous system feels that Patrick's environment is safe and secure, it has the opportunity to start to release all of this unfinished business. When this starts, he can perceive this as a threat and get overwhelmed again, causing the system to crash once more into overwhelm.

This is why Patrick has been experiencing periods

of being depressed and out of control. He's going up and down as his nervous system tries desperately to discharge and complete all those incomplete stress cycles. And he's clutching at anything that might help regulate him along the way.

It's a cruel irony that a person can spend their whole life seeking security, and as soon as they are safe, the nervous system takes it as a cue to start re-experiencing all of its earlier experiences of danger. Most people don't like this and try to stuff them back down. Overeating and binge-drinking are ways of stuffing unwanted material back down.

Then, his wife gets pregnant, on top of this risky internal reorganisation. His sense of safety begins to crumble and he becomes incredibly vulnerable. And worse, he's got nothing to medicate it anymore now that he's quit the drinking and pornography, and is trying to stop binge eating.

Treatment

Patrick had been using food, alcohol and pornography to give him temporary relief from his depression, but, in the end, these only caused him more stress, shame and guilt. We helped him to see this from the point of view of the story of the nervous system and his valid efforts to regulate himself.

With more awareness of this dynamic, Patrick can actually notice when the urge to use substances or behaviours begins. He can then notice what his triggers are and when he's struggling with his boundaries. This gives insight into where new boundaries need to be set, which will reduce the triggers hitting his system.

In traditional addiction treatment, people were

often told to stop drinking or taking drugs, but not shown how to find a substitute for this attempt to regulate their nervous system. This left them just as dysregulated as ever, with no strategy for reducing the dysregulation that caused their addictions in the first place.

If Patrick just gives up the unhealthy behaviour without noticing the triggers and setting boundaries, the triggers will keep coming at him, and he will eventually relapse into the original behaviour that once gave him relief. Even if he does manage to build a very strong safety bubble with firm boundaries and healthy behaviours, if he doesn't work on the baggage, he will remain at risk of getting retriggered again. The bubble might burst.

Containing his behaviour gave Patrick clarity in identifying exactly what was triggering him. From this, it became clear that one of Patrick's triggers was the overwhelming responsibility he felt from what was expected of him as a husband and a father.

Before he came to seek help, Patrick had always responded from a place of powerlessness. He didn't believe he had the right to say "no". Now, as he gained the tools to observe his system and notice when he gets triggered, he had the opportunity to experiment by saying "no" to things, or at least to find the courage to share, honestly, what he is feeling. This created the space to deal with his baggage and to do somatic work on completing these incomplete responses to threat from his childhood.

Patrick now knows how to contain his behaviour and set boundaries to reduce his triggers, and has worked on his baggage to reduce the risk of getting reactivated. He is doing well. Like many high achievers, he was determined to get better and he used his intelligence and discipline to learn the tools that would aid his recovery. He has embraced understanding human behaviour with an open mind and is working conscientiously to apply what he's learned to his everyday life.

He now has the chance to really start enjoying all the blessings that his life has to offer, a wonderful wife, new baby, a good job and great friends, instead of consistently sabotaging his happiness, health and success to get rid of them.

WHY IS OUR DAUGHTER ANOREXIC AND CAN SHE RECOVER?

Presenting Problem

Juliet is twenty. She's been at university for a year and is an average student, not excelling, but never struggling. At the beginning of her second year, three weeks into the term, she dropped out and came home, telling her parents she wasn't happy there. She has agreed with the university that she can take study leave and go back at any time, but she has told her parents that she doesn't feel that she can ever go back.

Juliet has not been eating. She's been confining herself to her room, and she appears completely listless and purposeless. Her parents have become increasingly alarmed by how thin Juliet has become, and they're concerned that she might be anorexic. The way they describe it, Juliet seems to have completely shut down. They're afraid that their daughter is in a very negative and dangerous downward spiral.

After six weeks of having her daughter at home,

doing nothing and seemingly wasting away, Juliet's mother asked us to assess her daughter. She has been trying to organise activities and projects for Juliet, but Juliet has rejected them all. She doesn't seem to want to engage with anyone. She's dropped all contact with her friends from school and university and has completely distanced herself from her siblings too. Her younger sister is doing extremely well in her final year at school and her older brother has just started working in London as a trainee lawyer.

Juliet's father has a high-pressure job, and commutes to London from their picturesque Surrey town every day, just as he has done for most of Juliet's life. He's not home much, but he makes all the right supportive noises. Juliet's mother is full of theories about what might be wrong with her daughter, but ultimately, she's extremely anxious and is just desperate to help Juliet get her life back on track.

The person who walked into the clinic for an initial assessment was a bright, articulate, seemingly confident young woman. She did look too thin, but otherwise, didn't outwardly display any behaviour that was cause for alarm. As we got talking, Juliet resolutely stuck to talking only about what had gone on in her last few months at university. She explained that she felt she was on the wrong course but didn't know what she wanted to do, which was why she had taken time out.

When gently pushed, she admitted that she had also had problems with her group of friends. They were very close in the first year of university, but, as soon as they had all gone back for the second year, Juliet immediately felt ostracised. These were the people she had thought were her best friends, but now she felt bullied and was sure people were gossiping about her.

Interestingly, Juliet completely challenged her mother's assessment of her. She said she was actually very busy doing things, like looking into different courses to see what might interest her. She was convinced that if she can just find the right course, and the right group of friends, then everything will be fine.

When we tried to get her to talk about some of the other issues that were worrying her mother, such as the lack of eating, Juliet became very defensive and insisted that nothing was wrong. She admitted she had lost a little weight recently but blamed the situation at university. She was adamant that she was trying to eat more in order to put on weight.

We then asked Juliet about her family life. At this point, she was quite abrupt and tense, unwilling to talk in any detail about it. Her view was that she had had a perfect childhood, that her family was lovely and that she got on very well with all of them.

The feeling I got, while talking to Juliet, was that I was on the receiving end of a performance of sorts. This is not uncommon in people who come for an assessment at the request of someone else, and perhaps understandably so. I suspected she was, on some level, terrified of revealing her true self. Curious, I asked her how she felt in the moment, how she felt about being in treatment.

She looked very sad for a moment. She said that while she was quite happy to be there, discussing her problems with us, she was only really doing it to please her parents. They were, she felt, totally overreacting. That was the point at which I felt the consultation had really begun.

Patient's History

Juliet described a fairly uneventful family life. Her parents had been married for a couple of years before their first baby, Tom, had come along. Before Tom was born, Juliet's mother had worked in an advertising agency, but she had given up work to look after the baby. They had moved out of London to a Surrey commuter town, which was where Juliet was born. Her sister came along two years later.

Juliet remembered an extremely happy childhood. She had lived in the same spacious and comfortable house all her life. Juliet's father had been through several high-pressure jobs on his way up the career ladder and travelled a lot on business. All three children were privately educated at a nearby school and had a good circle of friends. Juliet remembered happy family holidays abroad while they were growing up.

It was easy for me to see the areas where we needed to dig a little deeper. First of all, I asked Juliet if she knew how well her mother coped, having three young children to look after when her father was away so much for work. Her mother had just given up a career and moved to a commuter suburb, where she didn't initially have a support network.

Juliet seemed a little baffled by the question, as if she couldn't quite see it from her mother's perspective. She just said she was fine. I wanted to know about Juliet's relationship with her mother and older brother. I asked her what her earliest memories of that dynamic were. At this point, Juliet suddenly became much more animated. She talked about how well Tom and her mother got along, that Tom was always very busy with various activities, how Mum was always running around taking Tom places and organising his life. Juliet, it seemed, had simply observed or tagged along.

I asked Juliet if she felt Tom was something of a larger-than-life character, who always got a lot of attention. She agreed. Then I asked if her younger sister, Abigail, also faded into the shadows of Tom's spotlight. "Oh no, Abigail was a little princess!" said Juliet. She went on to describe how Abigail was always on show because she was such a sweetheart, and how everyone stopped to look at and admire baby Abigail. As they grew up, Abigail got her own way a lot and never allowed herself to be dragged around to all of Tom's activities in the way Juliet was.

I started to get a picture of how marginalised Juliet had been as a child, firstly seeming of lesser importance than her older, gregarious brother, and then slightly overlooked as a toddler because a new, gorgeous baby had arrived and was demanding all her mother's attention. At this point, as a different picture of her childhood began to dawn on Juliet, she opened up and launched into a long and convoluted story about her recent troubles with her friends at university. She described subtle, shifting dynamics within two or three friendship groups, how she seemed to find herself caught in the middle between these groups and subsequently left out of everything. She explained how she felt everyone had "their" group except for her and how she felt on the fringes of these groups. While everyone seemed busy, active and engaged with each other, Juliet was never sure which direction to go in.

As Juliet told the university story, I noticed she was the most passionate and engaged she'd been all session. I asked Juliet if she thought Tom and Abigail were both more like their mother and if she, Juliet, was more like her father. She seemed surprised by the question but was quick to agree that it was probably true. Then I asked her where her father was during most of her childhood experiences. Of course, she answered that he was away working, and that he was very busy. She acknowledged that this was necessary because he provided so well for the family.

Very carefully, we started to peel away the delicate layers of denial that Juliet had constructed, to get us to the truth about her emotional experience in her family structure. The reality was, Juliet felt consistently overwhelmed and overruled by her brother, and outshone by her little sister. She also felt misunderstood and marginalised by her mother. The only time Juliet ever felt truly comfortable was when her father was paying attention to her, which unfortunately, through his frequent absences, wasn't very often.

Juliet confessed that, in actual fact, her school life had been punctuated by quite severe episodes of social anxiety. She went through phases of feeling alienated from different friendship groups, to the point of feeling significantly bullied during one particular extended period in her last year of primary school, when she was ten. The problem continued at secondary school and her parents eventually moved her to a new school. But it seemed to follow her. She moved again for sixth form so that she could get a fresh start before doing her A' levels, but again, there were issues.

When Juliet went to university to study History of Art, she truly believed that the distance and change of culture in a new city would help give her a clean break. At first, she seemed to make some good friends and they formed a group. But about halfway through the first year, she fell out with one of the girls in the group over a boy. Suddenly she was out in the cold again, alienated and confused.

As she approached the end of her first year, feeling incredibly lonely, Juliet started to experience symptoms of Irritable Bowel Syndrome. She had been diagnosed with Irritable Bowel Syndrome after episodes of abdominal pains when she was nine and again when she was fourteen. Through the summer term of university, Juliet managed to make some new friends, who had been on the fringes of her original group. But she never felt completely secure. She stopped eating properly and became extremely anxious, finding it difficult to concentrate on her academic studies.

Juliet was sure that after a good summer break, and catching up with some of her old school friends at home, her second year at university would be easier. She convinced herself that she would be able to put all her problems behind her. But to her dismay, when she returned to university, all the old problems with the friendship dynamics came back. Soon, she was completely depressed and after four weeks, she went to see her tutor to ask for a study break. It was sometime after that that we first met Juliet.

Formulation

The dynamics of Juliet's childhood provide plenty of information to help identify her baggage. Tom was perhaps a replacement for everything Juliet's mother had just given up. Before she was pregnant, She had had an exciting life in London. She had a career and enjoyed a carefree and sociable life with her husband

and friends, and they had two disposable incomes. But suddenly, within the space of a year, Juliet's mother had given up her job, moved away from her friends and was a stay-at-home mum to a small baby. Now, with only one salary to rely on, the pressure was on her husband to provide, so he was often absent. Not surprisingly, Tom became the centre of her universe. She poured all her energy into him.

And then Juliet came along. And although she loved her second baby, Juliet's mother resented the distraction from Tom, the apple of her eye. While it Juliet was dearly loved and wanted, she was also a catalyst for waking up her mother's own baggage of loss. After all, this was a woman who had already lost her husband to longer hours and a big commute. She had lost her career and connection to her London friends. And now, the bubble that she had become with her firstborn was also lost, disrupted by the arrival of another baby.

This was a sad and completely unintentional situation. But it meant that from day one, Juliet could never quite get enough; not enough nourishment, because her mother, busy with Tom, sometimes delayed breastfeeding, and not enough physical affection, because her mother now had to split her attention between the two children yet couldn't bear to abandon Tom. Any young mammal has very basic needs. Automatically, baby mammals form a strong attachment with the primary caregiver, on whom they're completely dependent for shelter, warmth, food and water. In Juliet's case, this attachment was interrupted.

Juliet's mother later agreed that she did resent how needy her new baby was, because it took time away from her firstborn and the special relationship she'd enjoyed so much for two-and-a-half years. Breastfeeding Juliet had felt like the most unbearable chore because it meant she couldn't play with Tom. Yet she was ideologically committed to breastfeeding, thinking it was best for her baby. So imagine Juliet's experience of being fed, in the context of a young mammal. She would have picked up on this mood of resentment from her mother. This means that receiving one of the most basic needs for survival also became mixed in with the reality of not being wanted. Thus, receiving nourishment becomes linked to an experience of existential threat because a very young mammal cannot survive without this primary caregiver.

Juliet's nervous system is now hardwired to treat any attempt at connection with great caution. It won't take much at all to make her feel threatened. And her response to that threat is to revert to her infant experiences to regulate herself which could only have been to avoid feeding. The digestive system relies on the absence of threat to operate. If eating triggers the threat response, then it becomes impossible for the digestive system to have the relaxed functionality it was biologically destined to have. Medically unexplained symptoms relating to eating habits and the digestive tract are now very common.

The experiences Juliet described of social isolation, anxiety, bullying, digestive problems, and anorexia are all related to the combination of the young mammal's nervous system experiencing both nourishment and aggression at the same time in the early months of life. An organic recovery from such early nervous system dysregulation is possible. That would most likely involve acting out as a young child and discharging some of the baggage, but this was not always acceptable in Juliet's family or social circles.

Juliet was caught in a perfect storm of family dynamics, economic circumstances and a social culture that does not approve of visible emotional drama. The result was a logjam in her nervous system which played out throughout her childhood and had got more serious now as she embarked on adult life.

Treatment

We recommended that Juliet start her treatment by staying in our residential clinic. She needed to train her nervous system to feel safe in a community, so that she could feel regulated and not threatened as she re-learned how to form attachments and receive nourishment in all its forms. Remember how in her first session, she rejected help? We now know that this is because nourishment was a fundamental threat to her.

I felt that Juliet could only recover successfully in a completely safe environment, away from all of her old triggers. And if she did, she had a good chance of being ready to return to university the following September, fully able to make new friends and find a course she would truly enjoy.

Another benefit of residential treatment is that the social interaction of living with a group of residents will mirror the tensions in early family dynamics. This will offer clues as to where more work needs to be done to regulate the nervous system.

Juliet chose not to go into residential treatment. Instead she opted to work with a therapist in weekly outpatient sessions. Without the safety of the residential environment, this was not enough to teach her nervous system to respond better to a nurture and to discharge the baggage triggered by social relationships. After a number of consultations, even though it seemed at first as though she was embracing her treatment, Juliet ultimately regressed to the position that she took in her very first assessment.

Juliet's nervous system could not deal with the perceived threat of nourishment when she was offered care. This is a factor that can sabotage people's treatment time and time again. In refusing residential treatment, Juliet denied herself the nourishment which could have made her better. Her weekly attendance became intermittent over the following few months, and ultimately her commitment to the process was not sufficient for us to be able to help her.

Not every case study has a happy ending. But this one, despite our inability to help Juliet recover, serves an important lesson. Here is a seemingly normal, happy family. Juliet's recovery should, in theory, have been straightforward. But if your very first experience of receiving help is tainted with layers of difficult feelings and alarming biological responses, it becomes extremely hard to accept help in any context at any stage of later life.

Frequently, we find that people who have been let down or in some way undernourished in early life are suspicious or antagonistic towards the professionals who want to support their recovery. The therapeutic relationship itself never quite feels safe enough.

As for Juliet, I trust and believe that one day, she will find what she needs when the time is right for her. I hope that the work that she has done so far has planted the first seed of recovery. We will look forward to seeing that seed take root and grow.

FURTHER RESOURCES

Suggested Reading

Dr Bessel van der Kolk: *The Body Keeps the Score*

Dr Stephen Porges: *The Pocket Guide to the Polyvagal Theory*

Dr Peter Levine: *Waking the Tiger* and *In An Unspoken Voice*

Pia Mellody: *Facing Love Addiction* and *The Intimacy Factor*

Dr Janina Fisher: *Healing the Fragmented Selves of Trauma Survivors*

Dr Pat Ogden: *Trauma and the Body*

Dr Dan Seigel: *The Developing Mind* and *Brainstorm*

Dr Richard Schwartz: *Internal Family Systems Therapy*

Suggested Treatment Modalities

Somatic Experiencing

Sensorimotor Psychotherapy

EMDR

Materials Referenced in This Book

See Videos Referenced in this Book

Take the 28-Day Recovery Plan Test Online

Download the Printable 28-Day Recovery Plan

Buy the 28-Day Recovery Plan Workbook

Buy the Illustrations Flip-chart

Please visit www.theinvisiblelion.com for further links to these resources above.

INDEX

A

Abandonment, 116, 157
Abdomen, 239, 244, 247, 255-6
Abdominal Pain, 425
Ability Of
    Expression, 179
    Self-Reflection, 44
Absence of Threat, 427
Abuse, 159, 182, 184, 237, 240, 243
    Childhood, 208
    Substance, 98
    Verbal, 230, 393
Abusive
    Men, 39
    Psychologically, 391
    Relationship, 158
Accelerator, 14, 31, 35
Accumulated
    Baggage, 395, 400
    Dysregulation, 184
Accumulation of Resources, 214
Activation, 31, 43, 55, 70, 99, 138, 158, 162, 356
    And Sensations, 342
    And Threat, 34, 37
    Discharge Of, 70
    Of Unfinished Reaction, 262

Acute Stress Disorder, 100
Adaptation, 16, 17, 22
Addict, 193, 209
Addicted and Avoidant, 190
Addiction, 89, 97, 210, 389
    Pornography, 413-4
    Sugar, 413
    Treatment, 209, 419
Adult Attachment, 183
Adult Attention Deficit/
Hyperactivity Disorder
(ADHD/ADD), 99
Adrenaline, 4
Affairs, 405, 407
Aggression, 39, 41, 416, 430
Alcohol, 39, 97-8, 389, 394, 414, 418
Alzheimer's Disease, 97
Ambivalence, 178
American Psychiatric Association, 92-3
Anatomy, 67, 70, 175, 209
Anger, 157, 166, 168, 178, 188, 238
Anorexia, 421, 430
Antidepressants, 92, 96, 392
Antisocial Personality Disorder, 100
Anxiety, 3, 5, 107, 388, 391, 398, 401, 403, 414, 430

Arizona, 5-6
Attachment, 174, 429
    Adult, 183
    Avoidant, 178
    Disorder, 271
    Disorganised, 181-2
    Recovery, 180
    Research, 179
    Resistant, 177
    Secure, 176, 396
    Style, 175, 184, 191
    Theory, 179
Attention, 406
Attractions, 106, 406

B

Babies, 2, 68, 175, 178, 180, 182
    Attachment, 181, 183
    Regulation, 137, 174, 180
    Threat, 69
Behaviour, 145, 164, 208-9, 265
    And Health, 103
Bereavement, 100
Bible, 58
Biochemistry, 79, 80, 85-7, 114, 170
Biology, 57, 59
Bipolar Disorder, 99-100, 155
Blame, 61, 240, 242, 249, 251, 409
Blood Pressure, 30, 82
Body
    And Health Problems, 79
    Scan, 344-59
Borderline Personality Disorder, 66
Boundary, 124, 134, 136, 164, 181, 246, 401
    Management, 124
    Stabilisation, 132
Brain, 45, 70, 113, 198-9, 227
    Building Of, 17
    Executive, 200
    Mammal, 19-20, 45, 57, 198-9
    Reptile, 45, 57, 198, 205
Break Down, 4, 269
Breastfeeding, 428-9
Breathlessness, 83-4

C

Cairo, 127
Caregiver, 135, 174, 177, 212, 397
    Bond, 69
Catholic Confessional, 104
Choices, 2, 95, 127, 365
Clinical Case Studies, 387
Cognitive Behavioural Therapy (CBT), 63-4, 392
Conduct Disorder, 100
Constipation, 83
Containment, 129, 132, 134, 136, 164, 181

D

Dalai Lama, 272, 274
Dead Faint, 205
Depression, 99, 409, 413-4, 418
Developmental Trauma, 67-8
Diagnoses, 95, 101
Diagnostic and Statistical Manual of Mental Disorders (DSM), 92, 98
Dialogue, 197, 242, 252, 255
Diaphragm, 114
Diarrhoea, 83-4
Discharging, 261-2
Dissociative Disorder, 84
Distress, 61, 176, 212, 253, 306, 314
Dizziness, 84
Dreams, 185, 264
Dysregulation, 53, 57-8, 71, 77, 79, 140

E

Emotions, 19, 178, 238-9, 264, 265, 309, 317, 323, 329, 335
Empathy, 123, 241-3
Endocrine System, 30
Energy, 84, 86, 96, 113, 196
Evolution, 13, 20-3, 27, 33, 35, 118, 212, 272

F

Faintness, 84
Fantasy, 185
Fibromyalgia, 84, 87
Fisher, Dr Janina, 202, 207

INDEX

Fits, 83
Flight, 21, 24, 33, 35-8, 43, 75, 204, 210
    Response, 23, 85
Formulation, 396
Fragmentation, 208
Freeze Response, 15, 23, 33, 55, 118
Frozen Activation, 48, 50-1, 139
    Energy, 77
    Nervous System, 109

G

Gazelle, 31, 35-8, 41-7, 60-4, 205, 264, 285, 343, 360
Garden of Eden, 59, 269
General Aches and Pains, 84
Generalised Anxiety Disorder, 66, 83, 93, 99
Ghandi, 358
Goldilocks
    Model, 108
    Nervous System, 150
    Overreaction, 151, 161
    Reaction, 117, 203
    Relationship, 170-2, 181, 198
    Response, 199
    Underreaction, 164
Guilt, 238, 418

H

Headache, 83-4
Health Problem, 79
Healthcare, 104, 105, 140, 270, 271
    Future Of, 387
Help, 139, 204
History, 394, 406, 415, 424
Homeostasis, 30-1
Human, 22, 118
    Brain, 258, 264, 279, 343, 383, 398
Hung Parliament, 197, 199
Hypomanic Episode, 99
Hysteria, 82, 93

I

Imaginary Lion, 145-6, 207, 394
Integration, 138

Intelligence, 105, 214, 420
Intimacy, 38, 41, 412
Irritable Bowel Syndrome, 84, 91-2, 106, 114, 122, 427
Irrational Behaviour, 63

J

Jawless Fish, 15-6, 21-3, 33

L

Levine, Dr Peter, 20, 207, 264
Lion Analogy, 1, 11, 73
Love, 192
    Addict, 184-6, 190-1
    Avoidant, 187, 189

M

Mammal Brain, 19-20, 45, 57, 70, 77, 198-9, 203, 205, 224, 254
Matrix, 25
Medically Unexplained Symptoms, 83-6, 89-90
    Eating Habits and The Digestive Tract, 427
    Mental Health, 100
Medication, 4-5, 92, 96, 139
Medicine, 69, 82-3, 94, 104
    Physical, 87, 93, 100
Mellody, Pia, 184, 197, 207
Mental Disorder, 92
Mental Health, 5, 7, 104, 124, 145-6
    History, 92
    Unexplained Symptom, 90
Mindfulness, 69, 270
Myalgic Encephalomyelitis (ME), 87

N

Narcissism, 66
Natural Selection, 13-6
Neck Stiffness, 84
Negative
    Comment, 110
    Reaction, 262
Nervous Systems, 31, 98
    Access, 132

and Behaviour, 107
Dysregulation, 54-9, 68, 77
Definition, 80
Regulation, 174
Neurobiology, 70, 130, 175, 206, 209, 270-1
Non-Epileptic Attack Disorder, 84
Nightmare Disorder, 100
Numbness, 84

O

Observations, 36, 94-5
Obsessive Compulsive Disorder (OCD), 66, 100, 391, 398, 401, 403
Ogden, Dr Pat, 202, 211
Opioid Use Disorder Symptoms, 99
Orthodox Jew, 105
Over-Reactions, 63, 114, 189

P

Pain, 84, 93
    Disorder, 101
    Muscles or Joints, 83
Palpitations, 83-4
Panic
    Attack, 3, 101, 388
    Disorder, 99
Paralysis, 84
Paranoia, 208, 392, 398
Parkinson's Disease, 97
Personalities, 195, 208-19, 277
Prefrontal Cortex, 200
Polyvagal Theory, 23, 114
Population, 16-7, 21
Porges, Dr Stephen, 20, 23, 114, 207
Pornography, 411-3, 418
Postpartum, 99
Post-Traumatic Stress Disorder (PTSD), 64-6, 99, 286
Processing, 132
Psychiatric
    Disorder, 67
    Hospital, 4, 66, 139, 392
Psychologist, 66, 92
Psychology, 63, 94, 206

R

Reaction Styles, 150
Reactivity, 107
Recovery
    Plan, 277
    Spirit, 104
Relationship, 2, 39, 108, 153-4, 157, 158, 164, 165, 172, 176, 410
Religion, 70, 81, 269, 274
Resentment, 157, 169, 429
Residential Treatment, 411
Royal College of Psychiatrists, 83

S

Schizophrenia, 99
Schwartz, Dr Dick, 202
Seigel, Dr Dan, 175
Self-Awareness, 44, 62, 202, 213-4, 219, 269
Sensorimotor Psychotherapy, 138, 211
Separation Anxiety Disorder, 100
Sex, 40, 97, 389, 412
Sexuality, 411
Shakiness, 84
Shame, 238, 414, 418
Shutdown, 159, 179, 210
SIBAM, 264
Somatic Experience, 138, 264
Somatisation/ Somatoform Disorder, 84
Social
    Anxiety/Phobia, 98, 99, 426
    Engagement, 22-4, 75, 118, 203-8
Stabilisation, 132, 138
Stress, 66, 85-7, 91, 396
    Cycle, 400, 418
Substance Abuse, 98, 389
Sweating, 84

T

Tai Chi, 69
Teenagers, 210-1
Tension, 264
Therapy, 69

INDEX

Thinking Brain, 19, 202, 224
Threat, 68
    Cycle, 27, 42-6, 53-4, 67, 87
    Distorted Response, 77
    External, 62, 111, 417
    Internal, 62
    Response To, 222-3
    Self-Awareness, 212
Throat Tightness, 84
Time Travel, 62, 107, 254-5, 261-2, 351-381
Trauma, 8, 64, 66-8
Tremor, 84

U

Underreaction, 112
Understanding, 224
Unfinished Business, 48-9, 85, 210-1, 243, 396-7
Unprocessed Material, 159

V-Y

van der Kolk, Dr Bessel, 140
Virus, 90
Vulnerability, 106, 122, 159
X-Ray, 82
Yoga, 69, 138, 270, 401
YouTube, 112, 115, 126, 201

ANSWERS TO THE TEST

Day One	Day Two	Day Three	Day Four	Day Five
1 B	1 A	1 E	1 C	1 A
2 D	2 B	2 D	2 B	2 E
3 C	3 C	3 B	3 A	3 B
4 E	4 E	4 A	4 D	4 C
5 A	5 D	5 C	5 E	5 D
6 D	6 C	6 E	6 D	6 A
7 A	7 E	7 A	7 B	7 D
8 D	8 D	8 C	8 A	8 C
9 C	9 B	9 B	9 C	9 E
10 E	10 A	10 D	10 D	10 C

ABOUT THE AUTHOR

Benjamin is the Founder of NeuralSolution, Khiron House and Get Stable. He is an accredited psychotherapist, author and entrepreneur.

He has had a rich and varied career, combining his interests in psychology, the media and business. In his twenties he founded two small businesses before starting a family, training as a psychotherapist and writing his first book which led to presenting a television series for the BBC.

More recently he has combined his business experience, clinical training and media skills to set up Khiron House, a residential mental-health clinic, to lobby for more effective treatment in the public sector through his non-profit Get Stable and to found NeuralSolution which delivers nervous system informed technology for a variety of behavioural health problems.

He delivers workshops on this subject and continues to work for the recovery of nervous systems globally.

Printed in Great Britain
by Amazon